Kaleidoscope

NCTE Bibliography Series

Kaleidoscope

A Multicultural Booklist for Grades K–8

Rudine Sims Bishop, Editor,
and the Multicultural Booklist Committee
of the National Council of Teachers of English

National Council of Teachers of English
1111 W. Kenyon Road, Urbana, IL 61801-1096

Manuscript Editor: Jane M. Curran

Production Editor: Rona S. Smith

Interior Design: Doug Burnett

Cover Design: R. Maul

Cover Illustration: Ashley Bryan. From *All Night, All Day: A Child's First Book of African-American Spirituals.* Atheneum, 1991. © 1991 by Ashley Bryan. Reprinted by permission of the artist.

NCTE Stock Number: 25433-3050

Permissions acknowledgments for photographs begin on page 168.

It is the policy of NCTE in its journals and other publications to provide a forum for the open discussion of ideas concerning the content and the teaching of English and the language arts. Publicity accorded to any particular point of view does not imply endorsement by the Executive Committee, the Board of Directors, or the membership at large, except in announcements of policy, where such endorsement is clearly specified.

Library of Congress Cataloging-in-Publication Data

Kaleidoscope : a multicultural booklist for grades K–8/ Rudine Sims Bishop, editor, and the Multicultural Booklist Committee of the National Council of Teachers of English.
      p.   cm. — (NCTE bibliography series, ISSN 1051-4740)
   Includes index.
   ISBN 0-8141-2543-3 : $14.95
    1. Minorities—United States—Juvenile literature—Bibliography.
2. Afro-Americans—Juvenile literature—Bibliography. 3. Asian Americans—Juvenile literature—Bibliography. 4. Hispanic Americans—Juvenile literature—Bibliography. 5. Indians of North America—Juvenile literature—Bibliography. I. Bishop, Rudine Sims. II. National Council of Teachers of English. Multicultural Booklist Committee. III. Series.
Z1361.E4K34 1994
[E184.A1]
016.3058'00973—dc20   94-22268
                                                       CIP

The bottom line is this: You write in order to change the world, knowing perfectly well that you probably can't, but also knowing that literature is indispensable to the world. In some way, your aspirations and concern for a single man in fact do begin to change the world. The world changes according to the way people see it, and if you alter, even by a millimeter, the way a person looks or people look at reality, then you can change it.

James Baldwin, 1979 interview,
The New York Times Book Review

Contents

Acknowledgments   ix

Foreword   xi

Introduction   xiii

1. Poetry and Verse   1

2. The Arts   8

3. Ceremonies and Celebrations   12

4. People to Know and Places to Go   16

5. Concepts and Other Useful Information   25

6. Biography: Individuals Who Made a Difference   29

7. History: The Way We Were   40

8. Immigrants and Immigration: Coming to America   46

9. Folktales, Myths, and Legends: Old and New   48

    Origins: How and Why Things Came to Be   48

    Animals   53

    Wonder Tales: Romance, Magic, and the Supernatural   57

    Realistic Tales   66

    Collections   68

10. Books for the Very Young   72

11. Picture Books: Primary and Beyond   76

12. Fiction for Middle Readers   100

13. Novels for Older Readers   106

14. Anthologies: Gatherings of Poems and Stories   117

15. A Potpourri of Resources   121

Award-Winning Books   131

Directory of Publishers   141

Author Index   147

Illustrator Index   151

Subject Index   154

Title Index   160

Photo Credits   166

Editor   169

Acknowledgments

Many people had a hand in the completion of this booklist. Thanks to the publishers who generously sent review copies of their books, without which the job would have been a great deal more difficult, if not impossible.

This was indeed a group project. Members of the committee spent long hours reading and annotating books, a task more difficult than it appears. I thank them for that, and for their advice and support.

A number of other people stepped in to help clear up the backlog of books waiting to be annotated as the deadline for submission of the manuscript came and went. For little or no compensation, the following people generously gave their time, their support, their sometimes adamant opinions, their expert knowledge, and their skill at writing concise annotations. I am grateful to them all and extend my heartfelt thanks.

Patricia M. Dashiell, The Ohio State University
Laura E. Desai, The Ohio State University
Shu-Jy Duan, The Ohio State University
Filiz Shine Edizer, The Ohio State University
Jui-Yi Huang, The Ohio State University
Huey-Jen Lin, The Ohio State University
Mei-ying Liu, The Ohio State University
Melanie Myers, The Ohio State University
Christine Nees, Akron, Ohio
Nikki Nwosu, The Ohio State University
Alicia P. Rodriguez, University of Illinois at Urbana-Champaign
Mary E. Shorey, The Ohio State University
Elizabeth Smith, The Ohio State University
Luella Tapo, Columbus, Ohio
Cynthia Tyson, The Ohio State University/Columbus City Schools
Carol Wolfenbarger, The Ohio State University

Foreword

The National Council of Teachers of English is proud to publish five different booklists, renewed on a regular rotation, in its bibliography series. The five are *Adventuring with Books* (pre-K through grade 6), *Your Reading* (middle school/junior high), *Books for You* (senior high), *High Interest—Easy Reading* (junior/senior high reluctant readers), and *Kaleidoscope: A Multicultural Booklist for Grades K–8*. Conceived as resources for teachers and students alike, these volumes reference thousands of the most recent children's and young adults' trade books. The works listed cover a wide range of topics, from preschool ABC books to science fiction novels for high school seniors; from wordless picture books to nonfiction works on family stresses, computers, and mass media.

Each edition of an NCTE booklist is compiled by a group of teachers and librarians, under leadership appointed by the NCTE Executive Committee. Working with new books submitted regularly by publishers, the committee members review, select, and annotate the hundreds of works to be listed in their new edition. The members of the committee that compiled this volume are listed on one of the first pages.

Of course, no single book is right for everyone or every purpose, so inclusion of a work in this booklist is not necessarily an endorsement from NCTE. However, it is an indication that, in the view of the professionals who make up the booklist committee, the work in question is worthy of teachers' and students' attention, perhaps for its informative, perhaps its aesthetic, qualities. On the other hand, exclusion from an NCTE booklist is not necessarily a judgment on the quality of a given book or publisher. Many factors—space, time, availability of certain books, publisher participation—may influence the final shape of the list.

We hope that you will find this booklist useful and that you will collect the other booklists in the NCTE series. We feel that these volumes contribute substantially to our mission of helping to improve instruction in English and the language arts. We think you will agree.

Charles Suhor
Deputy Executive Director
National Council of Teachers of English

Introduction

This book is an annotated bibliography of selected books about or related to African Americans, Asian Americans, Hispanic Americans/Latinos, and Native Americans. It also lists books involving people and countries in Africa, Asia, South and Central America, and the Caribbean, as well as relevant books set in Mexico, Canada, or England. In addition, it includes works that focus on interracial and intercultural topics, issues, and relationships. The books, all of which were published in 1990, 1991, or 1992, are suitable for children from kindergarten through eighth grade. *Kaleidoscope* is intended to serve as a resource for teachers who wish to offer children books that reflect something of the diversity of American society.

An educated guess is that during the years 1990–92, five to six thousand new books were published per year, the total depending on how and whether one counts paperbacks and reissues. Judging from the publishers' catalogs, we received most of the relevant books from the major children's book publishers, and many from smaller presses. Altogether we were sent about six hundred books. If our estimates are correct, that means that the books we received for this list—books relating to people of color—constitute 3 to 4 percent of the fifteen to eighteen thousand new books published in those years. This is a welcome increase over past years, but still a small percentage compared to the proportion of people of color in the population, and in the schools.

Until quite recently in the history of English-language children's literature, children of color have been virtually invisible in books or, worse, visible only as stereotypes or objects of ridicule. Only in the past quarter century has children's literature from the major publishers begun to include children of color in a positive way in any appreciable numbers. In this last decade of the twentieth century, with one face toward the next milennium and, like two-headed Janus, with another toward the past, we have begun to recognize the harm that is visited on all our children when important segments of the population are rendered invisible in the literature sanctioned by their teachers and other adults in their lives.

Literature is one of the vehicles through which we adults transmit to children our values, our attitudes, our mores, our world views, our philosophies of life. The cumulative message inherent in years of schooling in which children seldom see anyone in a book who resembles themselves and who shares their cultural values, attitudes, and behaviors, or in which children see themselves portrayed as laughable stereotypes, is that these children do not count and are not valued by the society at large. We should not be surprised, therefore, when such schooling also results in negative attitudes toward that society and its institutions, and to literature itself.

The cumulative message for the children, mainly white and middle class, who see their own reflections almost exclusively, is that they are inherently superior, that their culture and way of life is the norm, and that people and cultures different from them and theirs are quaint and exotic at best, and deviant and inferior at worst. In a shrinking world where whites are in the minority, this attitude can lead to serious conflict. And in the United States of today, such an attitude can only reinforce and perpetuate the practices of discrimination and racism that have already marred the history of this nation, and that continue to be the most critical social issue this country must face.

Literature educates not only the head, but the heart as well. It promotes empathy and invites readers to adopt new perspectives. It offers opportunities for children to learn to recognize our similarities, value our differences, and respect our common humanity. In an important sense, then, children need literature that serves as a window onto lives and experiences different from their own, *and* literature that serves as a mirror reflecting themselves and their cultural values, attitudes, and behaviors. Until recently, children of color have had almost exclusively the book as window, while white, middle-class children have almost exclusively been offered the book as mirror. The current emphasis on multicultural children's literature seeks to correct that situation, and this book is intended as a contribution to that effort. We hope that the books listed in this bibliography and others reflecting America's cultural diversity will be read aloud, incorporated into the curriculum, and made available for children's independent reading.

How the Books Were Selected and Organized

From the books received, the committee selected nearly four hundred to annotate, based on a few principles and criteria. We tried, first, to choose well-written books that will appeal to children in kindergarten through eighth grade. We eliminated some excellent books because we thought they were more suitable to high school than middle or elementary school. In keeping with the rationale for developing the booklist, our two other main criteria were (1) that the book should contribute in a positive way to an understanding and appreciation of persons of color and their cultures, or (2) that the book should offer a positive vision of a diverse society and a multicultural world. Our intent was to bring new books to the attention of our readers. Therefore, we generally omitted reissues of books that had been previously published, although we included new editions that had been updated in some way, usually through new illustrations.

The chapters in this booklist emerged from the reading and annotating of the books. Nonfiction was divided into topics such as "The Arts," "Ceremonies and Celebrations," "History: The Way We Were," and "People to Know and Places to Go." In a few cases, particularly relevant fiction books were also listed under these topics. "Poetry and Verse," "Biography: Individuals Who Made a Difference," and "Folktales, Myths, and Legends: Old and New" each constituted a separate category. Fiction, for the most part, was divided by age level, beginning with the very young and advancing through middle school. The designation of age levels is always problematic. We either adopted the publishers' suggested age levels or tried to give a reasonable age-range estimate for the books. It is well to remember, however, that good literature has no real age limits, and that a book suggested for one level may well be enjoyed by readers older or younger. The subject index lists books under the appropriate sociocultural group as well as the appropriate subject matter for each book.

What's New? Current Themes and Topics

As we read and annotated the books, some themes and topics seemed to recur. Some were relevant across groups; others were related more specifically to one group or another. A discussion of a few of those themes and topics may be useful for teachers who are making decisions about incorporating multicultural literature into their own classrooms.

Among the books about people of African descent, there is now some attention to the diversity that is present within that group. These books can help to make students aware of the African diaspora and the similarities and differences that exist between and among Black peoples. Several books, for example, focus on Black people from the West Indies, the islands of the Caribbean. Because of the colonial relationship that existed between England and some of those islands, there is now a considerable Black population in England as well, and some of the newer books about Black people, such as *Amazing Grace* by Mary Hoffman, are not about African Americans, but about Black Britons. In addition, there are a few books of contemporary fiction set in Africa. Some, such as *Chain of Fire* by Beverley Naidoo, relate to racial strife in South Africa, but others, such as *Galimoto* by Karen Lynn Williams, are about the everyday lives of African children. Unfortunately, some authors refer to the setting only as "Africa," without being more specific, feeding into the erroneous impression of Africa as one undifferentiated geographical and sociocultural mass.

The early 1990s have also seen a good deal of attention given in children's books to slavery in the United States and to the continuing struggle for freedom during the civil rights movement of the 1960s, a hundred years after emancipation. Novels such as *Steal Away* by Jennifer Armstrong and *Letters from a Slave Girl: The Story of Harriet Jacobs* by Mary E. Lyons, biographies such as *Sojourner Truth: Ain't I a Woman?* by Patricia C. and Fredrick McKissack and *Rosa Parks: My Story* by Rosa Parks with Jim Haskins, and historical accounts such as *Mississippi Challenge* by Mildred Pitts Walter all help to tell the story of Black Americans as an essential part of American history.

Although this bibliography focuses on books for kindergarten through eighth grade, we also included several books intended for children a bit younger. Some schools include preschool centers, and some of the books might profitably be used in kindergarten. Some of these books feature individual children who are Black, Asian, or Native American. Others feature a variety of children of different backgrounds. The number of books for the very young featuring such children, while still small, seems to be increasing.

In keeping with the tendency of children's literature to reflect current and recent issues, several books—some fiction, some nonfiction—are related to immigrants and immigration. These newer books pay particular attention to immigrants from Korea and from Southeast Asia, especially Vietnam. Not surprisingly, other books involve people from Mexico and from South and Central America and often involve the issue of illegal immigration. They tell the stories of how and why people come to America and what their lives are like in this country.

Some of the books focusing on immigrants and immigration are in the form of photo essays or photo-illustrated books. This format is also prevalent in the "People to Know and Places to Go" chapter. At least ten of the books in that chapter are related to Native Americans. Diane Hoyt-Goldsmith, for example, has produced such books as *Totem Pole*, *Pueblo Storyteller*, and *Arctic Hunter*, each featuring an Indian child and his or her family and community and each illustrated with photographs by Lawrence Migdale. Most of what we received about contemporary Native Americans came in this form.

There is a small and welcome increase in the number of picture books with Hispanic/Latino characters. *Abuela* by Arthur Dorros, *Abuelita's Paradise* by Carmen Santiago Nodar, and *A Birthday Basket for Tía* by Pat Mora all feature contemporary Hispanics/Latinos (indeterminate, Puerto Rican, and Mexican American, respectively). Interestingly, those three books are also examplars of a prominent theme in the Hispanic picture books that we received—intergenerational relationships. Grandparents and other older relatives play an important role in these books. If not grandparents, then the immediate family is at the center of most of the Hispanic-related picture books that we received.

Another welcome mini-trend in books related to Hispanics is the publication of bilingual English/Spanish books, such as *Family Pictures/Cuardros de Familia* by Carmen Lomas Garza. There are also a few books in English and other languages, such as some Native American languages and some Asian languages. Such books recognize and respect the dual heritages of many of today's Americans.

Folktales account for about 20 percent of the total number of books. For three of the four general umbrella groupings—Asian American, Hispanic/Latino, and Native American—the largest number of books fall into this category. Included here are legends and myths and literary folktales; that is, original tales written in the folk tradition. It is important to note that in the case of Asian, African, and Latino folktales, the place of origin and the setting of the tales are outside the United States. This is significant because, although such stories offer a sense of some of the traditional values and mores of the people who created them, they have less to say about the lives of contemporary Asian Americans, African Americans, or Hispanic Americans/Latinos, particularly those who have been in this country for several generations. Although many of the Native American tales originated on this continent, they, too, offer insight into the traditional culture of Indian peoples, but little insight into the lives and experience of contemporary Native Americans. This is not to devalue folktales. The stories of our ancestors play an important role in helping us understand how we have come to be who we are, and they should be a part of our classrooms. In one sense, folktales offer an easy multiculturalism, but teachers and librarians seeking multicultural literature for today's classrooms and libraries will also want to search beyond the folktales for other materials that help us see ourselves in the contemporary world.

Issues and Concerns

Names and Peoples

It is quite convenient, and sometimes a useful shortcut, to speak of Asian Americans, Hispanic Americans/Latinos, and Native Americans. The labels do not serve us well, however, if we use them as if each one referred to one distinct monolithic group. It is important to note that included under those large umbrella groupings are different and distinct groups of people. Growing up Puerto Rican is not the same as growing up Mexican American, although both groups may be called Hispanic or Latino. It is also wrong to assume that Japanese Americans and Chinese Americans are interchangeable, or that there are no differences between the Navajos and the Iroquois, for example. We also need to remind ourselves that Chinese American, for instance, is different from Chinese; growing up in the United States is different from growing up in China, and if you are looking for books about contemporary Chinese Americans, books about Chinese living in Beijing will not do. We have tried, where possible, to designate the specific sociocultural group to which each book is related. As with the folktales, books about or set in the homelands from which our ancestors came to this country can help us to understand our cultural heritage, but when selecting books for the classroom it is well to keep these distinctions in mind so that the literature collection presents as full and accurate a picture as possible.

A different concern related to names is what terms to use for what groups. Do people want to be called Mexican American or Chicano? Hispanic American or Latino? Native American or American Indian? African American or Black? Answers to inquiries addressed to people who are members of those groups varied with the person being asked. Written references also varied, and sometimes the same person used terms interchangeably. Where possible, we tried to use the most specific name that we could find. For example, we tried to use the names of tribal groups when referring to Native Americans. When that was not possible, we used both Native American and Indian. The same is true of Hispanic American and Latino. We hope that if any readers are offended by our terminology, they will forgive the error on the basis that we made a good-faith effort.

Avoiding the Negative: Stereotypes, Inaccuracies, Funny Language

Some books were disqualified from this booklist because they were considered inappropriate in terms of their treatment of the people and places that were their focus. A listing of some of our concerns provides a beginning guide to the issues to which teachers might try to become sensitive and the problems that teachers might learn to avoid in their selections. The chapter titled "A Potpourri of Resources" can provide further information.

Stereotyped images in text or illustrations. Unfortunately, such images continue to exist, although their numbers seem somewhat diminished. One example that turned up more than once is the little Black girl with Topsy-like braids protruding willy-nilly from all over her head. This plantation image makes Black children objects of amusement and simply does not reflect today's reality. Another example came from a book set in China that offended the reviewer with its illustrations of people with slant eyes and buck teeth, a traditional negative caricature of Asian peoples. Teachers need also to be aware of stereotypes in the text, such as the Mexican American father who is described as "hot-tempered" and as behaving in foolish ways because he acts out of emotion rather than reason. Such a depiction reinforces the myth of the "hot-blooded Latin." Native American stereotypes found in some books include the noble savage, the Indian princess, and the brutal savage of old. The continued presence of these sorts of representations helps to perpetuate racism by reducing whole groups of people to a set of stereotypes that permit some people to avoid confronting them as fellow human beings.

Problems with language. We refer here to two kinds of problems. The first is the inaccurate, inappropriate, or demeaning use of language by the characters in a book. An example is the Japanese character who is consistently portrayed as pronouncing "Honolulu" as "Honoruru," making him appear linguistically incompetent and laughable. Another example would be the Indian who talks like Tonto (e.g., "Me Tonto. You Indian now."). A related concern is the use of language that is inappropriate to the time and place of the setting. For example, in one story set in nineteenth-century Japan, the Japanese characters remarked that all they could hear from the English-speaking characters was "Thee" and "Thou," yet the English-speaking characters spoke modern twentieth-century American English.

The other problem is inaccuracies in the use of a language other than English. This was particularly prevalent in books related to Hispanic peoples. There were many cases of incorrect vocabulary choices and misspelled words in books incorporating Spanish into the text.

Inaccuracies. Several books were rejected because there were inaccuracies in the pictures or text. A story from India was illustrated with clothing and architecture from a different time period than the one in which the story was set. A book set in Japan was omitted because there were inaccurate depictions of clothing, customs, and the setting.

Problems with perspective. Not all authors are sensitive to the perspectives of the people about whom they are writing; some are unable to move beyond their own ethnocentric viewpoint. One of the committee members had this to say about a book on Southeast Asians: "a European, colonistic view. . . . It treats the histories of these people as only beginning with contacts with the Western World. . . . I was appalled at the analogy made between Ho Chi Minh and George Washington. At the least it is historically incorrect; at the most it disregards totally the refugee's perspective of over a million Vietnamese-Americans. . . . the treatment of the people of Southeast Asia in the book is simplistic and condescending." Another example: In a story about Mexican Americans, a little girl sometimes wishes she had been born "gringa blond." She is ashamed of being Mexican American, of not being wealthy, of their rundown truck, and so on. Neither of these books is likely to contribute in a positive way to an understanding of the people and cultures portrayed.

Tokenism. A few books seemed to offer only tokenism. Such books might, for example, interject a Spanish word or name to give the impression that the book is relevant to Hispanic Americans. Or there might be a Black child as a member of a group in a story centered on someone else. Another example is the "color-me-gray" sort of indeterminate illustrations in which there is just enough shading to suggest that the characters may be persons of color, but no other clue to their racial or cultural identity is present.

Multicultural Literature in the Classroom

Teachers often ask how books such as the ones listed in this bibliography can be used in the classroom. The short answer is that they can be used in the same way as any other literature. There is no need to make these books appear alien or exotic. Nor is it necessary to treat fictional works as if they were textbooks on a given culture. Even though each book generates its own specific questions and discussion points, classroom book discussions often tend to get at a few basic things: the meaning that the readers make of a book, their emotional and intellectual responses to it, the relevance that they think it has to their own lives. Such discussion points are as appropriate for the books in this bibliography as they are for any other. When the literature program has a multicultural focus, all literature is treated as one small part of the human story. Specific teaching suggestions appear in some of the resources listed in "A Potpourri of Resources." There are, however, two general suggestions that can be offered here.

Make these books and others like them an integral part of the literature program. Select these books and others like them for read-aloud time, for independent reading, for literature study groups. Groups of books focusing on the same topic or theme can be read, compared, and discussed in relation to each other, providing opportunities for appreciating various perspectives on the same topic. Many books from these cultures focus on relationships in the family, for instance, offering opportunities for understanding how families are similar and different across social groups. Different versions of the same folktale appear in many different cultures. Certain motifs, such as the trickster, appear across cultures and can be examined for their similarities and differences. Author studies can introduce students to the writings of diverse peoples. Multicultural literature can be a natural part of any classroom literature program.

Use these books to enhance study in the content areas. Good teachers go beyond textbooks. Sometimes it requires a bit of imagination, but often books like the ones listed in this bibliography can enrich the curriculum. For example, the study of science or social studies is enhanced when students learn about some of the people who have made important contributions in their fields. When studying inventions, for instance, take a look at the life of Thomas Edison, but also remember Jim Haskins's book *Outward Dreams: Black Inventors and Their Inventions.* Mathematics can be enriched by examining counting systems from various cultures. For young children, merely using a counting book that features a Black child, for example, implies that the presence of such a child in a book is a normal thing to expect. It is not necessary to preach a sermon about differences (nor, incidentally, to pretend to be color blind).

On the other hand, many of these books offer opportunities to examine critically the society in which we live, and the values and assumptions that underlie conflicts, events, and behaviors. When such concerns are an inherent aspect of a book—either fiction or nonfiction—it is important that they be confronted and discussed. Certainly any study of history needs to include the perspectives of people who have traditionally been omitted or who have been seen only through the eyes of their oppressors or conquerors. The story of the "westward movement," for example, is usually studied from the perspective of the

European "settlers" who lived on the East Coast. What about the people who were already there on the plains? As another example, do the stories of cowboys include the vaqueros and the Black cowboys?

Incorporating these books into the existing curriculum is an important first step toward rethinking the curriculum so that multiculturalism or pluralism is at its core. At minimum we need to avoid the "holidays and celebrations" syndrome. To confine the use of literature about specific peoples to certain months or holidays—African Americans in January and February, Native Americans in November, Chinese at the Chinese New Year—serves only to keep people marginalized. A commitment to multiculturalism requires much more. It is our hope that this booklist will prove useful to the teachers who are its intended readers, and that it will be used in a way that helps to enrich the lives of the children who are its intended beneficiaries.

1 Poetry and Verse

1.1   Adoff, Arnold. **In for Winter, Out for Spring.** Illustrated by Jerry Pinkney. Harcourt Brace Jovanovich, 1991. ISBN 0-15-238637-8. 48p. 5–9 (est).

These poems follow Rebecca and her family—brother Aaron, mother, father, grandmother—through a year of changing seasons, changing weather, and special times together. They celebrate the small things (a butterfly, a mouse, fireflies) and the special moments (picking mulberries, playing in mud, digging holes for saplings). Arnold Adoff's poems need to be seen as well as heard, and Jerry Pinkney's watercolor paintings capture the moods of the poems and the emotions of this close-knit African American family.

1.2   Allison, Diane Worfolk. **This Is the Key to the Kingdom.** Illustrated by Diane Worfolk Allison. Little, Brown, 1992. ISBN 0-316-03432-0. 32p. 5–7.

An African American girl steps out of her urban neighborhood and into an imaginary kingdom in which she visits a small, green, flowering town and meets a friend. Then she returns to the city with its contemporary problems. But did she really imagine it all? The muted watercolors seem dream-like. See also *The Keys to My Kingdom: A Poem in Three Languages* by Lydia Dabovich (1.8) for a very different treatment of the same rhyme.

1.3   Berry, James. **When I Dance.** Illustrated by Karen Barbour. Harcourt Brace Jovanovich, 1991. ISBN 0-15-295568-2. 120p. 12 and up.

James Berry celebrates Black inner-city youths in Britain and their ties with Caribbean cultures in these fifty-nine poems. Cadence and rhythm are strong in the call-and-response and "work-song" poems written in Caribbean Nation Language. The poems are British, Caribbean, or mixed in voice. The varied and culturally rich collection lets the reader peek at the Black British youths' experiences on the street, relationships with friends and family, and feelings of joy and loneliness.

1.4   Bruchac, Joseph, and Jonathan London. **Thirteen Moons on Turtle's Back: A Native American Year of Moons.** Illustrated by

Thomas Locker. Philomel Books, 1992. ISBN 0-399-22141-7. 32p. 5–7.

This collection of poems was inspired by Native American legends. Chosen from various Indian cultures, the poems are introduced by an Abenaki grandfather explaining how the thirteen scales on the turtle's shell correspond to the thirteen moons of the year. Storyteller Joseph Bruchac, drawing on his Abenaki heritage, collaborates with poet Jonathan London to explain animals' actions and natural occurrences. Thomas Locker's dark, sometimes-harsh but dramatic paintings capture the mood of the seasons and depict sunsets and various scenes of twilight and nightfall in the wilderness. *Notable 1992 Children's Trade Books in the Field of Social Studies.*

1.5   Bryan, Ashley. **Sing to the Sun.** Illustrated by Ashley Bryan. HarperCollins, 1992. ISBN 0-06-020829-5. 32p. All ages.

These twenty-three poems sing not only to the sun, but to the sea, the wind, the birds, and life on a warm sunny Caribbean island. But while the poems celebrate steel drums, frangipani, and carnival, they also celebrate joy, love, beauty, and family. The feelings that they evoke will be recognized and shared by readers of all ages and backgrounds. Ashley Bryan's kaleidoscopic artwork make his first book of poetry sparkle. *Notable 1992 Children's Trade Books in the Field of Social Studies.*

1.6   Carlstrom, Nancy White. **Northern Lullaby.** Illustrated by Leo and Diane Dillon. Philomel Books, 1992. ISBN 0-399-21806-8. 32p. 4–8.

A Native American baby says goodnight to all those objects in nature that are important to the people of the North: the mountains, the rivers, the animals, the trees. This poetic lullaby is accompanied by striking full-page airbrush illustrations which personify earth and sky. The Dillons note that their illustrations portray the spirit of all native peoples from Alaska and do not represent one specific group.

1.7   Cassedy, Sylvia, and Kunihiro Suetake, translators. **Red Dragonfly on My Shoulder.** Illustrated by Molly Bang. HarperCollins, 1992. ISBN 0-06-022625-0. 32p. 5–10.

These thirteen haiku have been translated from the Japanese by the late Sylvia Cassedy and Kunihiro Suetake, a Japanese student of haiku. Each brief seventeen-syllable poem features a different animal—a fish, a crow, a frog, a cicada, a pony, and a cat are among the creatures represented. Each haiku is strikingly illustrated by one of Molly Bang's big, bold, and colorful collages containing such common items as cookies, beads, tinfoil, cloth, screws, clothespins, wire, feathers, buttons, shells, and, of course, paper. *ALA Notable Children's Books, 1993.*

1.8   Dabovich, Lydia. **The Keys to My Kingdom: A Poem in Three Languages.** Illustrated by Lydia Dabovich. Lothrop, Lee and Shepard Books, 1992. ISBN 0-688-09775-8. 32p. 5–7.

In this version of the traditional rhyme, the keys to the kingdom are paints and brushes. Follow a little girl on her imaginative journey, narrated in Spanish, French, and English, into the kingdom and the city, town, house, and room beyond. The colorful pen-and-ink drawings invite readers back to the pages again and again. See also *This Is the Key to the Kingdom* by Diane Worfolk Allison (1.2).

1.9   Demi, compiler (translated by Tze-si Huang). **In the Eyes of the Cat: Japanese Poetry for All Seasons.** Illustrated by Demi. Henry Holt, 1992. ISBN 0-8050-1955-3. 77p. All ages.

A collection of classic Japanese poetry presents the poets' keen observations about nature. Organized by the four seasons, the poems feature animals both wild and domestic. Gnats, frogs, monkeys, cats, bats, deer, wild boar—these and many others populate the pages of this small book. Demi's brightly colored illustrations add action to the poems.

1.10   Glenn, Mel. **My Friend's Got This Problem, Mr. Candler: High School Poems.** Photographs by Michael J. Bernstein. Clarion Books, 1991. ISBN 0-89919-833-3. 103p. 10 and up.

Fictional composites of students whom the author has taught over the years help this poetry collection address some of the typical problems that adolescents confront every day, from racism to uncaring teachers to teen pregnancy. The poignant poems are directed at Mr. Candler, the guidance counselor, over the period of a week and are accompanied by photographs. Some of the poems are about mature subjects, but middle school students will recognize themselves and their concerns as well. *Notable 1991 Children's Trade Books in the Field of Social Studies.*

1.11   Greenfield, Eloise. **Night on Neighborhood Street.** Illustrated by Jan Spivey Gilchrist. Dial Books for Young Readers, 1991. ISBN 0-8037-0778-9. 27p. 5 and up.

These seventeen poems celebrate life in a vibrant urban African American community. They describe such ordinary experiences as street games, bedtime, sleep-overs, and "fambly time," and they evoke such familiar emotions as joy, love, and nighttime fears. The focus is on both family and community. The poems vary in form and take added energy from the watercolor illustrations. They will speak to contemporary children in any neighborhood. *ALA Notable Children's Books, 1992; Coretta Scott King Writing Honor Book, 1992; Notable 1991 Children's Trade Books in the Field of Social Studies.*

1.12   Hale, Sarah Josepha. **Mary Had a Little Lamb.** Photographs by Bruce McMillan. Scholastic Hardcover Books, 1990. ISBN 0-590-43773-9. 32p. 3–7 (est).

In this contemporary interpretation of Sarah Josepha Hale's traditional verse, illustrated with color photographs, Mary is a young African American girl who wears glasses. The photographs were taken in Maine on a farm and at a racially mixed school. An afterword that includes the original verse and a page from a McGuffey reader help to complete the book. Be sure to look for Mary's lamb on the endpapers.

1.13   **The House That Jack Built.** Illustrated by Jenny Stow. Dial Books for Young Readers, 1992. ISBN 0-8037-1090-9. 28p. 5–8.

In this fresh version of the traditional rhyme, the "maiden all forlorn" and the other human characters are West Indians of African descent. The plants, animals, and architecture are all typical of the Caribbean. The collage illustrations reflect the colors of a sunny island day from bright morning through an orange and purple sunset and into a moonlit night.

1.14   Joseph, Lynn. **Coconut Kind of Day: Island Poems.** Illustrated by Sandra Speidel. Lothrop, Lee and Shepard Books, 1990. ISBN 0-688-09120-2. 32p. 6–12.

These thirteen poems evoke the sights and sounds of a "coconut kind of day" on the island of Trinidad. They follow a young girl from the morning song of the rooster to the night songs of the frogs, birds, and other animals. Her experiences include buying ice cream and helping the fishermen "pull seine," or pull in their fishing nets. Lynn Joseph has written the poems to keep her memories of home alive, and Sandra Speidel's illustrations capture the mood and convey the colors of a Caribbean island. *Notable 1990 Children's Trade Books in the Field of Social Studies.*

A.

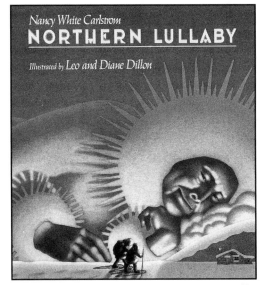

B.

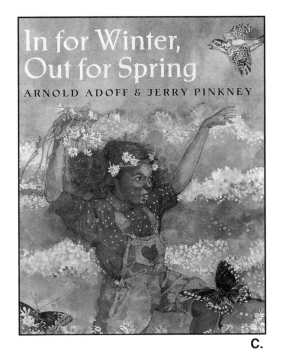

C.

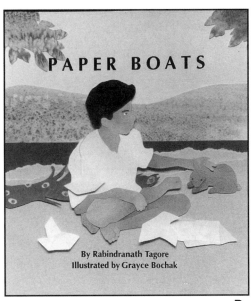

D.

A. *Father and Son* by Denizé Lauture; illustrated by Jonathan Green (see 1.15). **B.** *Northern Lullaby* by Nancy White Carlstrom; illustrated by Leo and Diane Dillon (see 1.6). **C.** *In for Winter, Out for Spring* by Arnold Adoff; illustrated by Jerry Pinkney (see 1.1). **D.** *Paper Boats* by Rabindranath Tagore; illustrated by Grayce Bochak (see 1.23).

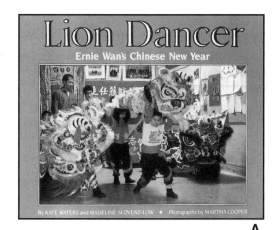

A.

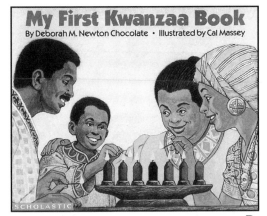

B.

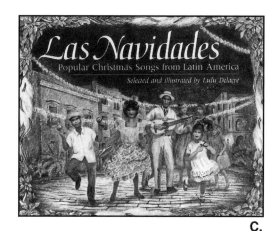

C.

D.

A. *Lion Dancer: Ernie Wan's Chinese New Year* by Kate Waters and Madeline Slovenz-Low; illustrated by Martha Cooper (see 3.9). **B.** *My First Kwanzaa Book* by Deborah M. Newton Chocolate; illustrated by Cal Massey (see 3.1). **C.** *Las Navidades: Popular Christmas Songs from Latin America* compiled and illustrated by Lulu Delacre (see 2.5). **D.** *Aïda* retold by Leontyne Price; illustrated by Leo and Diane Dillon (see 2.9).

1.15   Lauture, Denizé. **Father and Son.** Illustrated by Jonathan Green. Philomel Books, 1992. ISBN 0-399-21867-X. 32p. 6–9.

"Father and son / hand in hand / Up on the road / in the sun. . . ." In strong, simple words, this poem evokes the relationship between an African American father and son. They move up the road in perfect synchrony, "the soul of one / knowing the soul of the other," until at the end of the day, when it is time to go down the road again. Illustrator Jonathan Green sets the poem in the Gullah country of South Carolina, but children everywhere will understand the special bond between a child and his father.

1.16   Livingston, Myra Cohn. **Let Freedom Ring: A Ballad of Martin Luther King, Jr.** Illustrated by Samuel Byrd. Holiday House, 1992. ISBN 0-8234-0957-0. 32p. All ages.

Myra Cohn Livingston combines her poetry with the oratory of Martin Luther King Jr. to create this biographical tribute to the African American leader. Samuel Byrd's oil paintings are realistic representations of significant events in King's life. The final page gives specific dates for quotations from King's sermons and speeches as well as information about each scene depicted by the artwork.

1.17   Mado, Michio (translated by the Empress Michiko of Japan). **The Animals: Selected Poems.** Illustrated by Mitsumasa Anno. Margaret K. McElderry Books, 1992. ISBN 0-689-50574-4. 48p. All ages.

Twenty poems about animals are artfully presented in both Japanese and English versions. The poems catch the essence of a variety of animals and celebrate the wonder and joy of nature. The imagery is accessible to children. This is a delicate piece of bookmaking in which Anno's ornamental cut-paper animals echo the elegant sensitivity of the poetry.

1.18   Mathis, Sharon Bell. **Red Dog, Blue Fly: Football Poems.** Illustrated by Jan Spivey Gilchrist. Viking Penguin, 1991. ISBN 0-670-83623-0. 32p. 6–10.

These fourteen poems carry the reader through a football season. The players are elementary school boys—and one girl—and sometimes the going is rough. The action-filled poems reveal a variety of emotions, from beginners' jitters to the elation of winning the championship. The African American voices ring true, and Jan Spivey Gilchrist captures both the action and the

emotions in her lively watercolor illustrations. Young partici-
pants in team sports will recognize themselves in these poems.

1.19   Nye, Naomi Shihab, compiler. **This Same Sky: A Collection of
        Poems from around the World.** Four Winds Press, 1992. ISBN
        0-02-768440-7. 212p. 8–13 (est).

        This collection of 129 poems from sixty-eight countries resulted
        from Naomi Shihab Nye's request, during the Gulf Crisis, for
        poems celebrating people and life outside the United States.
        Readers are treated to a rich variety of form, rhythm, and voice.
        Nye achieves her goal of showing American children that others
        around the world share many experiences and "this same sky."
        Notes about the poets, a map indicating their homelands, a
        bibliography, and indexes to the poets by name and country are
        valuable extras. *ALA Notable Children's Books, 1993.*

1.20   Slier, Deborah, editor. **Make a Joyful Sound: Poems for Chil-
        dren by African-American Poets.** Illustrated by Cornelius Van
        Wright and Ying-Hwa Hu. Checkerboard Press, 1991. ISBN 1-
        56288-000-4. 108p. 3–12.

        Langston Hughes, Eloise Greenfield, Nikki Giovanni, Gwen-
        dolyn Brooks—these are some of the familiar African American
        poets whose work appears in this book. They are joined by some
        less familiar voices, such as Useni Eugene Perkins and Alfred
        Woods. This collection, illustrated in color and in black and
        white, is a useful resource for busy teachers. Ignore the errone-
        ous inclusion of Lee Bennett Hopkins as an African American
        poet.

1.21   Soto, Gary. **A Fire in My Hands: A Book of Poems.** Scholastic
        Hardcover Books, 1990. ISBN 0-590-45021-2. 64p. 10 and up.

        These twenty-three poems, according to Gary Soto's foreword,
        "keep alive the small moments which add up to a large moment:
        life itself." They derive from Soto's experiences growing up as a
        Mexican American in the San Joaquin Valley of California. Each
        poem is preceded by an anecdote that places the poem in con-
        text. At the end of the book, in a useful section titled "Questions
        and Answers about Poetry," Soto answers questions frequently
        asked of poets. *Notable 1991 Children's Trade Books in the Field of
        Social Studies.*

1.22   Soto, Gary. **Neighborhood Odes.** Illustrated by David Diaz.
        Harcourt Brace Jovanovich, 1992. ISBN 0-15-256879. 68p. 7 and
        up.

These twenty-one poems evoke an ordinary Mexican American neighborhood, but readers of all backgrounds will recognize and enjoy the humor, the joy, the familiarity of everyday experiences. Señor Leal's goat steals his pipe; one child writes a letter to the mayor about a pesky brother; another child feels ownership of "his" library when he reads thirty books for the summer read-a-thon. Gary Soto brings to life this neighborhood and the people who live there. *Notable 1992 Children's Trade Books in the Field of Social Studies.*

1.23   Tagore, Rabindranath. **Paper Boats.** Illustrated by Grayce Bochak. Caroline House, 1992. ISBN 1-878093-12-6. 32p. 6–10.

Rabindrath Tagore, India's Nobel Prize–winning essayist, poet, and playwright, provides a simple and eloquent poem about a young boy who launches paper boats and hopes that they will reach people in another country. The paper illustrations accurately highlight the simplicity of the piece and the Indian countryside. Tagore's work is widely read and admired across India.

1.24   Yolen, Jane, editor. **Street Rhymes around the World.** Illustrated by Seventeen International Artists. Boyds Mills Press/Wordsong, 1992. ISBN 1-878093-53-3. 40p. 4–10.

This anthology of children's street rhymes and counting songs from seventeen countries has three features that set it apart from similar collections. First, the illustrations are drawn by artists from the respective countries. Second, most of the rhymes have been transliterated to maintain their original sounds. Third, each country has a full two-page layout to enable simultaneous appreciation of rhymes and accompanying artwork. Teachers could easily incorporate the rhymes from this unique book into a multicultural celebration in the classroom.

2 The Arts

2.1 Barboza, Steven. **I Feel like Dancing: A Year with Jacques d'Amboise and the National Dance Institute.** Photographs by Carolyn George d'Amboise. Crown, 1992. ISBN 0-517-58455-7. 48p. All ages. Nonfiction.

Illustrated with color photographs, this book describes, month by month, a school year of preparations for the National Dance Institute's Event of the Year. Led by Jacques d'Amboise, who is known as the Pied Piper of Dance, a multiethnic group of New York City children put together a spectacular dance event called "Chakra: A Celebration of India." The text includes photographs of the event in which a thousand children took part.

2.2 Bryan, Ashley, compiler. **All Night, All Day: A Child's First Book of African-American Spirituals.** Illustrated by Ashley Bryan. Atheneum, 1991. ISBN 0-689-31662-3. 48p. All ages (est). Nonfiction.

This is another in the set of collections of African American spirituals compiled by Ashley Bryan. Some familiar songs— "This Little Light of Mine," "O When the Saints Go Marching In"—are interspersed with lesser-known ones in this introduction to twenty of these uniquely African American creations. A closing note suggests that this collection "could really be called Spirituals for the Young and ALL!" Bryan's jewel-toned illustrations sparkle like sunlit stained glass. The book includes piano accompaniment and guitar chords. *Coretta Scott King Illustration Honor Book, 1992.*

2.3 Burgie, Irving. **Caribbean Carnival: Songs of the West Indies.** Illustrated by Frané Lessac. Tambourine Books, 1992. ISBN 0-688-10778-0. 30p. 4 and up. Nonfiction.

This collection of Caribbean folk songs begins with Harry Belafonte's signature, "Day-O." It includes twelve other songs of varying types, including play songs and ballads. The music, along with Frané Lessac's colorful, two-dimensional illustrations, conjures up images of palm trees, banana boats, cool blue waters, and hot sand. Musical arrangements for voice, piano, and guitar accompany the pictures. An afterword by writer Rosa Guy provides a useful historical context. *Notable 1992 Children's Trade Books in the Field of Social Studies.*

2.4 Cummings, Pat, complier and editor. **Talking with Artists: Conversations with Victoria Chess, Pat Cummings, Leo and Diane Dillon, Richard Egielski, Lois Ehlert, Lisa Campbell Ernst, Tom Feelings, Steven Kellogg, Jerry Pinkney, Amy Schwartz, Lane Smith, Chris Van Allsburg and David Wiesner.** Bradbury Press, 1992. ISBN 0-02-724245-5. 96p. 8 and up. Nonfiction.

Pat Cummings has compiled and edited conversations with fourteen contemporary artists, several of whom are African Americans. Each entry begins with a brief autobiographical sketch, followed by a question-and-answer format describing sources of inspiration, techniques, materials, family and pets, and how that artist got to do his or her first book. This work doubles as an art catalog, describing sample illustrations by each artist by name, medium, and size. Childhood photos of each artist will captivate young readers. This will be practical, inspirational, and useful in many ways in the classroom. *ALA Notable Children's Books, 1993; Boston Globe–Horn Book Nonfiction Award, 1992; NCTE Orbis Pictus Honor Book, 1993.*

2.5 Delacre, Lulu, compiler. **Las Navidades: Popular Christmas Songs from Latin America.** Illustrated by Lulu Delacre. Scholastic Hardcover Books/Lucas Evans Books, 1990. ISBN 0-590-43548-5. 33p. All ages (est). Nonfiction.

This bilingual (Spanish-English) edition of twelve traditional songs traces the celebration of the Christmas season—Las Navidades—in Latin America from Christmas Eve to the Epiphany in January. The songs are mostly from Puerto Rico, Delacre's native country; however, reference is made in footnotes to Christmas customs and traditions from various other Latin American countries, including Mexico, Venezuela, and the Dominican Republic. Musical scores are provided at the end of the book. The illustrations depict scenes typical of the holiday season.

2.6 Haskins, James. **Black Dance in America: A History through Its People.** Thomas Y. Crowell, 1990. ISBN 0-690-04659-6. 232p. 11 and up. Nonfiction.

This photo-illustrated survey of the history of Black dance in America begins with a description of the practice of "dancing the slaves" on ships for exercise. Tracing the roots of dance to Africa, author James Haskins focuses on people who have adapted and perpetuated the ancient dance forms and developed them into such varieties as ballet, tap, and jazz. Dancers introduced include Bert Williams, Bill "Bojangles" Robinson, Katherine Dunham, Chubby Checker, and Gregory Hines, as well as companies, schools, and choreographers. This is a solid companion to James Haskins's *Black Music in America* and *Black Theater in America*. *Best Books for Young Adults, 1991; Coretta Scott King Writing Honor Book, 1991.*

2.7   Langstaff, John, compiler and editor. **Climbing Jacob's Ladder: Heroes of the Bible in African-American Spirituals.** Illustrated by Ashley Bryan. Margaret K. McElderry Books, 1991. ISBN 0-689-50494-2. 30p. 4 and up. Nonfiction.

Old Testament heroes are the focus of the songs in this collection. The spirituals celebrate the triumph of good over evil, kindness over selfishness, and hope over hopelessness. Songs such as "Rock-a My Soul" and "Go Down Moses" capture the determination of the oppressed to liberate themselves. The illustrations are notable for their style and color as well as for the depiction of the biblical heroes as people of African descent. Musical scores for piano, guitar, and voice are provided for each spiritual.

2.8   Medearis, Angela Shelf, compiler. **The Zebra-Riding Cowboy: A Folk Song from the Old West.** Illustrated by María Cristina Brusca. Henry Holt, 1992. ISBN 0-8050-1712-7. 32p. All ages. Nonfiction.

In this Western folksong, an "educated fellow" shows up at the camp and asks to borrow a horse. Thinking he is just a greenhorn, the cowboys give him the wild Zebra dun and expect to have some fun at the stranger's expense. But the cowboys are in for a big surprise. An afterword places the song in historical context and explains the casting of the stranger as African American and the presence of African American and Hispanic cowboys. The musical score appears on the endpapers.

2.9   Price, Leontyne, reteller. **Aïda.** Illustrated by Leo and Diane Dillon. Harcourt Brace Jovanovich/Gulliver Books, 1990. ISBN 0-15-200405-X. 32p. 10 and up. Nonfiction.

One of the best known opera singers to perform the role of the Egyptian Princess Aïda is Leontyne Price, the African American diva. Illustrated with paintings of Egyptian friezes, her retelling of Giuseppe Verdi's opera "Aïda" captures the drama of war, palace intrigue, and tragic forbidden love. An appended "Storyteller's Note" adds a special curtain call. The picture book format notwithstanding, the lengthy text makes this book suitable for older readers. *ALA Notable Children's Books, 1991; Coretta Scott King Illustration Award, 1991.*

2.10   Sullivan, Charles, editor. **Children of Promise: African-American Literature and Art for Young People.** Harry N. Abrams, 1991. ISBN 0-8109-3170-2. 126p. 10 and up (est). Nonfiction.

This anthology for older readers includes literature and art selected to tell the history of African Americans from the time of slavery to the twentieth century. It includes such poets and writers as James Baldwin, Gwendolyn Brooks, and W. E. B. DuBois juxtaposed with the art of people like Romare Bearden, Jacob Lawrence, and William H. Johnson. It also includes work by Walt Whitman, Thomas Jefferson, Winslow Homer, and other prominent whites whose lives or works touched on African American life and history. *Best Books for Young Adults, 1992.*

3 Ceremonies and Celebrations

3.1   Chocolate, Deborah M. Newton. **My First Kwanzaa Book.** Illustrated by Cal Massey. Scholastic/Cartwheel Books, 1992. ISBN 0-590-45762-4. 28p. 5–8 (est). Nonfiction.

"When Mama says, 'It's Kwanzaa time,' Daddy flies our red, black and green flag." In this introductory book, an unnamed boy describes the family's preparations for and activities during the seven days of Kwanzaa, a holiday celebrated in December to honor African American history and culture. An afterword provides factual information about the origins of the holiday. The book also includes an explanation of Nguzo Saba, or the "seven principles" of Kwanzaa, and a glossary of Swahili words used during Kwanzaa. Colorful illustrations in acrylics and colored pencil extend the text.

3.2   Clifton, Lucille. **Everett Anderson's Christmas Coming.** Illustrated by Jan Spivey Gilchrist. Henry Holt, 1991. ISBN 0-8050-1549-3. 28p. 4–8. Fiction.

"Everett Anderson / loves the sound / of Merry Christmases / all around." In simple, lyrical verse, Lucille Clifton expresses the excitement of a little African American boy at Christmastime— from December 20th to Christmas Day. Everett lives in the housing projects with his mother and, like many children in many places, finds joy in the season. Newly reissued with red-bordered color illustrations by Jan Spivey Gilchrist, this book will connect with any youngster who just cannot wait until Christmas day.

3.3   Dorros, Arthur. **Tonight Is Carnaval.** Illustrated by the Club de Madras Virgin del Carmen of Lima, Peru. Dutton's Children's Books, 1991. ISBN 0-525-44641-9. 28p. 5 and up. Fiction.

Set in the Andes Mountains and narrated by a young Peruvian boy, this story tells of the boy's eager preparation for and anticipation of Carnaval, a celebration occurring just before Lent. The text is illustrated with folk-art wall hangings called *arpilleras*, created and designed by members of a cooperative in Lima, Peru. A glossary of Spanish terms is at the end of the text as are explanations of aspects of the pictures that might be confusing to young readers. *Notable 1991 Children's Trade Books in the Field of Social Studies.*

3.4   Hoyt-Goldsmith, Diane. **Totem Pole.** Photographs by Lawrence Migdale. Holiday House, 1990. ISBN 0-8234-0809-4. 32p. 8–12. Nonfiction.

David, a young member of the Tsimshian tribe in Washington, takes pride in being the son of a woodcarver. Aided by color photographs, he describes his father's step-by-step process of carving a totem pole for the neighboring Klallam tribe and the ceremonies that accompany the raising of the pole. The book makes clear that while the Tsimshian Indians maintain their ancient customs, they are also quite contemporary. A glossary and index are included. *Notable 1990 Children's Trade Books in the Field of Social Studies.*

3.5   Joseph, Lynn. **An Island Christmas.** Illustrated by Catherine Stock. Clarion Books, 1992. ISBN 0-395-58761-1. 30p. 4–8. Fiction.

"De first day of Christmas holidays . . . ," Rose yells, "Is beach time!" But first she must help with the sorrell drink, and the black currant cake, and the decorations, and the gifts. The whole family joins in this Trinidadian Christmas celebration. An author's note gives information about Trinidad and Tobago and their Christmas customs. In spite of Catherine Stock's depiction of Rosie in Topsy-like braids, the book works as a lively celebration of an important family and community tradition in a place where Christmas is never white. *Notable 1992 Children's Trade Books in the Field of Social Studies.*

3.6   Peters, Russell M. **Clambake: A Wampanoag Tradition.** Photographs by John Madama. Lerner, 1992. ISBN 0-8225-2651-4. 48p. 8–11. Nonfiction.

This book is part of the We Are Still Here series focusing on contemporary Native Americans. In this photo essay, written by members of the Wampanoag tribe in southern Massachusetts, Steven Peters, a twelve-year-old Wampanoag, is learning how to prepare and host a traditional *appanaug,* or clambake. The book follows him through the preparations and the clambake itself, and then leaves him getting ready to play baseball the next day. A word list, pronunciation guide, and bibliography are included. See also *People of the Breaking Day* by Marcia Sewall

(7.13). *Notable 1992 Children's Trade Books in the Field of Social Studies.*

3.7   Porter, A. P. **Kwanzaa.** Illustrated by Janice Lee Porter. Carolrhoda Books, 1991. ISBN 0-87614-668-X. 56p. 5–7. Nonfiction.

This book in the On My Own series accurately describes the purposes and principles surrounding the African American Kwanzaa celebration. Written much like an easy reader, the text is simple enough for early readers, but detailed enough to include Swahili phrases as well as the concepts of African American pride and self-esteem. Realistic watercolors complement the informational text. This book would be particularly helpful for those without background knowledge of Kwanzaa or those wanting to start their own Kwanzaa celebration.

3.8   Rosen, Michael J. **Elijah's Angel: A Story for Chanukah and Christmas.** Illustrated by Aminah Brenda Lynn Robinson. Harcourt Brace Jovanovich, 1992. ISBN 0-15-225394-7. 32p. 8 and up. Fiction.

Michael, a nine-year-old Jewish boy, makes friends with Elijah, an elderly African American barber and woodcarver. One year when Christmas and Chanukah fall at the same time, Elijah gives Michael a carved angel. Michael fears he cannot keep a "graven image," but his parents help him understand the true meaning of Elijah's angel. Elijah Pierce was a renowned woodcarver from Columbus, Ohio, and both the writer and the illustrator were inspired by him and his work. *Notable 1992 Children's Trade Books in the Field of Social Studies.*

3.9   Waters, Kate, and Madeline Slovenz-Low. **Lion Dancer: Ernie Wan's Chinese New Year.** Photographs by Martha Cooper. Scholastic Hardcover Books, 1990. ISBN 0-590-43046-7. 30p. 4–10 (est). Nonfiction.

Ernie Wan, the young narrator, lives in New York's Chinatown and invites us to celebrate the Chinese New Year with his family. The many color photographs detail the preparations for this important holiday and the rituals associated with it. For example, we learn about the old belief that wearing something new renders a person unrecognizable to the evil spirits. The highlight of the holiday is Ernie's performance of the dramatic lion dance in the New Year's parade. *Notable 1990 Children's Trade Books in the Field of Social Studies.*

3.10   Wood, Ted (with Wanbli Numpa Afraid of Hawk). **A Boy Becomes a Man at Wounded Knee.** Walker, 1992. ISBN 0-8027-8175-6. 46p. 8–10. Nonfiction.

Wanbli Numpa Afraid of Hawk relates the story of his participation in the Big Foot Memorial Ride on the 100th anniversary of the massacre of over 350 Lakota (Sioux) Indians at Wounded Knee in the Badlands of South Dakota. For Wanbli Numpa, the difficult journey on horseback is an initiation into manhood. Color photographs capture the important details and the cold December landscapes as the Lakota honor their ancestors and try to "mend the sacred hoop" of their lives. An introduction tells the story of Wounded Knee. *Notable 1992 Children's Trade Books in the Field of Social Studies.*

4 People to Know and Places to Go

4.1   Beirne, Barbara. **A Pianist's Debut: Preparing for the Concert Stage.** Photographs by Barbara Beirne. Carolrhoda Books, 1990. ISBN 0-87614-432-6. 56p. 9–12 (est). Nonfiction.

This book is part of a series depicting young children in roles that could lead to future careers. Leah Yoon, an eleven-year-old Korean American pianist, spends many hours a day practicing the piano. She aspires to be a concert pianist and moves with her grandmother from California to New York in order to attend the Julliard School of Music. The book gives glimpses of her daily life and the role of family members in supporting her piano playing.

4.2   Berck, Judith. **No Place to Be: Voices of Homeless Children.** Houghton Mifflin, 1992. ISBN 0-395-53350-3. 148p. 10 and up. Nonfiction.

Through the words, poems, and stories of homeless children, author Judith Berck presents a devastating account of homeless youth in New York City. The book is meticulously researched and includes chapters that focus on the problems that arise when homeless families are forced to live in shelters or welfare hotels—finding privacy, getting an education, family separations, health risks, identity, and stress. *ALA Notable Children's Books, 1992.*

4.3   Brusca, María Cristina. **On the Pampas.** Illustrated by María Cristina Brusca. Henry Holt, 1991. ISBN 0-8050-1548-5. 32p. 5–8. Nonfiction.

The author shares childhood memories of an unforgettable summer on her grandparents' ranch on the pampas (grasslands) of Argentina. María Cristina Brusca and a younger cousin join in the work of the gauchos (cowboys): caring for horses, lassoing calves, herding cattle. They also enjoy the social life of the countryside: listening to stories, attending an outdoor party, singing, and dancing. Brusca's watercolor illustrations depict these regional scenes and more. The inside cover contains a map and a "pictionary" of Spanish words, including a pronunciation guide. *Notable 1991 Children's Trade Books in the Field of Social Studies.*

4.4 Ekoomiak, Normee. **Arctic Memories.** Illustrated by Normee Ekoomiak. Henry Holt, 1990. ISBN 0-8050-1254-0. 32p. All ages. Nonfiction.

Normee Ekoomiak, an Inuk born near James Bay in Arctic Quebec, shares his childhood with readers through his art and this bilingual (Inuktitut/English) text. Yes, he slept in an *iglu* in winter, but his memories are also full of active play and of a severe and demanding natural world inhabited by snowy owls, polar bears, seals, and geese, as well as by rarer spirits such as the Sedna (the mermaid sea goddess) and the narwhal (son of the Sedna). Acrylic and appliqué illustrations take us into the world of Ekoomiak's past, a world permanently changed by the erection of a large hydroelectric dam. *NCTE Orbis Pictus Honor Book, 1991; Notable 1990 Children's Trade Books in the Field of Social Studies.*

4.5 Haskins, Francine. **I Remember "121."** Illustrated by Francine Haskins. Children's Book Press, 1991. ISBN 0-89239-100-6. 32p. 5–7. Nonfiction.

Using brightly colored, stylized illustrations, Francine Haskins introduces readers to an African American family of the 1950s. Centered on the house in Washington, D.C., where she grew up, this autobiographical picture book recalls large family dinners, Howdy-Doody, the birth of a baby brother, her father's days off, and other details of Francine's daily life from age three to age nine. Contemporary children can still find something to connect with in this look at a traditional extended family.

4.6 Haskins, Jim. **Count Your Way through India.** Illustrations by Liz Brenner Dodson. Carolrhoda Books, 1990. ISBN 0-87614-414-8. 32p. 7–10 (est). Nonfiction.

Part of the Count Your Way series, this book introduces readers to counting from one to ten in the Hindi language. The focus is on introducing various aspects of India, including banyan trees, the flag of India, Mohandas Gandhi, the Taj Mahal, the Diwali festival of lights, the countries bordering India, the spices of Indian cooking, wildlife in India, and Ravana. The text and color illustrations serve as an introduction to an East Indian culture, and many U.S. children will enjoy counting to ten in a new language.

4.7   Hauptly, Denis J. **Puerto Rico: An Unfinished Story.** Atheneum, 1991. ISBN 0-689-31431-0. 133p. 12 and up. Nonfiction.

Replete with names, dates, laws, and other details, this book focuses on the status of Puerto Rico and whether it should remain a commonwealth, become a state, or become an independent nation. Author Denis Hauptly presents a detailed and balanced treatment of the history of the island from before the time of Columbus, through its colonization by both Spain and the United States, to the present day. He discusses the options for the future that must be determined by the Puerto Rican people.

4.8   Hewett, Joan. **Laura Loves Horses.** Photographs by Richard Hewett. Clarion Books, 1990. ISBN 0-89919-844-9. 40p. 7–10. Fiction.

Having a father who works at a California boarding and riding stable and living right next to the stable have fueled Laura Santanna's desire not only to ride but to compete in horse shows. This book chronicles some of eight-year-old Laura's early riding adventures as well as her experiences at her first horse show. Horseback-riding enthusiasts will enjoy reading about her experiences as well as looking at the full-color pictures.

4.9   Hoig, Stan. **People of the Sacred Arrows: The Southern Cheyenne Today.** Cobblehill Books, 1992. ISBN 0-525-65088-1. 130p. 10 and up. Nonfiction.

This volume offers an honest and sympathetic view of contemporary Cheyenne Indians in Oklahoma. Stan Hoig tells something of the Cheyenne's history, especially the injustices that they have suffered at the hands of whites. The focus, however, is on today and the ways in which the Cheyenne manage to live in two worlds, overcoming injustices and keeping their traditions and values alive. Hoig briefly profiles the work of individual Cheyennes and ends on a hopeful note. Black-and-white photographs and old prints complement the readable text.

4.10   Hoyt-Goldsmith, Diane. **Arctic Hunter.** Photographs by Lawrence Migdale. Holiday House, 1992. ISBN 0-8234-0972-4. 32p. 8–12. Nonfiction.

Reggie lives in Alaska above the Arctic Circle. In June, he and his family go to their camp to hunt and fish in the traditional Inupiaq way. Then they return to their village and live the modern way—with supermarkets, pizza, and video games. With the help of color photographs, Reggie describes his life as a proud Inupiaq, how his people have changed with the times, and how they still keep the old traditions. Section titles are in English and in Inupiak. A glossary and index are included. See also *Eskimo Boy: Life in an Inupiaq Eskimo Village* by Russ Kendall (4.14). *Notable 1992 Children's Trade Books in the Field of Social Studies.*

4.11 Hoyt-Goldsmith, Diane. **Pueblo Storyteller.** Photographs by Lawrence Migdale. Holiday House, 1991. ISBN 0-8234-0864-7. 32p. 8–12. Nonfiction.

April, a young Cochiti Indian girl who lives with her grandparents in the Cochiti Pueblo near Santa Fe, New Mexico, describes the life and customs of her people. Her grandparents are potters who make, among other things, storyteller figurines. As in Diane Hoyt-Goldsmith's companion volumes, *Totem Pole* (3.4) and *Artic Hunter* (4.10), the text and photographs offer a clear sense of modern Native Americans keeping old traditions alive while living thoroughly modern lives. An index, glossary, and pronunciation guide are helpful, as are the informative photo captions. See also *Pueblo Boy: Growing Up in Two Worlds* by Marcia Keegan (4.13) and *Children of Clay: A Family of Pueblo Potters* by Rina Swentzell (4.24). *Notable 1991 Children's Trade Books in the Field of Social Studies.*

4.12 Hunter, Latoya. **The Diary of Latoya Hunter: My First Year in Junior High.** Crown, 1992. ISBN 0-517-58511-1. 131p. 10–12. Nonfiction.

Twelve-year-old Latoya Hunter records, in her diary named Janice, the events of her first year of junior high school in the Bronx. For her, it is a difficult year: she experiences conflict with her mother; her visit "back home" to Jamaica is a big disappointment; her "first love" turns sour. On the other hand, she is a bridesmaid at her brother's wedding and a loving aunt to her new nephew. Her perceptive and sensitive observations will strike a familiar chord with many pre-adolescents.

4.13 Keegan, Marcia. **Pueblo Boy: Growing Up in Two Worlds.** Photographs by Marcia Keegan. Cobblehill Books, 1991. ISBN 0-525-65060-1. 48p. 7–9 (est). Nonfiction.

Timmy Roybal is ten, and in many ways he is typical of contemporary American boys his age. Although he lives in the ancient Pueblo village of San Ildefonso in New Mexico, he rides a bike to school, does school work on a computer, loves sports, and enjoys fishing. At the same time he is learning about his Pueblo Indian heritage and traditions and is participating in the tribal rituals and ceremonies of his people. Color photographs depict Timmy's daily activities in two worlds. See also *Pueblo Storyteller* by Diane Hoyt-Goldsmith (4.11) and *Children of Clay: A Family of Pueblo Potters* by Rina Swentzell (4.24). *Notable 1991 Children's Trade Books in the Field of Stocial Studies.*

4.14   Kendall, Russ. **Eskimo Boy: Life in an Inupiaq Eskimo Village.** Photographs by Russ Kendall. Scholastic Hardcover Books, 1992. ISBN 0-590-43695-3. 40p. 5–7 (est). Nonfiction.

Norman Kokeok is a seven-year-old Inupiaq Eskimo living in the island village of Shishmaref, Alaska. This book describes for young readers what his life is like. It emphasizes how much Norman is like "typical" American seven year olds, although it shows how the harsh climate affects village life. The book includes a glossary of Inupiaq Eskimo words and an afterword with information about modern-day Eskimos. Color photographs will appeal to young readers. See also *Arctic Hunter* by Diane Hoyt-Goldsmith (4.10). *Notable 1992 Children's Trade Books in the Field of Social Studies.*

4.15   Knight, Margy Burns. **Talking Walls.** Illustrations by Anne Sibley O'Brien. Tilbury House, 1992. ISBN 0-88448-102-6. 34p. 8–10. Nonfiction.

From endpaper to endpaper, *Talking Walls* takes the reader on an international tour of the world's walls, from the Great Wall of China to the Berlin Wall. Was the wall built to divide or unite? What does the wall say about the language, conflicts, and religions of a people? Can we imagine a world without walls? The vibrantly colored pastel illustrations vividly portray voices of the talking walls as they impact on children globally.

4.16   Lewington, Anna, adapter. **Antonio's Rain Forest.** Photographs by Edward Parker. Carolrhoda Books, 1993. ISBN 0-87614-749-X. 48p. 7–10. Nonfiction.

Antonio José is an eight-year-old boy who lives in the Amazon rain forest of Brazil. He describes everyday life there, where his father is a rubber tapper. He also makes the case for preserving the rain forest and his family's way of life. Photographs, maps, and drawings help tell the story, while interspersed expository text adds factual material. The book also explains the political

A.

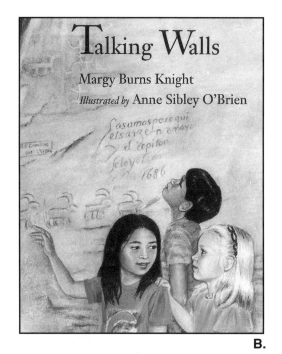

B.

C.

A. *Chi-hoon: A Korean Girl* by Patricia McMahon; photographs by Michael F. O'Brien (see 4.18). **B.** *Talking Walls* by Margy Burns Knight; illustrated by Anne Sibley O'Brien (see 4.15). **C.** *Himalaya: Vanishing Cultures* by Jan Reynolds; photographs by Jan Reynolds (see 4.21).

A.

B.

C.

A. *Count Your Way through India* by Jim Haskins; illustrated by Liz Brenner Dodson (see 4.6). **B.** *A Family in Taiwan* by Ling Yu; photographs by Chen Ming-jeng (see 4.27). **C.** *Arctic Memories* written and illustrated by Normee Ekoomiak (see 4.4).

context in which Antonio's family lives. A glossary and index are included.

4.17   Lomas Garza, Carmen (as told to Harriet Rohmer). **Family Pictures/Cuadros de Familia.** Illustrated by Carmen Lomas Garza. Children's Book Press, 1990. ISBN 0-89239-050-6. 31p. 7 and up. Nonfiction.

Through the art and text of *Family Pictures*, artist Carmen Lomas Garza weaves together a rich cultural fabric that tells of her childhood in the border town of Kingsville, Texas, including detailed scenes of her Hispanic American family and community. Fourteen "story pictures" chronicle her life from age five to age twelve, when she knew she wanted to become an artist. Presented in English and Spanish, *Family Pictures* is long on instructional possibilities that span the elementary school curriculum. *ALA Notable Children's Books, 1991.*

4.18   McMahon, Patricia. **Chi-hoon: A Korean Girl.** Photographs by Michael F. O'Brien. Boyds Mills Press/Caroline House, 1993. ISBN 1-56397-026-0. 48p. 8–10. Nonfiction.

"All Korean children are expected to keep a diary." Kim Chi-hoon, an eight-year-old girl living in Seoul, is no exception. Excerpts from her diary help to frame this account of a week in the life of Chi-hoon and her family. Color photographs and extensive text introduce the details of daily life in this modern city. American readers will find many similarities to their own lives, as well as many differences.

4.19   Mennen, Ingrid, and Niki Daly. **Somewhere in Africa.** Illustrated by Nicolaas Maritz. Dutton Children's Books, 1992. ISBN 0-525-44848-9. 32p. 6–8 (est). Fiction.

Ashraf knows that somewhere in Africa lions and zebras and crocodiles live in the wild, but he has met them only between the pages of his favorite book. He lives in a large, bustling city, and as he treks to the library to "stalk the shelves" of the "jungle of books," the reader accompanies him in taking in the colorful urban sights and sounds. The authors and artist, all from Cape Town, South Africa, pay tribute to their city and also correct a commonly held misconception about the continent of Africa. *Notable 1992 Children's Trade Books in the Field of Social Studies.*

4.20   Regguinti, Gordon. **The Sacred Harvest: Ojibway Wild Rice Gathering.** Photographs by Dale Kakkak. Lerner, 1992. ISBN 0-8225-2650-6. 48p. 8–11. Nonfiction.

Part of the We Are Still Here series about Native Americans today, this book follows Glen Jackson Jr. as he learns to harvest wild rice. Glen lives on an Ojibway reservation in northern Minnesota. For the Ojibway, wild rice is a sacred food, and in learning to harvest it, Glen is carrying on the traditions of his people. Photographs provide much of the information for this book, which also includes a word list and suggestions for further reading. Author Gordon Regguinti is a member of the Leech Lake Band of Ojibway. *Notable 1992 Children's Trade Books in the Field of Social Studies.*

4.21   Reynolds, Jan. **Himalaya: Vanishing Cultures.** Photographs by Jan Reynolds. Harcourt Brace Jovanovich, 1991. ISBN 0-15-234465-9. 30p. 8–11 (est). Nonfiction.

Yangshi, a young Sherpa living in a Himalayan village, introduces readers to the origin of the Sherpa people, drinking *chia*, buying food and trading goods at the market, and going to the monastery to meet the Lama and spin the prayer wheels. Readers will experience a taste of what life is like in the Tibetan highlands of the Himalayas and will gain an understanding of one of the world's vanishing cultures. *Notable 1991 Children's Trade Books in the Field of Social Studies.*

4.22   Reynolds, Jan. **Sahara: Vanishing Cultures.** Photographs by Jan Reynolds. Harcourt Brace Jovanovich, 1991. ISBN 0-15-269959-7. 30p. 8–11. Nonfiction.

Through the story of the daily life of a boy named Manda, author Jan Reynolds describes the contemporary social customs of the nomadic Tuareg people of the Sahara. Readers are introduced to real personalities through the eyes and experiences of Manda and his family. The Tuareg culture comes to the reader in the voice of a storyteller and is strengthened by vivid, realistic photographs. Like its companion, *Himalaya* (4.21), this book offers an empathetic understanding of one of the world's vanishing cultures. *Notable 1991 Children's Trade Books in the Field of Social Studies.*

4.23   Schmidt, Diane. **I Am a Jesse White Tumbler.** Photographs by Diane Schmidt. Albert Whitman, 1990. ISBN 0-8075-3444-7. 40p. All ages. Nonfiction.

"Last year we did 570 shows and went to twenty different states." Being a member of the Jesse White Tumblers, a team mostly made up of African American youngsters from the

Cabrini-Green housing project in the inner city of Chicago, is an exciting part of Kenyon Conner's life. The mover and shaker behind the team is Jesse White, a former teacher who is an Illinois state representative. In this photo essay, Kenyon helps us see just how impressive these dedicated and talented young people really are.

4.24   Swentzell, Rina. **Children of Clay: A Family of Pueblo Potters.** Photographs by Bill Steen. Lerner, 1992. ISBN 0-8225-2654-9. 40p. 8–10. Nonfiction.

An extended family of Tewa Indian potters from the Santa Clara Pueblo in New Mexico follow ancient customs to create their distinctive pottery. Led by Gia (mother) Rose, they gather the clay, clean it, shape it, dry it, polish it, fire it, and sell some of the pieces. The author is herself a Santa Clara potter, and her text, with many Tewa words interspersed, has the ring of authenticity. Color photographs make the pottery process accessible to young readers. A word list and bibliography are included in this book in the We Are Still Here series about Native Americans today. See also *Pueblo Storyteller* by Diane Hoyt-Goldsmith (4.11) and *Pueblo Boy: Growing Up in Two Worlds* by Marcia Keegan (4.13).

4.25   Thompson, Peggy. **City Kids in China.** Photographs by Paul S. Conklin. HarperCollins, 1991. ISBN 0-06-021655-7. 144p. 10 and up (est). Nonfiction.

The author and photographer provide the flavor of life from a child's point of view in present-day Changsha, a city located in central China. Captivating black-and-white photographs depict people shopping in open-air markets, the noodle maker frying noodles, and the barber giving a shave outdoors. Special events and individuals are highlighted in boxes. The index aids the beginning researcher in this highly informative and entertaining book.

4.26   Wells, Ruth. **A to Zen: A Book of Japanese Culture.** Illustrated by Yoshi. Picture Book Studio, 1992. ISBN 0-88708-175-4. 24p. 7 and up. Nonfiction.

Ichi, ni, san (1, 2, 3). Open this sophisticated alphabet book—with the spine on the right—and meet modern Japan, its language, and its culture. The topic on each page is given in Japanese—on the right, read from top to bottom—and in English. Learn about *aikido, origami, sushi,* and *yen.* Meet a *daruma,* a doll that can help you meet a goal. Savor the colorful illustrations, originally done in detailed batik, that make this book an informative work of art. *Notable 1992 Children's Trade Books in the Field of Social Studies.*

4.27 Yu, Ling. **A Family in Taiwan.** Photographs by Chen Ming-jeng. Lerner, 1990. ISBN 0-8225-1685-3. 32p. 10 and up (est). Nonfiction.

The appealing photographs immediately draw the reader into the life of twelve-year-old Fang-hsin and her family in Taipei, Taiwan. On each page, readers see the family members pictured in their daily routines at home, school, and work. Celebrations of special holidays are also depicted. In addition, facts about Taiwan and its geography are presented at the front and back of the book.

5 Concepts and Other Useful Information

5.1 Emberley, Rebecca. **Taking a Walk: A Book in Two Languages/Caminando: Un Libro en Dos Lenguas.** Illustrated by Rebecca Emberley. Little, Brown, 1990. ISBN 0-316-23640-3. 28p. 4–6.

This book invites the young child to take a walk—through the neighborhood, to the school and playground, down the street, across the bridge, by the park, and back home. Scenes and objects along the way are shown in simple, colorful forms. The text consists of identifying labels and a sentence or phrase at the bottom of the page, all in English and Spanish. Older learners of either English or Spanish as a second language might also find this book useful.

5.2 Falwell, Cathryn. **Shape Space.** Illustrated by Cathryn Falwell. Clarion Books, 1992. ISBN 0-395-61305-1. 32p. 4–8.

A young African American gymnast opens a box only to find bright, vibrant, colorful geometric shapes. She empties the box of rectangles, triangles, semicircles, circles, and squares and, after a brief contemplation, decides to dance, rock, step, stack, wear, and share the shapes. Following a romp with a "shapely" friend, the gymnast returns the shapes to the box and sits on top. Author Cathryn Falwell's playful, sometimes-rhyming verse, along with her full-color illustrations, creates a whimsical exploration into geometric shapes.

5.3 Garne, S. T. **One White Sail.** Illustrated by Lisa Etre. Green Tiger Press, 1992. ISBN 0-671-75579-X. 26p. 3–6.

Rhythmic verse and bright watercolor paintings make this counting book attractive and appealing. We see one white sail at sunrise, and go through the day to "ten boats asleep 'neath a pale island moon." Although the numerals are not included, the pictured people can be easily counted. (Unfortunately the "three girls walking / with baskets of bread" look more like women than girls.) Even children beyond the "counting book" age can enjoy this book for its vivid pictures of island life.

5.4 Greenspun, Adele Aron. **Daddies.** Illustrated by Adele Aron Greenspun. Philomel Books, 1991. ISBN 0-399-22259-6. 48p. 4–6.

With a hug and a kiss on the front cover, *Daddies* introduces the special relationship between fathers and children across cultures. From the first hello to a baby through the teaching, guiding, and playing of childhood, *Daddies* celebrates the loyalty, devotion, and joy that can make a special bond between a father and child. The black-and-white photographs accompany a poetic text to depict an array of emotions experienced by fathers and their children.

5.5 Hausherr, Rosmarie. **What Instrument Is This?** Scholastic Hardcover Books, 1992. ISBN 0-590-44644-4. 38p. 5–10.

Color photographs of multicultural children holding instruments, their faces full of curiosity, are coupled with the lead-in caption that asks: "What instrument is . . . ?" For each of the eighteen instruments, the answer is revealed on the following page in a black-and-white photograph, along with information about the instrument, its construction, and its use. From cover to cover, including the glossary and final notes, music is portrayed as a source of joy for everyone—young and old, the physically and mentally challenged, male and female.

5.6 Jenness, Aylette. **Families: A Celebration of Diversity, Commitment, and Love.** Photographs by Aylette Jenness. Houghton Mifflin, 1990. ISBN 0-395-47038-2. 47p. 7 and up.

The changes in the "traditional" family unit are compellingly presented in this black-and-white photo essay. Seventeen young people from varied cultures describe in the first person their ideas of family structure and its joys and challenges. The book begins by asking, "Families—what are they?" The answer lies in the faces, voices, and artwork of the adults and children that participated in this special project of the Children's Museum of Boston. *Notable 1990 Children's Trade Books in the Field of Social Studies.*

5.7 Lankford, Mary D. **Hopscotch around the World.** Illustrated by Karen Milone. Morrow Junior Books, 1992. ISBN 0-688-08420-6. 48p. 5–10.

"Hopscotch has been played throughout history in almost every country of the world," according to author Mary Lankford. This book presents nineteen versions of hopscotch, with diagrams and directions for play. The variants come from places as diverse as Aruba and China, Nigeria and Alaska. Although patterns vary and the object to be thrown takes different shapes and different names, the basic rules are similar worldwide. A map and a bibliography are included. Many illustrations give a brief sense of a particular country's climate, geography, or local archeology. *Notable 1992 Children's Trade Books in the Field of Social Studies.*

5.8   Linden, Ann Marie. **One Smiling Grandma: A Caribbean Counting Book.** Illustrated by Lynne Russell. Dial Books for Young Readers, 1992. ISBN 0-8037-1132-8. 26p. 4–8.

"One smiling grandma in a rocking chair / Two yellow bows tied on braided hair." This rhymed and rhythmical counting book evokes the flavor of a Caribbean island. A young Afro-Caribbean girl introduces readers to steel drums, flying fish, conch shells, mongooses, and other island sights, sounds, and tastes. The brightly colored acrylic paintings of people, animals, and objects to count give a sense of warmth and sunshine.

5.9   MacKinnon, Debbie. **My First ABC.** Photographs by Anthea Sieveking. Barron's Educational Series, 1992. ISBN 0-8120-6331-7. 28p. 2–5.

This alphabet book is illustrated with photographs of children from many ethnic groups. Each child's name and the object featured begin with the same letter, allowing for both upper-case and lower-case letters (such as "Allison's apple"). Entries like "Cathy's car" and "David's doll" prevent gender bias. Ample white space keeps the layout uncluttered, while bright borders around text and pictures serve to both separate and unify the elements on the page.

5.10   McMillan, Bruce. **Eating Fractions.** Photographs by Bruce McMillan. Scholastic Hardcover Books, 1991. ISBN 0-590-43770-4. 30p. 2–7.

One African American boy, one white boy, and a shaggy dog take us on a delicious fractional journey. Starting with bananas and ending with pizza, the threesome eat their way through the simplest fractional units—halves, thirds, and fourths. The full-color photographs introduce the basic mathematical concepts of fractions and reinforce the concepts of friendship and sharing. Recipes are also included, with tips for child involvement with the cooking. *ALA Notable Children's Books, 1993.*

5.11 Miller, Mary Beth, and George Ancona. **Handtalk School.** Photographs by George Ancona. Four Winds Press, 1991. ISBN 0-02-700912-2. 32p. 4–11.

What is the sign for shower? teacher? juice? Jen, Johnnie Ma, Jeff, Tara, and Shira introduce readers to American Sign Language (ASL) and the world of the deaf. We are led through a routine day for Jen—at home, at school, and preparing for the Thanksgiving play. Shira even calls home using the Telephone Device for the Deaf (TDD). The full-color photographs make it possible for readers to see the signs and try their "hand" at signing.

5.12 Morris, Ann. **Tools.** Photographs by Ken Heyman. Lothrop, Lee and Shepard Books, 1992. ISBN 0-688-10171-2. 32p. 3–7.

Through full-color photographs and simple text, this book explores tools, both familiar and unfamiliar, used in daily life around the world. An axelike adz from Bali, tweezers used by a shoemaker in Peru, and a brush used by an artist in China are some of the many tools represented in this book. An index briefly explains the context and use of each tool, and a map helps children to locate all the countries mentioned.

5.13 Rosenberg, Maxine B. **Brothers and Sisters.** Photographs by George Ancona. Clarion Books, 1991. ISBN 0-395-51121-6. 32p. 8–10.

Brothers and sisters from three different families share their feelings about their siblings. Jessica, a biracial child and the oldest of three, is responsible for her younger sisters. Justin, the youngest of two boys, found a real friend in his older brother. Brian, an African American middle child, appreciates his sisters but wishes for a brother. These children's narratives reveal the essence of daily interactions of brothers and sisters. The full-color photographs enhance this portrayal of the strong bonds between siblings.

6 Biography: Individuals Who Made a Difference

6.1 Adler, David A. **A Picture Book of Jesse Owens.** Illustrated by Robert Casilla. Holiday House, 1992. ISBN 0-8234-0966-X. 32p. 5–8. Nonfiction.

Jesse Owens was the hero of the 1936 Olympic Games in Berlin, proving Hitler was wrong to believe that Blacks were inferior. In this contribution to his Picture Book Biography series, David Adler re-creates Owens's life story from his birth as the son of sharecroppers, through his career as a track star and the disappointments that followed, to his death in 1980. The watercolor illustrations capture the action and drama of Owens's life. An author's note and chronology provide additional information.

6.2 Adler, David A. **A Picture Book of Simón Bolívar.** Illustrated by Robert Casilla. Holiday House, 1992. ISBN 0-8234-0927-9. 32p. 8–10 (est). Nonfiction.

The early nineteenth century was a time of rebellion and war in South America as the Spanish-ruled colonies fought for independence from Spain. Simón Bolívar, a Venezuelan by birth, played a key role in freeing five of the republics from Spanish rule. This book recounts some of the political and military accomplishments that earned Bolívar the title of *El Libertador* (the Liberator) and recognition as "the Second Washington of the New World." Unfortunately, the book contains misspellings ("Caracus" for "Caracas" and "Lebertador" for "Libertador") and an implied connection between physical features and behavior (blond hair and blue eyes to indicate a quiet manner, dark curly hair and black eyes to indicate a loud and difficult person).

6.3 Collier, James Lincoln. **Duke Ellington.** Macmillan, 1991. ISBN 0-02-722985-8. 140p. 10 and up. Nonfiction.

Duke Ellington always knew he was someone special. He grew up in a middle-class Black family in Washington, D.C., and even though he was a self-taught pianist and composer, he became one of the world's best known musicians. This biography traces his development from the leader of a small local band to the creator of the Sacred Concerts. Although the book offers insight into Ellington's personality, it focuses almost exclusively on his music and his career; it will appeal mostly to jazz fans or others interested in music. *Notable 1991 Children's Trade Books in the Field of Social Studies.*

6.4   Crews, Donald. **Bigmama's.** Illustrated by Donald Crews. Greenwillow Books, 1991. ISBN 0-688-09951-3. 32p. 5 and up. Nonfiction.

Young Donald Crews and his family ride the train south to Florida to spend the summer at Bigmama's farm. As soon as they arrive, the children in this African American family shed their shoes and go off to explore and make sure everything is the same as always. Satisfied, they all sit down to a big family dinner and close the day looking at millions of stars. This is an autobiographical celebration of a past time remembered, but today's young readers will understand. See also *Shortcut* by Donald Crews (11.12). *ALA Notable Children's Books, 1992.*

6.5   Demi. **Chingis Khan.** Illustrated by Demi. Henry Holt, 1991. ISBN 0-8050-1708-9. 54p. 8 and up. Nonfiction.

Based upon both historical documents and folklore, this is Demi's unique interpretation of the life of the Mongol leader and military genius Chingis Khan, the king of the spirit of light. The details contained in the book enable readers to see him both as a legendary figure who, at the height of his power, was supreme master of the largest empire ever created in the lifetime of one man, and also as a man of emotions and weakness. The watercolor illustrations, decorated with gilt, evoke images of a past golden kingdom.

6.6   Denenberg, Barry. **Nelson Mandela: "No Easy Walk to Freedom."** Scholastic Hardcover Books, 1991. ISBN 0-590-44163-9. 164p. 10 and up. Nonfiction.

The cause of Blacks in South Africa came to the attention of the world in part because of the efforts of Nelson Mandela. This biography of the uncompromised leader of the African National Congress is also a history of the Black struggle for freedom. Barry Denenberg makes clear the hardships that South African Blacks face in their daily lives and the extreme sacrifices that many have made for the cause. Illustrated with photographs, the book includes a chronology, bibliography, and index. See also *Nelson Mandela: Voice of Freedom* by Libby Hughes (6.15).

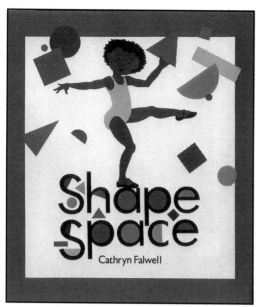

A.

B.

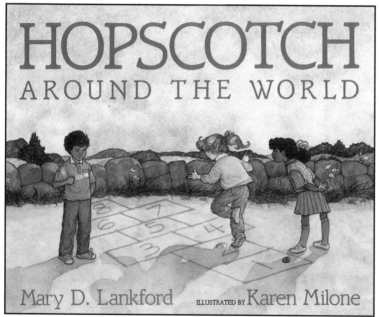

C.

A. *Shape Space* written and illustrated by Cathryn Falwell (see 5.2). **B.** *Eating Fractions* written and with photographs by Bruce McMillan (see 5.10). **C.** *Hopscotch around the World* by Mary D. Lankford; illustrated by Karen Milone (see 5.7).

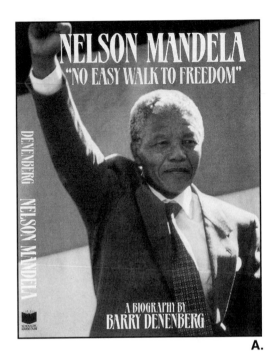

A.

B.

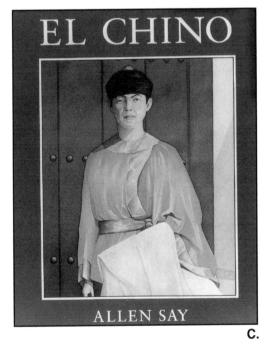

C.

D.

A. *Nelson Mandela: "No Easy Walk to Freedom"* by Barry Denenberg (see 6.6). **B.** *Diego* by Jonah Winter (translated by Amy Price); illustrated by Jeanette Winter (see 6.28). **C.** *El Chino* written and illustrated by Allen Say (see 6.23). **D.** *L'il Sis and Uncle Willie: A Story Based on the Life and Paintings of William H. Johnson* by Gwen Everett; illustrated by William H. Johnson (see 6.7).

6.7 Everett, Gwen. **Li'l Sis and Uncle Willie: A Story Based on the Life and Paintings of William H. Johnson.** Illustrated by William H. Johnson. Rizzoli International Publications/National Museum of American Art, Smithsonian Institution, 1991. ISBN 0-8478-1462-9. 32p. 7–10. Fiction.

The paintings of African American artist William H. Johnson are the illustrations for this fictional story based on actual events in Johnson's life. Born in South Carolina, Johnson lived in Europe for twelve years, married a Danish weaver, and returned to the United States with the outbreak of World War II. Told from the perspective of his niece, "Li'l Sis," the story focuses on Johnson's visit to his South Carolina home when Li'l Sis was six. Her authentic-sounding voice, along with the paintings, offers an engaging introduction to Johnson's art and African American culture. *ALA Notable Children's Books, 1993; Notable 1992 Children's Trade Books in the Field of Social Studies.*

6.8 Fradin, Dennis Brindell. **Hiawatha: Messenger of Peace.** Margaret K. McElderry Books, 1992. ISBN 0-689-50519-1. 40p. 11 and up. Nonfiction.

When you hear the name Hiawatha, you probably think of Longfellow's poem. *That* Hiawatha is an imagined character. The real Hiawatha probably lived in the 1400s. He was the peacemaker who helped create the Iroquois Federation of five tribes in what is now New York. Some historians believe the U.S. Constitution used ideas taken from the laws of the Iroquois Federation. Hiawatha's life story is re-created from available data and illustrated with photographs. *Notable 1992 Children's Trade Books in the Field of Social Studies.*

6.9 Golenbock, Peter. **Teammates.** Illustrated by Paul Bacon. Harcourt Brace Jovanovich/Gulliver Books, 1990. ISBN 0-15-200603-6. 32p. 7–10. Nonfiction.

When Jackie Robinson became the first African American on a major league baseball team, he had to put up with racist behavior from fans and other players alike. He knew that if he fought back, he would be dropped, and no other "Negro" would be allowed to play for many years. One day his Dodger teammate Pee Wee Reese decided to do the right thing and stand up for Robinson. Illustrated with paintings and vintage photographs, this moving story brings to life a dramatic moment in sports history. *Notable 1990 Children's Trade Books in the Field of Social Studies.*

6.10   Hart, Philip S. **Flying Free: America's First Black Aviators.**
            Lerner, 1992. ISBN 0-8225-1598-9. 64p. 10 and up. Nonfiction.

At one time in our history, even the skies were racially segre-
gated! This book tells the story of the pioneer Black pilots who
had to overcome not only the common dangers associated with
flying airplanes but also racism and discrimination. It profiles
four individual pioneers of the 1920s and 1930s, a group of
Chicago flyers, and the famous Tuskegee Airmen. A final four-
page chapter looks at the current status of Black flyers. The book
provides an introduction to a little known aspect of African
American life. *Notable 1992 Children's Trade Books in the Field of
Social Studies.*

6.11   Haskins, James. **Thurgood Marshall: A Life for Justice.** Henry
            Holt, 1992. ISBN 0-8050-2095-0. 149p. 11 and up. Nonfiction.

As a lively cutup of a youngster, Thurgood Marshall was fre-
quently sent to the school basement to memorize the U.S. Constitution. Little did his teachers know how important that activity would be in the life of the first African American Supreme
Court justice. This biography recounts Marshall's lifelong fight
for civil rights and justice, gives background information on
many of his famous cases, and emphasizes his importance to the
struggle for equal treatment under the law. It includes a bibliography, but no photographs. *Notable 1992 Children's Trade Books in
the Field of Social Studies.*

6.12   Haskins, Jim. **Against All Opposition: Black Explorers in
            America.** Walker, 1992. ISBN 0-8027-8138-1. 86p. 10 and up.
            Nonfiction.

Estevanico, Du Sable, York, Beckwourth, and Henson are among
the historical figures introduced in this collection of biographical accounts of Black explorers. Author Jim Haskins begins with
a historical context that relates information about pre-Colum-
bian African explorations to the "New World" and that provides
evidence of Black presence in civilizations around the world.
Biographies of space explorers Guion Bluford and Ronald
McNair round out the survey. Portraits, photographs, and reproductions add to the appeal of this volume. See also *Reflections of
a Black Cowboy: Book Four, Mountain Men* by Robert H. Miller
(6.18). *Notable 1992 Children's Trade Books in the Field of Social
Studies.*

6.13 Haskins, Jim. **One More River to Cross: The Stories of Twelve Black Americans.** Scholastic Hardcover Books, 1992. ISBN 0-590-42896-9. 215p. 10 and up. Nonfiction.

Who was the first American woman to earn a million dollars? Who is the "winningest coach" in college football? Who invented a way to make emergency blood transfusions possible? Madame C. J. Walker, Eddie Robinson, and Charles Drew are three of the twelve African Americans featured in this collection. It profiles four women and eight men, from Crispus Attucks to Ron McNair, who overcame many obstacles to make important contributions to American life. A bibliography and index are included. *Best Books for Young Adults, 1993; Notable 1992 Children's Trade Books in the Field of Social Studies.*

6.14 Haskins, Jim. **Outward Dreams: Black Inventors and Their Inventions.** Walker, 1991. ISBN 0-8027-6994-2. 101p. 10 and up. Nonfiction.

These brief biographies recount the ingenuity and creativity of African American inventors as well as their struggles to overcome obstacles to success. Beginning with inventions patented during the colonial period, the book concludes with inventors of the 1990s whose creations are important components to communications and to future space endeavors. A valuable appendix lists "Inventions by Blacks; 1834–1900" and includes the dates and numbers of their patents. *Notable 1991 Children's Trade Books in the Field of Social Studies.*

6.15 Hughes, Libby. **Nelson Mandela: Voice of Freedom.** Dillon Press, 1992. ISBN 0-87518-484-7. 144p. 10 and up. Nonfiction.

Illustrated with black-and-white photographs, this biography of Nelson Mandela begins with his release from prison and goes back to trace his life from childhood to the present. Author Libby Hughes lived in South Africa for ten years, and that experience provided an insider's perspective on the political and social context in which Mandela operates. Hughes includes details that help highlight Mandela's life in this People in Focus book. A bibliography and index are also included. See also *Nelson Mandela: "No Easy Walk to Freedom"* by Barry Denenberg (6.6).

6.16 Lyons, Mary E. **Sorrow's Kitchen: The Life and Folklore of Zora Neale Hurston.** Charles Scribner's Sons, 1990. ISBN 0-684-19198-9. 158p. 12 and up. Nonfiction.

Mixing the words and stories of Zora Neale Hurston with her own, Mary Lyons weaves an engaging yarn about the life of this talented and once-forgotten writer. The lyrical writing style of the author complements the generous dose of folklore and stories written by Hurston. The well-researched text will provide good reading for mature readers. Included are reproductions of many photographs taken throughout Hurston's life and now located in such places as the Library of Congress and rare book collections. See also *Jump at de Sun: The Story of Zora Neale Hurston* by A. P. Porter (6.21). *Recommended Books for Reluctant Young Adult Readers, 1991.*

6.17   McKissack, Patricia C., and Fredrick McKissack. **Sojourner Truth: Ain't I a Woman?** Scholastic Hardcover Books, 1992. ISBN 0-590-44690-8. 188p. 9 and up. Nonfiction.

Sojourner Truth was born a slave in 1797 in New York. By the time she died eighty-six years later, she had become a famous abolitionist who had traveled the country to tell the truth about slavery and about women's rights. This well-documented and clearly written biography will hold readers' attention with its straightforward style. It includes many photographs and reproductions of historical documents, biographical sketches of "people Sojourner knew," an index, and a bibliography. *ALA Notable Children's Books, 1993; Best Books for Young Adults, 1993; Boston Globe–Horn Book Nonfiction Award, 1993; Coretta Scott King Writing Honor Book, 1993.*

6.18   Miller, Robert H. **Reflections of a Black Cowboy: Book Four, Mountain Men.** Illustrated by Richard Leonard. Silver Burdett Press, 1992. ISBN 0-382-24082-0. 81p. 9–12. Nonfiction.

Esteban, Jean Baptiste Pointe Du Sable, Jim Beckwourth, George McJunkin—each of these Black men played an important role in United States history. In this book, "The Old Cowboy" narrates the exploits of the Moroccan slave who became an explorer in the Southwest, the Haitian trader who founded Chicago, the blacksmith who temporarily became a Crow Indian chief, and the cowboy who discovered an important archeological site. Written in an easy, informal style incorporating much dialogue, the book contains a bibliography and a few black-and-white sketches. See also *Against All Opposition: Black Explorers in America* by Jim Haskins (6.12).

6.19 Morey, Janet Nomura, and Wendy Dunn. **Famous Asian Americans.** Cobblehill Books, 1992. ISBN 0-525-65080-6. 170p. 10 and up. Nonfiction.

This collection of short biographical sketches of fourteen famous Asian Americans will provide great insight into the hardships that these individuals faced in their struggles to succeed. They are a diverse group, representing a variety of Asian and Asian American cultural heritages: China, Japan, Korea, Vietnam, Cambodia, and the Philippines. Senator Daniel Inouye, writer Maxine Hong Kingston, architect I. M. Pei, and illustrator Jose Aruego may be familiar names to some readers. A foreword provides useful context. The book is illustrated with numerous black-and-white photographs. *Notable 1992 Children's Trade Books in the Field of Social Studies.*

6.20 Parks, Rosa (with Jim Haskins). **Rosa Parks: My Story.** Dial Books, 1992. ISBN 0-8037-0673-1. 192p. 12 and up (est). Nonfiction.

When the bus driver told Mrs. Rosa Parks to give up her seat to a white man, the African American woman refused. It was December 1, 1955, and her arrest led to the Montgomery, Alabama, bus boycott and the rise to prominence of Martin Luther King Jr. Mrs. Parks became known as the mother of the civil rights movement. This autobiography places her act of courage in the context of a lifetime devoted to the struggle for equal rights. The book has the ring of nearly eighty years of oral history. See also *The Year They Walked: Rosa Parks and the Montgomery Bus Boycott* by Beatrice Siegel (7.14). *ALA Notable Children's Books, 1993; Best Books for Young Adults, 1993; Recommended Books for Reluctant Young Adult Readers, 1993.*

6.21 Porter, A. P. **Jump at de Sun: The Story of Zora Neale Hurston.** Carolrhoda Books, 1992. ISBN 0-87614-667-1. 96p. 8–11. Nonfiction.

Zora Neale Hurston grew up in an all-Black town in Florida in the early twentieth century. Thrust out on her own early in life, she always remembered her mother's encouragement: "Jump at de sun!" Even though she was always in need of money, Hurston almost always found ways to fulfill her soaring ambitions. This well-written biography brings to life the determined "free spirit" who became an anthropologist, folklorist, and the author of *Their Eyes Were Watching God.* See also *Sorrow's Kitchen: The Life and Folklore of Zora Neale Hurston* by Mary E. Lyons (6.16).

Notable 1992 Children's Trade Books in the Field of Social Studies; Recommended Books for Reluctant Young Adult Readers, 1993.

6.22   Sabin, Louis. **Roberto Clemente: Young Baseball Hero.** Illustrated by Marie DeJohn. Troll Associates, 1992. ISBN 0-8167-2509-8. 48p. 6–9. Nonfiction.

An engaging story that focuses more on the childhood and upbringing of legendary baseball player Roberto Clemente than on his professional career, this biography is certain to appeal to a wide range of readers. By giving details of life in his native Puerto Rico and centering on the values and dignity with which Clemente's parents raised him, the book introduces young readers to the island and its culture. See also *Pride of Puerto Rico: The Life of Roberto Clemente* by Paul Robert Walker (6.27).

6.23   Say, Allen. **El Chino.** Illustrated by Allen Say. Houghton Mifflin, 1990. ISBN 0-395-52023-1. 32p. 7–12 (est). Nonfiction.

"In America, you can be anything you want to be." Billy Wong wants to be a professional athlete, and his father's words are his inspiration. Although trained as an engineer, Wong becomes fascinated by bullfighting and, against the odds, becomes one of Spain's most famous matadors, "El Chino." Allen Say's vivid watercolors capture the style and grace of this Chinese American bullfighter. He uses the transition from black and white to color for dramatic effect. *Notable 1990 Children's Trade Books in the Field of Social Studies.*

6.24   Senna, Carl. **Colin Powell: A Man of War and Peace.** Walker, 1992. ISBN 0-8027-8181-0. 150p. 10 and up. Nonfiction.

General Colin Powell, the first African American chairman of the Joint Chiefs of Staff, grew up in Harlem, the son of hard-working Jamaican immigrants. Beginning with college ROTC, he overcame many obstacles to become one of the most highly respected men in the nation, the strategist behind Desert Storm, and a potential candidate for vice president of the United States. Informative details add to the story of the general and his times, and a bibliography and source notes verify the author's research.

6.25   Stanley, Fay. **The Last Princess: The Story of Princess Ka'iulani of Hawai'i.** Illustrated by Diane Stanley. Four Winds Press, 1991. ISBN 0-02-786785-4. 40p. 7 and up (est). Nonfiction.

When Princess Ka'iulani was born in 1875, people expected her to become queen of the Kingdom of Hawai'i. She spent many years preparing for her royal duties, but she never ascended the throne. Fay Stanley relates the story of Hawaii's last princess and her valiant fight against the powerful U.S. government, which toppled the monarchy and annexed Hawaii in 1898. This sympathetic portrait is enhanced by daughter Diane Stanley's realistic paintings. Notes on the Hawaiian language and an index are included. *Notable 1991 Children's Trade Books in the Field of Social Studies.*

6.26　Uchida, Yoshiko. **The Invisible Thread.** Julian Messner, 1991. ISBN 0-671-74163-2. 136p. 10 and up (est). Nonfiction.

In this autobiography, the late author of *Journey to Topaz* and *A Jar of Dreams* relates what it was like to grow up as a Japanese American during the 1930s and 1940s. Yoshiko Uchida, who was a Nisei, or a Japanese American born in the United States, grew up in Berkeley, California. Her family was among those Japanese Americans taken to concentration camps after the Pearl Harbor bombing. In straightforward prose, Uchida evokes both the horror of that experience and the strengths that helped these Americans come through their ordeal without having their spirits destroyed. See also *The Journey: Japanese Americans, Racism, and Renewal* by Sheila Hamanaka (7.6).

6.27　Walker, Paul Robert. **Pride of Puerto Rico: The Life of Roberto Clemente.** Harcourt Brace Jovanovich/Odyssey Books, 1991. ISBN 0-15-263420-7. 157p. 9–12. Nonfiction.

Certain to delight baseball lovers, this biography of Roberto Clemente, the Puerto Rican right fielder for the Pittsburgh Pirates, offers insights into his life and values. Clemente suffered many indignities because of his Spanish accent and dark skin, but his spirit, his love for baseball, and the support from family and friends helped him become one of the greatest baseball players ever. Clemente died at age thirty-eight on a mission to help the victims of the Nicaraguan earthquake of 1972. See also *Roberto Clemente: Young Baseball Hero* by Louis Sabin (6.22).

6.28　Winter, Jeanette (text by Jonah Winter; translated by Amy Price). **Diego.** Illustrated by Jeanette Winter. Alfred A. Knopf/Borzoi Books, 1991. ISBN 0-679-81987-2. 32p. 5–8. Nonfiction.

When Diego Rivera was a boy, he drew everywhere, even on the walls. He also made five thousand toy soldiers all by himself. As a man, Rivera became one of Mexico's best-known artists. His famous murals celebrate working people all over the world.

With simple text—in both English and Spanish—and engaging illustrations, this book focuses on the artist's childhood and early adulthood. Sadly, the book does not include any examples of Rivera's own work. And note that the book gives the date of Rivera's death as November 24, 1957, but other sources list it as November 25, 1957. *Notable 1991 Children's Trade Books in the Field of Social Studies; Parents Choice Award, 1991.*

6.29   Wisniewski, David. **Sundiata: Lion King of Mali.** Illustrated by David Wisniewski. Clarion Books, 1992. ISBN 0-395-61302-7. 32p. 7 and up (est). Nonfiction.

Striking cut-paper pictures illuminate this picture book biography of Sundiata, the thirteenth-century king of Mali in West Africa. Distilled from the accounts of *griots*, keepers of the oral tradition, the book recounts the legendary exploits of the chosen heir who was forced into exile by jealous rivals after his father's death. Seven years later, upon hearing that his homeland had been attacked, the eighteen-year-old Sundiata gathered an army, vanquished the invaders, and reclaimed his throne. A cut-paper map and an author's note provide valuable additional information. *ALA Notable Children's Books, 1993; Notable 1992 Children's Trade Books in the Field of Social Studies.*

6.30   Yep, Laurence. **The Lost Garden.** Julian Messner, 1991. ISBN 0-671-74159-4. 117p. 10 and up. Nonfiction.

Laurence Yep, author of *Dragonwings* and numerous other books, relates his memories of growing up as a Chinese American. From the time he was a child, he felt like an outsider: "the Chinese American raised in a black neighborhood, . . . too American to fit into Chinatown, . . . too Chinese to fit anywhere else . . . the clumsy son of the athletic family. . . ." Writing allowed Yep to put together the pieces of the puzzle of himself. This is an insightful examination of how he came to be who he is as a writer and as a person.

6.31   Zheng Zhensun and Alice Low. **A Young Painter: The Life and Paintings of Wang Yani—China's Extraordinary Young Artist.** Photographs by Zheng Zhensun. Scholastic Hardcover Books/Byron Preiss–New China Pictures Books, 1991. ISBN 0-5990-44906-0. 80p. 8 and up (est). Nonfiction.

The life of this Chinese child prodigy evokes admiration and awe, from her first bold strokes at age three to the youngest ever one-person show at the Smithsonian Institution at the age of fourteen. The many examples of Wang Yani's Zen-like ink paintings of animals delight the eye. For Wang, art simply flows naturally: "I think painting is something very simple. You just paint what you think about." Her development as an artist is likely to captivate readers. *ALA Notable Children's Books, 1992.*

7 History: The Way We Were

7.1 Aaseng, Nathan. **Navajo Code Talkers.** Walker, 1992. ISBN 0-8027-8183-7. 114p. 10 and up. Nonfiction.

During World War II, when the marines needed a code to communicate secret messages, they called on the Navajo code talkers, a special group of marines who went on to play a major role in the U.S. victory over Japan. Using the Navajo language, the code talkers created a code that could not be broken by the enemy. This book, illustrated with archival photographs, dramatically tells the story of these little known and mostly unsung men.

7.2 Arnold, Caroline. **The Ancient Cliff Dwellers of Mesa Verde.** Photographs by Richard Hewett. Clarion Books, 1992. ISBN 0-395-56241-4. 64p. 8–12. Nonfiction.

For ten centuries, the Anasazi group of the Pueblo Indians lived in what is now the Four Corners area of the Southwest. When they abandoned their community sometime around 1300, they left evidence of a complex culture and civilization, the most striking feature of which are the cliff dwellings in Mesa Verde National Park in Colorado. Based on archeological data and illustrated with color photographs, this book describes what daily life might have been like for the Anasazi. A glossary is included. See also *The Village of Blue Stone* by Stephen Trimble (7.15).

7.3 Cox, Clinton. **Undying Glory: The Story of the Massachusetts 54th Regiment.** Scholastic Hardcover Books, 1991. ISBN 0-590-44170-1. 167p. 8 and up. Nonfiction.

The men of the all-Black 54th Massachusetts regiment were among the most valiant soldiers in the Civil War. Even though they faced racial discrimination and lower wages than whites, they remained undaunted. Their valor and skill in the face of astounding odds impressed even their detractors. Using photographs and primary source materials, Clinton Cox recounts the story of these young men who helped to liberate Black people.

Moviegoers may remember this as the *Glory* regiment. *Notable 1991 Children's Trade Books in the Field of Social Studies.*

7.4   Freedman, Russell. **An Indian Winter.** Illustrated by Karl Bodmer. Holiday House, 1992. ISBN 0-8234-0930-9. 88p. 10 and up (est). Nonfiction.

The Mandan Indians were a proud and prosperous people when German Prince Alexander Philipp Maximilian and Swiss artist Karl Bodmer wintered with them in the Missouri River Valley in what is now North Dakota in 1833–34. The Mandan and their neighbors, the Hidatsas, generously permitted the two men to share their daily lives, cultural events, and routine activities. Russell Freedman has used the journals and artwork of these two travelers to create a moving portrait of a people who were nearly destroyed by the ravages of small pox and the white man's greed. *ALA Notable Children's Books, 1993; Best Books for Young Adults, 1993; Notable 1992 Children's Trade Books in the Field of Social Studies.*

7.5   Fritz, Jean, Katherine Paterson, Patricia McKissack, Fredrick McKissack, Margaret Mahy, and Jamake Highwater. **The World in 1492.** Illustrated by Stefano Vitale. Henry Holt, 1992. ISBN 0-8050-1674-0. 168p. 9 and up. Nonfiction.

This book is an important addition to traditional American history books. It not only highlights fifteenth-century Europe and Columbus's epic voyage, but it also describes other great civilizations existing in 1492, including ones in Asia, Africa, Australia and Oceania, and the Americas. Through the narratives of these popular authors, plus maps, drawings, artwork, and artifacts, the volume offers an overview of the rich histories and customs of the varied peoples living at that time, and in so doing it begins to provide an important context for understanding the period. *ALA Notable Children's Books, 1993; Notable 1992 Children's Trade Books in the Field of Social Studies.*

7.6   Hamanaka, Sheila. **The Journey: Japanese Americans, Racism, and Renewal.** Illustrated by Sheila Hamanaka. Orchard Books, 1990. ISBN 0-531-08449-3. 40p. 10 and up. Nonfiction.

During World War II, members of Sheila Hamanaka's family, U.S. citizens of Japanese ancestry, were imprisoned in concentration camps in the United States. Hamanaka painted the mural on which this book is based to reflect that event and the history of Japanese Americans in general. The mural depicts the racism endured by Japanese Americans, their struggle to end discrimination, and their hopes for the future. Closeup photographs of sections of the mural are accompanied by explanatory text. The full five-panel mural is reproduced at the end of the text. See also *The Invisible Thread* by Yoshiko Uchida (6.26). *Jane Addams Honor Book, 1991; Best Books for Young Adults, 1991; Notable 1990 Children's Trade Books in the Field of Social Studies; Recommended Books for Reluctant Young Adult Readers, 1991.*

7.7   Haskins, Jim. **The Day Martin Luther King, Jr., Was Shot: A Photo History of the Civil Rights Movement.** Scholastic, 1992. ISBN 0-590-43661-9. 96p. 8–12. Nonfiction.

Beginning and ending this book with an assessment of the lasting significance of the work of Dr. Martin Luther King Jr., Jim Haskins traces the history of the civil rights movement from slavery through modern times. Haskins has divided the book into twenty-three short chapters that focus on specific issues and eras in the movement, such as "The Abolitionist Movement" and "On from Selma." Illustrated with archival photographs and drawings, this book is a useful historical piece.

7.8   Hernández, Xavier (translated by Kathleen Leverich). **San Rafael: A Central American City through the Ages.** Illustrated by Jordi Ballonga and Josep Escofet. Houghton Mifflin, 1992. ISBN 0-395-60645-4. 62p. 10 and up. Nonfiction.

Through the history of a fictional city, Xavier Hernández traces the growth and development of what could be any Central American city from 1000 B.C. to the present day. Illustrated with detailed black-and-white drawings, including alternating double-page spreads, this informative book shows how the city would have evolved through fourteen stages, from a small settlement into a late-twentieth-century metropolis. It also describes the uncertain future that the city faces in the twenty-first century.

7.9   Jacobs, Francine. **The Tainos: The People Who Welcomed Columbus.** Illustrated by Patrick Collins. G. P. Putnam's Sons, 1992. ISBN 0-399-22116-6. 107p. 10 and up. Nonfiction.

With a perspective rarely available to younger readers, this book is a thoroughly researched and sympathetic portrait of the Taino Indians who welcomed Columbus on his arrival in the Caribbean in 1492. It provides an unrelenting saga of the cruelty, greed, and barbarism of the Spaniards that resulted in the almost complete annihilation of the Tainos within fifty years of the Spaniards' arrival, and it presents Columbus as a vain and arrogant man who lusted only for gold. See also *Encounter* by Jane Yolen (11.79) and *Morning Girl* by Michael Dorris (13.10). *Notable 1992 Children's Trade Books in the Field of Social Studies, 1992.*

7.10   Katz, William Loren. **Breaking the Chains: African-American Slave Resistance.** Atheneum, 1990. ISBN 0-689-31493-0. 208p. 11 and up. Nonfiction.

With chapters such as "The Battle for Family and Knowledge," "Runaways and Maroons," and "The Bayonets of Freedom," William Loren Katz chronicles the history of African American slave resistance, beginning with the slave trade in Africa and continuing through the Civil War and liberation. To authenticate his text, Katz uses a variety of sources, including journals and books of such well-known figures as Frederick Douglass, lesser-known slave narratives, and works of slaveholders. The book is illustrated with reproductions of historical drawings and documents. *Best Books for Young Adults, 1991.*

7.11   Myers, Walter Dean. **Now Is Your Time! The African-American Struggle for Freedom.** HarperCollins, 1991. ISBN 0-06-024371-6. 292p. 10 and up (est). Nonfiction.

This is an impassioned presentation of African American history from the seventeenth century to the present. Illustrated with historical photographs and documents, the book is a combination of history, biography, and autobiography. African American history is told through the stories of "freedom fighters" over three centuries, woven into accounts of important historical events, famous and otherwise. Walter Dean Myers also traces part of his own ancestry and connects it to the larger history. His style makes the book a good choice for reading aloud. *ALA Notable Children's Books, 1991; Best Books for Young Adults, 1992; Coretta Scott King Writing Award, 1992; NCTE Orbis Pictus Honor Book, 1992.*

7.12   Rappaport, Doreen. **Escape from Slavery: Five Journeys to Freedom.** Illustrated by Charles Lilly. HarperCollins, 1991. ISBN 0-06-021632-8. 124p. 9–12. Nonfiction.

"Slave escapes occurred from the earliest times after enslaved Africans were first brought to America in 1619." So begins this book that historically documents five accounts of successful slave escapes on the Underground Railroad. It includes the story of Eliza, who escaped across a river on melting ice; Dosha, who helped his sisters Camelia and Selena outsmart the sheriff; and Henry Brown, who shipped himself out of slavery in a box. Focusing on individual acts of courage, the stories are drawn from sources such as *Reminiscences of Levi Coffin* and William Still's *The Underground Rail Road,* both published in the 1870s. *Notable 1991 Children's Trade Books in the Field of Social Studies.*

7.13   Sewall, Marcia. **People of the Breaking Day.** Illustrated by Marcia Sewall. Atheneum, 1990. ISBN 0-689-31407-8. 48p. 8 and up (est). Nonfiction.

This book takes the reader back in time to the seventeenth century when the Wampanoag Indians thrived in what is now southeastern Massachusetts. With watercolor paintings and a poetic text, Marcia Sewall describes the seasonal activities—hunting, fishing, planting, harvesting—and the customs, values, and traditions of the people who were there when the Pilgrims arrived. This is a companion book to Sewall's *The Pilgrims of Plimouth.* A glossary and a list of Wampanoag words are included. See also *Clambake: A Wampanoag Tradition* by Russell M. Peters (3.6). *Notable 1990 Children's Trade Books in the Field of Social Studies.*

7.14   Siegel, Beatrice. **The Year They Walked: Rosa Parks and the Montgomery Bus Boycott.** Four Winds Press, 1992. ISBN 0-02-782631-7. 104p. 9–12. Nonfiction.

This is an account of the Montgomery, Alabama, bus boycott and the persons associated with it. It includes biographical information about Rosa Parks and Dr. Martin Luther King Jr. and carefully details the events surrounding this landmark civil rights action. The book also includes photographs of incidents that occurred during and after the boycott. This account, divided into eleven chapters, can be read aloud to younger students or read independently by older readers interested in learning more about these civil rights figures. See also *Rosa Parks: My Story* by Rosa Parks with Jim Haskins (6.20). *Notable 1992 Children's Trade Books in the Field of Social Studies.*

7.15   Trimble, Stephen. **The Village of Blue Stone.** Illustrated by Jennifer Owings Dewey and Deborah Reade. Macmillan, 1990. ISBN 0-02-789501-7. 62p. 10 and up (est). Nonfiction.

Stephen Trimble has composed a picture of daily life, in 1100 A.D., of Anasazi pueblo dwellers in what is now the Four Corners area

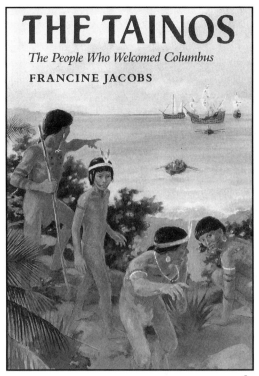

A.

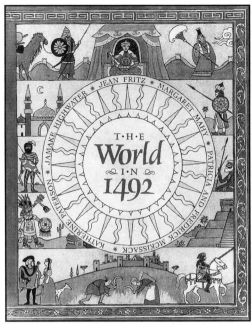

B.

C.

A. *The Tainos: The People Who Welcomed Columbus* by Francine Jacobs; illustrated by Patrick Collins (see 7.9). **B.** *The World in 1492* by Jean Fritz, Katherine Paterson, Patricia McKissack, Fredrick McKissack, Margaret Mahy, and Jamake Highwater; illustrated by Stefano Vitale (see 7.5). **C.** *The Journey: Japanese Americans, Racism, and Renewal* written and illustrated by Sheila Hamanaka (see 7.6).

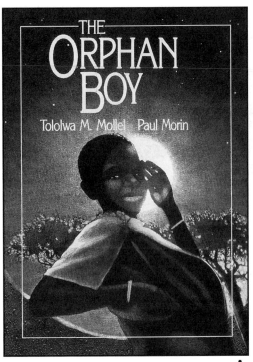

A.

B.

C.

D.

A. *The Orphan Boy: A Maasai Story* by Tololwa Mollel; illustrated by Paul Morin (see 9.11). **B.** *Lee Ann: The Story of a Vietnamese-American Girl* by Tricia Brown; photographs by Ted Thai (see 8.2). **C.** *Ma'ii and Cousin Horned Toad: A Traditional Navajo Story* written and illustrated by Shonto Begay (see 9.21). **D.** *Moon Rope: A Peruvian Tale* written and illustrated by Lois Ehlert; translated by Amy Prince (see 9.4).

of the American Southwest. The book re-creates a year in the "village of blue stone," describing a culture that has been preserved to this day. The book appears to be well researched, drawing on archeological data and the knowledge of other experts. Included is an index, glossary, and bibliography. Black-and-white drawings provide additional information. See also *The Ancient Cliff Dwellers of Mesa Verde* by Caroline Arnold (7.2). *Notable 1990 Children's Trade Books in the Field of Social Studies.*

7.16 Walter, Mildred Pitts. **Mississippi Challenge.** Bradbury Press, 1992. ISBN 0-02-792301-0. 205p. 11 and up. Nonfiction.

This is the story of the struggle for voting rights undertaken by African Americans living in Mississippi. The first part of the book relates the brutal history of race relations in Mississippi from the time of slavery through the first half of the twentieth century. Part two chronicles the extraordinary efforts of Fannie Lou Hamer and other courageous men and women to establish the Mississippi Freedom Democratic Party and to challenge both state and federal power structures to obtain the rights of citizenship. *Coretta Scott King Writing Honor Book, 1993.*

8 Immigrants and Immigration: Coming to America

8.1   Anastos, Phillip, and Chris French. **Illegal: Seeking the American Dream.** Photographs by Phillip Anastos and Chris French. Rizzoli International Publications, 1991. ISBN 0-8478-1367-3. 128p. 10 and up. Nonfiction.

Illegal is unique in several ways: its authors are not professional writers, but two high school students; its focus is Hispanic immigrant children, not adult refugees; and its setting is Brownsville, Texas, a port of entry not often mentioned in children's literature about the refugee experience. The result is a fresh, sincere look at a pressing social issue. The text by Phillip Anastos and Chris French is straightforward and informative; their photographs are simple yet illuminating. The foreword itself makes for worthwhile reading. *Best Books for Young Adults, 1992.*

8.2   Brown, Tricia. **Lee Ann: The Story of a Vietnamese-American Girl.** Photographs by Ted Thai. G. P. Putnam's Sons, 1991. ISBN 0-399-21842-4. 48p. 6–8. Nonfiction.

This photo essay shows the family life and school life of a middle-class Vietnamese American child. Lee Ann Trang enjoys and appreciates both what she experiences in America and what she learns about her Vietnamese heritage from her parents and community members. Her experiences are different from many Vietnamese American children, however. Her school offers English as a second language and has a Vietnamese community liaison person. Text and pictures combine to show Lee Ann's life as similar to that of many children in middle- and upper-income American families.

8.3   Grenquist, Barbara. **Cubans.** Franklin Watts, 1991. ISBN 0-531-11107-5. 64p. 10 and up. Nonfiction.

Tracing the Cuban American community from the early history of Cuba to the community's place in the United States today, this book in the Recent American Immigrants series includes vignettes of heroic escapes from the island and successful acculturation to the United States. Author Barbara Grenquist attempts to be both comprehensive and neutral, but the difficulty of articulating complex historical issues to young readers is evident in the book's handling of some controversial topics.

8.4   Kuklin, Susan. **How My Family Lives in America.** Illustrated by Susan Kuklin. Bradbury Press, 1992. ISBN 0-02-751239-8. 32p. 4–7. Nonfiction.

In this photo essay about three children from African American, Puerto Rican, and Chinese American backgrounds, author Susan Kuklin uses the children's words to describe their everyday lives and shows how their heritage is transmitted in their daily activities. Each of the featured children has at least one parent who was born outside of the United States. The book provides affirming portraits of the children and their communities and concludes with a recipe from each family.

8.5   O'Connor, Karen. **Dan Thuy's New Life in America.** Lerner, 1992. ISBN 0-8225-2555-0. 40p. 9–12. Nonfiction.

This is a photo essay about Dan Thuy, a thirteen-year-old Vietnamese American girl, and her family, who have been in San Diego for just four months. Some general historical and cultural background information about Vietnam is woven into the text. Combining black-and-white photographs, interviews, and people's own thoughts and opinions, author Karen O'Connor offers a detailed and informative chronicle of one family, part of the increasing population of Vietnamese immigrants in the southwestern United States.

8.6   Poynter, Margaret. **The Uncertain Journey: Stories of Illegal Aliens in** *El Norte.* Atheneum, 1992. ISBN 0-689-31623-2. 163p. 12 and up. Nonfiction.

The stories of twelve illegal immigrants to the United States—from Mexico, Central America, South America, and the Caribbean—are told in a detailed, moving manner. Several pages of photographs complement these modern tales, reflecting faces and scenes from the lives of today's undocumented workers. How the author came to know the stories and their central characters is not revealed. Unfortunately, numerous spelling and grammatical errors in the book's Spanish phrases are distracting to the reader of Spanish (e.g., *el mosca (la mosca), vamanos (vámonos),* and *mi miños (mis miños).*

9 Folktales, Myths, and Legends: Old and New

Origins: How and Why Things Came to Be

9.1 Anderson, David A./SANKOFA, reteller. **The Origin of Life on Earth: An African Creation Myth.** Illustrated by Kathleen Atkins Wilson. Sights Productions, 1991. ISBN 0-9629978-5-4. 32p. 7 and up.

This creation myth comes from the Yoruba people of Nigeria. Obatala, an *orisha,* or agent, of the supreme god Olorun, descends from the sky on a gold chain and, assisted by other *orishas*, creates the earth with sand, an egg, nuts, and seeds. He also creates people, and Olorun breathes into them the breath of life. The striking feature of this book is the illustrations—silhouetted figures dressed in colorful and exquisite West African clothing, set against backgrounds reminiscent of tie-dyed fabric. *Coretta Scott King Illustration Award, 1993.*

9.2 Charles, Donald. **Chancay and the Secret of Fire: A Peruvian Tale.** Illustrated by Donald Charles. G. P. Putnam's Sons/Whitebird Books, 1992. ISBN 0-399-22129-8. 32p. 5–8 (est).

When Chancay catches an enormous colorful fish, he thinks it is too beautiful to eat, and so he returns it to the water. The fish, really a Spirit of Father Earth, grants Chancay one wish in return for his kindness. Chancay wants fire to relieve his people from the cold, but first he must prove that he is strong and brave, as well as kind. The eye-catching illustrations for this original tale are inspired by ancient Peruvian art.

9.3 Dixon, Ann, reteller. **How Raven Brought Light to People.** Illustrated by Jim Watts. Margaret K. McElderry Books, 1992. ISBN 0-689-50536-1. 32p. 5–9.

In this adaptation of an Alaskan Tlingit Indian legend, Raven the trickster transforms himself into the grandson of the great chief who selfishly hoards the sun, moon, and stars. How Raven tricks the chief and obtains light for the people makes an exciting story. On a secondary note, the story also explains the origin of the raven's color. James Watts's illustrations are rich with Native

American designs. See also *The Story of Light* by Susan L. Roth (9.14) and *Raven's Light: A Myth from the People of the Northwest Coast* by Susan Hand Shetterly (9.15).

9.4   Ehlert, Lois (translated by Amy Prince). **Moon Rope: A Peruvian Tale/Un Lazo a La Luna: Una Leyenda Peruana.** Illustrated by Lois Ehlert. Harcourt Brace Jovanovich, 1992. ISBN 0-15-255343-6. 32p. 4–8.

If you could have anything in the world, what would it be? For Mole it is worms, but for Fox it is a trip to the moon. In this adaptation of a Peruvian tale, Fox convinces Mole to join him in a climb to the moon on a woven grass rope. If readers go out on a moonlit night, they may find out what happened to both animals. The text is in English and Spanish. The stylized silvery illustrations will hold the attention of young listeners. *ALA Notable Children's Books, 1993.*

9.5   Gerson, Mary-Joan, reteller. **Why the Sky Is Far Away: A Nigerian Folktale.** Illustrated by Carla Golembe. Little, Brown/Joy Street Books, 1992. ISBN 0-316-30852-8. 32p. 4–8.

According to this ancient Nigerian pourquoi tale, in the beginning the sky was the source of all food. It was so close that people could reach up and pluck a piece whenever they were hungry. Wastefulness threatened their bounty, and for a while everyone was careful not to take more than they could use. But one woman, Adese, was never satisfied, and her greed sealed the fate of all the people in the land. Strikingly illustrated in contrasting black and bright colors, this is a timely tale relevant to today's environmental concerns. *Notable 1992 Children's Trade Books in the Field of Social Studies.*

9.6   Goble, Paul. **Love Flute.** Illustrations by Paul Goble. Bradbury Press, 1992. ISBN 0-02-736261-2. 32p. 6 and up.

This love story relates the origin of the love flute used by Plains Indian males in their courtship rituals. A shy young man, unable to express his affection for the girl whom he loves, leaves camp in sadness, not caring what happens to him. But unseen powers are watching over him, and after a four-day journey, he receives a gift that solves his problems. References and notes in the beginning of the book and drawings of various love flutes provide valuable information. *ALA Notable Children's Books, 1993; Notable 1992 Children's Trade Books in the Field of Social Studies.*

9.7 Hong, Lily Toy, reteller. **How the Ox Star Fell from Heaven.** Illustrated by Lily Toy Hong. Albert Whitman, 1991. ISBN 0-8075-3428-5. 32p. 4–8 (est).

In this retelling of a Chinese folktale, an ox star is sent on a mission to earth. Mistakenly, he misreads the imperial edict from the heavens, and as his punishment, the ox star is banished and sent back to earth to become a beast of burden. Ironically, this celestial blunder becomes an earthly blessing in disguise. Children will enjoy this read-aloud book accompanied by the bright, bold illustrations.

9.8 Knutson, Barbara, reteller. **How the Guinea Fowl Got Her Spots: A Swahili Tale of Friendship.** Illustrated by Barbara Knutson. Carolrhoda Books, 1990. ISBN 0-87614-416-4. 32p. 5–8.

When Nganga the Guinea Fowl and her big friend Cow go off to the green hills to eat grass and seeds, they both keep an eye out for Lion. One day when Lion is about to attack Cow, fearless Nganga thwarts Lion's plans and saves Cow's life. Later Cow finds a way to return the favor. This simply told Swahili tale of how Nganga gets her protective coloration makes a good read-aloud. The scratchboard illustrations include many African designs. *Notable 1990 Children's Trade Books in the Field of Social Studies.*

9.9 Lewis, Richard. **All of You Was Singing.** Illustrated by Ed Young. Atheneum, 1991. ISBN 0-689-31596-1. 30p. 8 and up.

The sky, earth, wind, and sun are the central forces in this lyrical retelling of an Aztec myth about the earth's creation and how music was brought to earth. The sky entreats the wind to steal music away from the sun so that the earth can shed its silence. The wind's mission is accomplished only after the sky and sun engage in a clash of power. The striking artwork conveys the diverse imagery of this poetic myth. *ALA Notable Children's Books, 1992; Notable 1991 Children's Trade Books in the Field of Social Studies.*

9.10 Martin, Francesca. **The Honey Hunters: A Traditional African Tale.** Illustrated by Francesca Martin. Candlewick Press, 1992. ISBN 1-56402-086-X. 28p. 4–8.

The song of the honey guide bird—"Che, che! Cheka, che! If you want honey, follow me!"—is irresistible to a young boy and a cumulative parade of wild animals, all of whom love honey. This pourquoi tale from the Ngoni of East Africa explains what happened to change the animals from friends to enemies. The delicate, elaborately detailed illustrations are good for close examination, and the uncomplicated narrative style makes for good reading aloud or telling.

9.11   Mollel, Tololwa M. **The Orphan Boy: A Maasai Story.** Illustrated by Paul Morin. Clarion Books, 1990. ISBN 0-89919-985-2. 32p. All ages.

An old man, lonely and searching for a star, is surprised to find instead Kileken, an orphan boy. In the days following, Kileken makes life prosperous for the old man in spite of a drought. In return, he asks only the old man's unquestioning trust. When curiosity causes betrayal, the boy must return home as Venus, called Kileken by the Maasai of East Africa. Glowing, batik-like paintings, pencil sketches, and bead-like decorations, combined with poetically descriptive language, depict the Maasai people, animals, landscape, and legend. *ALA Notable Children's Books, 1993; Notable 1991 Children's Trade Books in the Field of Social Studies.*

9.12   Mollel, Tololwa M. **A Promise to the Sun: An African Story.** Illustrated by Beatriz Vidal. Little, Brown/Joy Street Books, 1992. ISBN 0-316-57813-4. 32p. 6–10.

Why do bats fly only at night? When a severe drought hits the land of the birds, they choose the bat to go in search of rain. The Moon, the Stars, the Clouds, and the Winds say they cannot help, but the Sun agrees to bring rain in return for a cool quiet place to rest at the end of each day. After a bountiful harvest, the birds refuse to fulfill the bat's promise of a nest for the sun, leaving the bat to suffer the consequences. Illustrations in watercolor, acrylic, and crayon accompany this African tale. *Notable 1992 Children's Trade Books in the Field of Social Studies.*

9.13   Oughton, Jerrie. **How the Stars Fell into the Sky: A Navajo Legend.** Illustrated by Lisa Desimini. Houghton Mifflin, 1992. ISBN 0-395-58798-0. 32p. All ages.

On the first day, First Woman decides that the people need to know the laws. At the suggestion of First Man, she begins to use her jewels, the stars, to write the laws in the night sky. When curious Coyote offers to help, First Woman accepts, but Coyote's patience gives out long before the work is done and, in haste, he ruins her careful plans. Poetic language and dramatic illustrations make this Navajo creation myth suitable for a wide range of readers. *Notable 1992 Children's Trade Books in the Field of Social Studies.*

9.14 Roth, Susan L. **The Story of Light.** Illustrated by Susan L. Roth. Morrow Junior Books, 1990. ISBN 0-688-08676-4. 32p. 6–8.

"It was dark before the sun came. The animal people couldn't see. . . ." They meet to decide how to get some light from the sun. Possum tries but singes the hair off his tail; Buzzard burns a bald spot on top of his head. Then it is tiny Spider's turn. She cannot possibly succeed—she is too old, too small, and a woman! How Spider proves the other animals wrong is the story of light. Susan Roth makes effective use of contrasting black, white, and yellow to illuminate this Cherokee myth. See also *How Raven Brought Light to People* by Ann Dixon (9.3) and *Raven's Light: A Myth from the People of the Northwest Coast* by Susan Hand Shetterly (9.15). *Notable 1990 Children's Trade Books in the Field of Social Studies.*

9.15 Shetterly, Susan Hand, reteller. **Raven's Light: A Myth from the People of the Northwest Coast.** Illustrated by Robert Shetterly. Atheneum, 1991. ISBN 0-689-31629-1. 32p. 6–10.

Where did the earth come from? Raven dropped a small stone onto the water, and it grew. Where did the animals and people come from? Raven dropped them from the sack around his neck. It was all beautiful, but it was all still dark. Raven could see only by starlight. This creation story from four Pacific Northwest peoples tells how Raven, the trickster, was able to steal light from day. See also *How Raven Brought Light to People* by Ann Dixon (9.3) and *The Story of Light* by Susan L. Roth (9.14). *Notable 1991 Children's Trade Books in the Field of Social Studies.*

9.16 Van Laan, Nancy, adapter. **The Legend of El Dorado: A Latin American Tale.** Illustrations by Beatriz Vidal. Alfred A. Knopf/Borzoi Books, 1991. ISBN 0-679-90136-1. 36p. 7 and up.

The legend of El Dorado (or the Gilded Man), with its much-sought treasures, is explained in this glowingly colorful adaptation taken from the Chibcha Indians of what is now Colombia. After the king's wife and daughter are lured beneath the waters of Lake Guatavita by the serpent who lives there, the king pays him homage each year with gold and jewels. Text and illustrations together portray a peaceful kingdom where the king rules while waiting to be reunited with his family. *Notable 1991 Children's Trade Books in the Field of Social Studies.*

9.17 Williams, Sheron. **And in the Beginning. . . .** Illustrated by Robert Roth. Atheneum, 1992. ISBN 0-689-31650-X. 40p. 6–10.

In this original creation story, Mahtmi, the Blessed One, creates the first man from the dark soil of Mount Kilimanjaro in East Africa. This original being, Kwanza ("the first one"), tires of his particular spot on earth and goes exploring. When he returns, he discovers that Mahtmi has created many other humans. Mahtmi then gives the jealous Kwanza a gift that marks him as special. Colloquial language adds an intimacy to the telling, and the watercolor illustrations reflect the mood. *Notable 1992 Children's Trade Books in the Field of Social Studies.*

Animals

9.18 Aardema, Verna. **Anansi Finds a Fool: An Ashanti Tale.** Illustrated by Bryna Waldman. Dial Books for Young Readers, 1992. ISBN 0-8037-1165-4. 32p. 4–8.

In this Ashanti tale from Ghana, the legendary trickster Anansi is up to his usual antics. He is looking for a fool—a fishing partner to do all the hard work. But Bonsu, Anansi's partner, has some tricks of his own, and at the end of their venture, Anansi discovers that the fool he has found is not the one he was expecting to find. The full-color illustrations reflect the humor of the story, which, with its sound effects, makes a good read-aloud. A glossary of names is included. See also *Anansi Goes Fishing* by Eric A. Kimmel (9.25). *Notable 1992 Children's Trade Books in the Field of Social Studies.*

9.19 Aardema, Verna, reteller. **Borreguita and the Coyote: A Tale from Ayutla, Mexico.** Illustrated by Petra Mathers. Alfred A. Knopf/Borzoi Books, 1991. ISBN 0-679-90921-4. 32p. 5–8.

In this retelling of a Mexican folktale, Borreguita (Spanish for "little lamb") tricks Coyote three times and succeeds in defeating his plans to eat her. Outsmarted and physically bruised by Borreguita, Coyote learns not to bother her again. Vividly colored illustrations capture the wiliness of the ewe lamb and the gullibility of the hungry coyote. Playful words convey the sounds of the animal characters and their actions. A brief glossary of Spanish terms is included with this trickster tale, but note that *Esta bien* means "It's all right" or "That's all right," rather than "that is good." *Notable 1991 Children's Trade Books in the Field of Social Studies.*

9.20   Aardema, Verna, reteller. **Traveling to Tondo: A Tale of the Nkundo of Zaire.** Illustrated by Will Hillenbrand. Alfred A. Knopf/Borzoi Books, 1991. ISBN 0-679-90081-0. 36p. 5–8.

Traveling to Tondo for his wedding takes a long, long time for Bowane, the civet cat who waits for his friends to accompany him. When they eventually arrive—after he has waited for the palm nuts to ripen, a snake to be digested, a tree trunk to rot— Bowane's bride-to-be can no longer be his bride. Will Hillenbrand's expressive paintings and silhouettes add to the hilarity of this absurd tale. The cumulative structure and the repetitious language make this tale from the Nkundo of Zaire a natural read-aloud choice. *ALA Notable Children's Books, 1992; Notable 1991 Children's Trade Books in the Field of Social Studies.*

9.21   Begay, Shonto. **Ma'ii and Cousin Horned Toad: A Traditional Navajo Story.** Illustrated by Shonto Begay. Scholastic Hardcover Books, 1992. ISBN 0-590-45391-2. 32p. 5–8.

When Ma'ii the lazy coyote becomes hungry, he goes to visit Horned Toad, his hardworking cousin. Horned Toad is too polite to refuse Ma'ii, but greedy Ma'ii's appetite is out of control. When Horned Toad demands that Coyote work to earn his food, Coyote decides to trick his cousin out of the farm. Ma'ii swallows Horned Toad, but the coyote soon discovers that Horned Toad has some tricks of his own. The illustrations capture the humor of this Navajo trickster tale. An afterword and glossary of Navajo words are included.

9.22   Belpré, Pura. **Perez and Martina: A Puerto Rican Folktale/Perez y Martina.** Illustrated by Carlos Sánchez. Viking Penguin, 1991. ISBN 0-670-84166-8 (0-670-84167-6, Spanish ed.). 64p. 3–8.

A traditional Puerto Rican folktale with its origins in Spain, this is the story of Martina, a Spanish Cockroach whose suitors woo her with a variety of sounds. Martina finally settles on Perez the Mouse because of the beautiful way in which he speaks to her. But Perez meets an untimely demise when he falls into a rice pudding that Martina is cooking for him as a Christmas surprise.

9.23   Compton, Patricia A., reteller. **The Terrible EEK: A Japanese Tale.** Illustrated by Sheila Hamanaka. Simon and Schuster Books for Young Readers, 1991. ISBN 0-671-73737-6. 32p. 5 and up.

One night as the wind and rain batter their small thatched house, a father admits to his son that the thing he fears most is a "terrible leak." The wolf lurking outside is frightened at the thought of something so fierce. The thief on the roof hears "terrible eek" and is frightened, too. Through a cumulative series of mishaps, the thief, the wolf, a tiger, and a monkey all become involved in a hilarious and humorously illustrated search for the elusive terrible leak in this Japanese tale.

9.24   Goble, Paul. **Dream Wolf.** Ilustrated by Paul Goble. Bradbury Press, 1990. ISBN 0-02-736585-9. 32p. All ages.

This original folktale recalls the once-close relationship between Plains Indian peoples and wolves. Bored with their berry-picking chores, young Tiblo and his little sister Tanksi wander away from camp. Trying to reach the top of the hills, they lose track of time, and night finds them far from home and lost. They are not alone, however. Wolf sees to their safety and, in return, is honored by the Indians. Detailed illustrations and simple text provide a glimpse of historical Plains Indian culture. The text has been rewritten in this revised edition of *The Friendly Wolf* (1974). *Notable 1990 Children's Trade Books in the Field of Social Studies.*

9.25   Kimmel, Eric A., reteller. **Anansi Goes Fishing.** Illustrated by Janet Stevens. Holiday House, 1992. ISBN 0-8234-0918-X. 32p. 4–9.

This humorous retelling of an Anansi trickster tale also explains the origin of the spider web. Anansi the spider thinks that he can trick Turtle into doing all the work of catching fish. All Anansi will have to do is eat. But Turtle has some tricks of his own. The story of who gets to work and who gets to eat will keep readers laughing, as will the brightly animated illustrations. See also *Anansi Finds a Fool: An Ashanti Tale* by Verna Aardema (9.18).

9.26   Lester, Julius, reteller. **Further Tales of Uncle Remus: The Misadventures of Brer Rabbit, Brer Fox, Brer Wolf, the Doodang, and Other Creatures.** Illustrated by Jerry Pinkney. Dial Books, 1990. ISBN 0-8037-0611-1. 148p. All ages.

In the third of his Uncle Remus books, Julius Lester retells thirty-four African American folktales. Brer Rabbit and his friends get into and out of all kinds of mischief, playing tricks on one another and on their common enemies. Lester retains a narrator, similar to Chandler's Uncle Remus, but his narration is full of references to contemporary life. Most of the tales are humorous, and children young and old can enjoy hearing them read aloud. Jerry Pinkney's illustrations give the animals an almost human quality. *ALA Notable Children's Books, 1991; Notable 1990 Children's Trade Books in the Field of Social Studies.*

9.27 McDermott, Gerald. **Zomo the Rabbit: A Trickster Tale from West Africa.** Illustrated by Gerald McDermott. Harcourt Brace Jovanovich, 1992. ISBN 0-15-299967-1. 32p. 5–8.

Zomo the Rabbit is not big or strong, but he is very clever. He wants to be more than clever, however; he wants to be wise. He asks Sky God for help, but Sky God will not give Zomo wisdom until he completes three impossible tasks. How can little Zomo obtain the scales of Big Fish, the milk of Wild Cow, and the tooth of Leopard? This funny West African story with its vivid stylized paintings and simple text will appeal to a wide audience.

9.28 Mollel, Tololwa M. **Rhinos for Lunch and Elephants for Supper! A Maasai Tale.** Illustrated by Barbara Spurll. Clarion Books, 1991. ISBN 0-395-60734-5. 32p. 4–8.

"Who is there?" asks the hare when she returns to her cave home and finds it occupied. "A monster . . . ! I eat rhinos for lunch and elephants for supper! Come in if you dare!" answers a booming voice from inside the cave. What's a poor frightened hare to do? This one enlists the aid of her friends. Their encounters with the intruder, and the way in which the "monster" is revealed—and by whom—make a humorous story, rendered even funnier by the colorful bordered illustrations. The folktale comes from the Maasai of East Africa.

9.29 Sierra, Judy. **The Elephant's Wrestling Match.** Illustrated by Brian Pinkney. Lodestar Books, 1992. ISBN 0-525-67366-0. 32p. 5–8.

Who is brave enough and strong enough to wrestle with the mighty elephant? The monkey sends out the challenge on his talking drum, and the leopard, the crocodile, and the rhinoceros each take a turn, but the elephant is too much for each of them. Then a bat accepts the challenge and proves that victory does not always go to the mighty. The text is spare and rhythmical, making this story a good read-aloud. Brian Pinkney's scratchboard illustrations capture the action and the humor of this story from Cameroon.

9.30 Stiles, Martha Bennett, reteller. **James the Vine Puller: A Brazilian Folktale.** Illustrated by Larry Thomas. Carolrhoda Books, 1992. ISBN 0-897614-775-9. 28p. 5–8.

James the turtle enjoys life in his Brazilian jungle, eating coconuts and seaweed. But one day the elephant declares himself king of the jungle and refuses to allow James to eat his coconuts. Then the whale declares himself king of the ocean and forbids James seaweed. What can he do? Like a classic trickster, James uses his wits to outsmart both animals and to restore harmony to his domain. The Arawak Indians of Brazil use this version of an African tale to explain high tides.

Wonder Tales: Romance, Magic, and the Supernatural

9.31   Argueta, Manlio (translated by Stacey Ross). **Magic Dogs of the Volcanoes/Los Perros Mágicos de los Volcanes.** Illustrated by Elly Simmons. Children's Book Press, 1990. ISBN 0-89239-064-6. 32p. 5–10 (est).

The *cadejo*—mythic dogs of the El Salvador volcanoes—protect the nearby villagers from harm and danger. When greedy landlords attempt to destroy the *cadejos* and make the villagers work harder, the volcanoes conspire to erupt, saving both the *cadejos* and the villagers from the landlords and their lead soldiers. The text is written in both Spanish and English. The brightly colored folk-art style illustrations are a fitting accompaniment to this original pacifist tale based on folkloric material.

9.32   Birdseye, Tom, adapter. **A Song of Stars: An Asian Legend.** Illustrated by Ju-Hong Chen. Holiday House, 1990. ISBN 0-8324-0790-X. 32p. 5 and up.

The love between Chauchau, the celestial weaver, and Newlang, the handsome herdsman, is so great that the Emperor of Heaven decrees that they should be married. Unfortunately, the two are so devoted to each other that they neglect their other duties. As a punishment, they must live apart from each other and can meet only once a year on the seventh day of the seventh month. On the assigned date, Newlang has trouble crossing the Great Milky Way to see Chauchau. Who will come to their aid? An author's note explains how the myth is celebrated in both China and Japan. *Notable 1990 Children's Trade Books in the Field of Social Studies.*

9.33   Blanco, Alberto (translated by Barbara Paschke). **The Desert Mermaid/La Sirena del Desierto.** Illustrated by Patricia Revah. Children's Book Press, 1992. ISBN 0-89239-106-5. 32p. 7–9 (est).

This original "folktale," in both English and Spanish, carries a strong message about the need to "remember the songs of our ancestors." A mermaid living in an oasis in the Sonora Desert of Mexico learns from an Indian on a magic horse that the other mermaids have disappeared because they forgot their songs. The mermaid's quest for the ancient songs leads her eventually to the sea, where she finds exactly what she needs. The unusual illustrations were created by a tapestry artist.

9.34 Brusca, María Cristina, and Tona Wilson, retellers. **The Blacksmith and the Devil/El Herrero y el Diablo.** Illustrated by María Cristina Brusca. Henry Holt, 1992. ISBN 0-8050-1954-5 (0-8050-2411-5, Spanish ed.). 40p. 7 and up.

Juan Pobreza, an Argentine blacksmith, is poor, but he never turns anyone away for lack of money. One day he shoes the mule of a poor gaucho who claims to be San Pedro. In return, San Pedro grants him three wishes, but a disbelieving Juan impulsively squanders them. Then Mr. Wetcoals, who is a devil, appears, and Juan makes a Faustian bargain with him. When it comes time to pay up, Juan's frivolous wishes come in handy. He outsmarts the devil and lives a long life, but when he finally dies, he discovers that he may well have outsmarted himself. María Cristina Brusca's watercolors enhance the humor of this South American tale.

9.35 Dee, Ruby, reteller. **Tower to Heaven.** Illustrated by Jennifer Bent. Henry Holt, 1991. ISBN 0-8050-1460-8. 32p. 6–10.

Each day, while pounding her pestle, Yaa talks to the sky god Onyankopon. In her enthusiasm, she accidentally hits him with her pestle once too often, so Onyankopon moves far away into the heavens. Yaa misses her daily talks and has the village build a tower of mortar so that she can climb up to reach Onyankopon. But the tower is just one mortar short. If they just take one from the bottom. . . . Brightly colored illustrations reflect the humor of this West African tale.

9.36 Demi. **The Magic Boat.** Illustrated by Demi. Henry Holt, 1990. ISBN 0-8050-1141-2. 32p. 4–8.

In return for saving his life, an old man gives kind-hearted Chang a magic boat that grows big or small on command. During a flood, Chang rescues an ant, a bee, a crane, and the trickster Ying. While the others become helpful friends to Chang, Ying steals the magic boat and runs off to the emperor to make himself rich. This story tells how Chang and his friends go about getting the boat back. Detailed illustrations featuring red and gold reflect the Chinese setting of this tale.

9.37 Drummond, Allan. **The Willow Pattern Story.** Illustrated by Allan Drummond. North-South Books, 1992. ISBN 1-55858-172-3. 32p. 8 and up (est).

This love story explains the blue and white landscape design found on willow ware. A Chinese mandarin plans to marry his daughter Koong Shee to an old merchant. But she falls in love with Chang, the servant who manages her father's business and cares for the garden, and the two lovers run away together. Koong Shee's embittered father searches long years, and when he finds the couple, he exacts his punishment. Although the story is set in China, the china pattern was designed and first produced in England nearly two hundred years ago, which may explain some inaccuracies in the pictured costumes. *Notable 1992 Children's Trade Books in the Field of Social Studies.*

9.38 French, Fiona. **Anancy and Mr. Dry-Bone.** Illustrated by Fiona French. Little, Brown, 1991. ISBN 0-316-29298-2. 28p. 5–8 (est).

This original tale is based on Jamaican Anancy stories and is set in the Caribbean. Anancy, who is a poor man, wants to marry Miss Louise, who is very clever and beautiful, but who has never laughed in her life. Mr. Dry-Bone, who is rich, also wants to marry her. Miss Louise will marry the one who can make her laugh. Which one succeeds—and how—makes an entertaining story. The black silhouettes against colorful backgrounds add interest to this simply told tale.

9.39 Goble, Paul. **Iktomi and the Buffalo Skull: A Plains Indian Story.** Illustrated by Paul Goble. Orchard Books/Richard Jackson Books, 1991. ISBN 0-531-08511-2. 32p. 5–7.

Iktomi's vanity and curiosity again get the best of him in this tale about the Plains Indian trickster and his misadventures. Iktomi, dressed to impress the girls, hears music coming from a sacred buffalo skull, where mice are having a powwow. He falls asleep with his head in the skull, and the mice nibble off his hair. Iktomi is in serious trouble, and only his wife can help. The strong line and vivid colors of Paul Goble's illustrations complement this humorous story. See also Goble's *Iktomi and the Ducks: A Plains Indian Story* (9.40).

9.40 Goble, Paul, reteller. **Iktomi and the Ducks: A Plains Indian Story.** Illustrated by Paul Goble. Orchard Books/Richard Jackson Books, 1990. ISBN 0-531-08483-3. 32p. 5–7.

In Paul Goble's third Iktomi tale, the Plains Indian trickster dupes a flock of ducks and kills them for dinner. Coyote, in turn, tricks Iktomi and steals all but one of the roasting ducks, which he fills with coals. Again, Iktomi's greed and conceit prove detrimental to him. This retelling, as with the other Iktomi tales, has various typefaces and sizes to represent the story line, Iktomi's thoughts, and audience asides. This keeps the story moving, as do the bold, colorful, and distinctive illustrations. See also Goble's *Iktomi and the Buffalo Skull: A Plains Indian Story* (9.39).

9.41 Hillman, Elizabeth. **Min-Yo and the Moon Dragon.** Illustrated by John Wallner. Harcourt Brace Jovanovich, 1992. ISBN 0-15-254230-2. 32p. 6–10.

The heroine of this story set in China is a little girl named Min-Yo. The moon is falling, and if someone cannot think of a solution, the earth is doomed. Because of Min-Yo's agility and small size, the emperor requests that she climb the cobweb staircase to visit the moon dragon. Together Min-Yo and the dragon devise a way to save the earth and, at the same time, make the night sky sparkle. Watercolors illuminate this magical journey.

9.42 Hooks, William H. **The Ballad of Belle Dorcas.** Illustrated by Brian Pinkney. Alfred A. Knopf/Borzoi Books, 1990. ISBN 0-394-94645-6. 32p. 9 and up (est).

The daughter of a white slave owner and a house slave, Belle Dorcas, is "free issue." But she is not free to marry the slave Joshua, the man whom she loves. When a new master threatens to sell Joshua, Belle seeks help from the conjure woman and agrees to "give up Joshua to keep him." The conjure woman's spell keeps the lovers together for all time—at a very high price. Brian Pinkney's evocative drawings convey the power of the magic and the dignity of the characters. *Notable 1990 Children's Trade Books in the Field of Social Studies.*

9.43 Ikeda, Daisaku (translated by Geraldine McCaughrean). **The Snow Country Prince.** Illustrated by Brian Wildsmith. Alfred A. Knopf/Borzoi Books, 1990. ISBN 0-679-91965-1. 28p. 7 and up.

As winter arrives in Snow Country, Mariko and Kazuo begin looking after swans. The Snow Prince thanks them and advises, "whatever happens, don't give up." When the children's father

A.

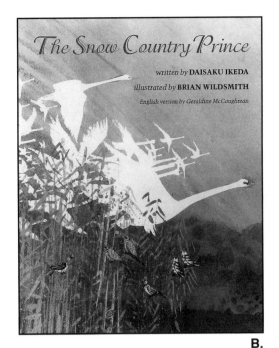

B.

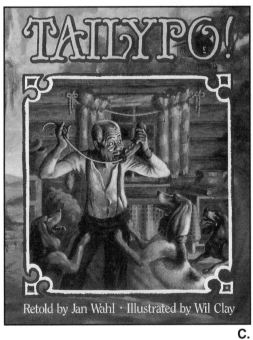

C.

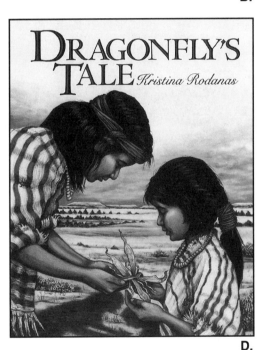

D.

A. *Tower to Heaven* retold by Ruby Dee; illustrated by Jennifer Bent (see 9.35). **B.** *The Snow Country Prince* by Daisaku Ikeda (translated by Geraldine McCaughrean); illustrated by Brian Wildsmith (see 9.43). **C.** *Tailypo!* retold by Jan Wahl; illustrated by Wil Clay (see 9.58). **D.** *Dragonfly's Tale* written and illustrated by Kristina Rodanas (see 9.52).

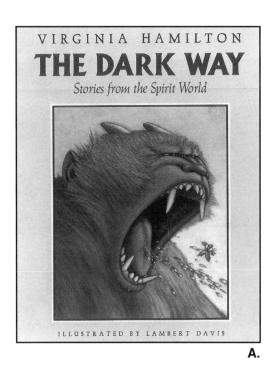

A.

B.

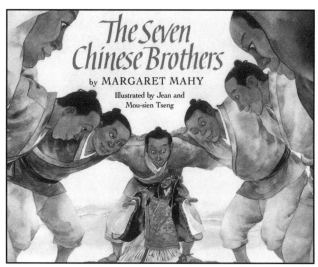

C.

A. *The Dark Way: Stories from the Spirit World* retold by Virginia Hamilton; illustrated by Lambert Davis (see 9.72). **B.** *Lightning inside You, and Other Native American Riddles* edited by John Bierhorst; illustrated by Louise Brierley (see 9.69). **C.** *The Seven Chinese Brothers* by Margaret Mahy; illustrated by Jean and Mou-sien Tseng (see 9.45).

is injured while away, their mother must go off to care for him. Alone, the children continue caring for an injured swan and sending pictures of their daily activities to their parents. The advice of the Snow Prince proves to be invaluable through the winter and into the spring, which brings the return of their parents. Brian Wildsmith's illustrations for this Japanese tale are vibrant.

9.44 Lacapa, Michael, reteller. **The Flute Player: An Apache Folktale.** Illustrated by Michael Lacapa. Northland, 1990. ISBN 0-87358-500-3. 48p. 7 and up.

"Listen!" It is not the wind, but the sound of a flute. Long ago a certain young man would play his flute in the canyon, and the young woman whom he loves would send a leaf down the river to signal her pleasure. When he goes on an extended hunting trip without her knowledge, she thinks that he no longer cares, and she becomes inconsolable. What happens when he returns makes a sad and romantic story, retold and illuminated by an Apache-Hopi artist.

9.45 Mahy, Margaret. **The Seven Chinese Brothers.** Illustrated by Jean and Mou-sien Tseng. Scholastic Hardcover Books, 1990. ISBN 0-590-42055-0. 36p. 6–10 (est).

Set in the time of the first emperor of China, Chin Shi Huang, this is the story of seven brothers, each possessing a unique power. When Third Brother repairs a great gaping hole in the Great Wall in one afternoon, the emperor feels threatened and sentences him to death. But his brothers come to his rescue, and the emperor finds that carrying out the sentence is not easy. Further, he learns that cruelty does not pay. Rich in historical detail, the watercolor illustrations heighten interest. *ALA Notable Children's Books, 1991; Notable 1990 Children's Trade Books in the Field of Social Studies.*

9.46 Martin, Rafe. **The Rough-Face Girl.** Illustrated by David Shannon. G. P. Putnam's Sons, 1992. ISBN 0-399-21859-9. 32p. 5 and up.

This Algonquin version of a Cinderella tale is retold in the words of a storyteller and in boldly dramatic illustrations. Many women wish to marry the rich and powerful Invisible Being, but his sister decrees that "only the one who can see him can marry him." The Rough-Face Girl, scarred from the cook fires that her sisters force her to tend, easily passes the test of the Invisible

Being's sister and proves once more that true beauty lies within. Note that at least one Native American critic has pointed out discrepancies between the text and pictures, such as a tipi for a wigwam and a crown instead of a cap, which recalls the "Indian Princess" stereotype.

9.47   Martinez, Alejandro Cruz (text by Rosalma Zubizarreta, Harriet Rohmer, and David Schecter). **The Woman Who Outshone the Sun: The Legend of Lucia Zenteno/La Mujer que Brillaba Aún Más que el Sol: La Leyenda de Lucía Zenteno.** Illustrated by Fernando Olivera. Children's Book Press, 1991. ISBN 0-89239-101-4. 32p. 7 and up.

When Lucia Zenteno arrives at the village accompanied by an iguana, her long unbraided hair outshines the sun. The river falls in love with Lucia's hair, and when Lucia bathes, the river flows through her hair until she combs it out. Fearful and intolerant of Lucia's differences, the villagers drive her out, but they soon have reason to regret their actions. Based on a poem by Alejandro Cruz Martinez, the poetic text of this Zapotec Indian legend from Mexico is in both English and Spanish. *ALA Notable Children's Books, 1992.*

9.48   Mayer, Marianna. **Golden Swan: An East Indian Tale of Love from** *The Mahabharata.* Illustrated by Robert Sauber. Bantam Skylark Books/Timeless Tales, 1990. ISBN 0-553-07054-1. 64p. 8 and up.

A young king named Nala falls in love with the beautiful princess Damayanti as he listens to an enchanting song about her sung by traveling minstrels. He sends a golden swan to her distant home to express his love. When it comes time for Damayanti to select a husband and she chooses Nala, this angers one of her suitors, Kali, the snake-eyed god of misfortune. He begins a course of vengeance that strips Nala of all his fortunes and separates the couple. Yet, true love endures. Damayanti's great loyalty to her husband ensures a happy ending to this classical story from India. Inspired by *The Mahabharata*, this tale is a masterful blend of myth and legend.

9.49   Paterson, Katherine. **The Tale of the Mandarin Ducks.** Illustrated by Leo and Diane Dillon. Lodestar Books, 1990. ISBN 0-525-67283-4. 40p. 7 and up (est).

A greedy lord in ancient Japan cages a magnificent drake, separating him from his mate. When the grieving drake loses its luster, the lord banishes the duck to a kitchen corner. Eventually the kitchen maid Yasuko and the servant Shozo release the duck, and as punishment, the lord sentences them to die. But the drake and his mate find a way to intervene and repay the couple for their kindness. The Dillons' Japanese-inspired paintings are perfect complements to Katherine Paterson's original Japanese folktale. *ALA Notable Children's Books, 1991; Boston Globe–Horn Book Picture Book Award, 1991; Notable 1990 Children's Trade Books in the Field of Social Studies.*

9.50   Pattison, Darcy. **The River Dragon.** Illustrated by Jean and Mousien Tseng. Lothrop, Lee and Shepard Books, 1991. ISBN 0-688-10427-4. 32p. 7–10 (est).

A Chinese blacksmith is betrothed to the daughter of a wealthy goldsmith, but the father is dissatisfied with the matchmaker's choice. At each prenuptial banquet, the father purposely serves the favorite foods of the dragon who guards the River Dragon's bridge, intending that the blacksmith will be devoured as he returns home. Fortunately, the blacksmith, aided by the "fortune cookie" clues, outsmarts the dragon and proves that he is a worthy husband-to-be. The dramatic watercolors capture the dragon's ferocity in this modern original tale that draws on some Chinese lore.

9.51   Rappaport, Doreen, reteller. **The Journey of Meng: A Chinese Legend.** Illustrated by Yang Ming-Yi. Dial Books for Young Readers, 1991. ISBN 0-8037-0896-3. 32p. 10 and up.

Meng Jiangnu's husband has been conscripted to help build the Great Wall of China. After he appears to her in a dream, she courageously sets out to find him. Magic helps her in her travels, but it is too late—her husband is dead. Meng Jiangnu is taken before the emperor, who insists that she become his. She makes a bargain with the emperor but finds that she cannot bring herself to keep her promise. Somber hues and misty watercolors illustrate this tragic story of love and courage for mature readers. *Notable 1991 Children's Trade Books in the Field of Social Studies.*

9.52   Rodanas, Kristina. **Dragonfly's Tale.** Illustrated by Kristina Rodanas. Clarion Books, 1991. ISBN 0-395-57003-4. 32p. 5–7.

In this Zuni Indian tale, Ashiwi villagers waste the bounty given them by the Corn Maidens. The resulting famine drives the villagers away, but they unwittingly leave behind two children. To soothe his frightened sister, the boy makes a cornstalk toy, which comes to life and intercedes with the Corn Maidens on the children's behalf. When the Ashiwi return, the surprise that awaits them teaches them an important lesson. Earth tones and splashes of red and blue predominate in this tale from the American Southwest.

9.53   San Souci, Robert. **Sukey and the Mermaid.** Illustrated by Brian Pinkney. Four Winds Press, 1992. ISBN 0-02-778141-0. 32p. 6 and up.

Mermaids are rare, and the rarest kind are Black mermaids. As Sukey rests by the sea, her plaintive song is answered by the beautiful and kind Mama Jo. When Sukey shares the Black mermaid's gifts with her ma and step-pa, "Mister Hard-Times," the greedy man wants more. Both Sukey and her step-pa get all they deserve from this awesome creature. Brian Pinkney's scratchboard illustrations add homey details and elements of wonder to this suspenseful African American folktale. *ALA Notable Children's Books, 1993.*

9.54   So, Meilo, reteller. **The Emperor and the Nightingale.** Illustrated by Meilo So. Bradbury Press, 1992. ISBN 0-02-786045-0. 24p. 7–9 (est).

The nightingale's song is so wonderful that the Chinese emperor is moved to tears. He places her in a golden cage and listens daily until someone sends him a mechanical nightingale that is prettier than the real one and that sings just as well. The real bird escapes, but the emperor is content with the mechanical bird—until it wears out. Years later, the emperor, old and sick, learns the value of true beauty and true friendship. This adaptation of Hans Christian Andersen's story is illustrated in vibrant colors.

9.55   Torre, Betty L., reteller. **The Luminous Pearl: A Chinese Folktale.** Illustrated by Carol Inouye. Orchard Books, 1990. ISBN 0-531-08490-6. 27p. 7–10 (est).

In this Chinese folktale, the Dragon King's beautiful daughter seeks a husband who is honest and brave. To win her hand, two brothers are sent to retrieve the luminous pearl from the Eastern Sea. The elder brother returns with a shining pearl. The younger brings a magic dipper to save a flooded village, and when the waters recede, he discovers an oyster with a black pearl. The princess knows, however, that appearances are deceiving. Watercolor paintings make the magic seem possible.

9.56 Volkmer, Jane Anne, reteller (translated by Lori Ann Schatschneider). **Song of the Chirimia: A Guatemalan Folktale/La Musica de la Chirimia: Folklore Guatemalteco.** Illustrated by Jane Anne Volkmer. Carolrhoda Books, 1990. ISBN 0-87614-423-7. 40p. 8 and up.

A Mayan princess promises to marry a suitor if he learns to sing like the birds. Unfortunately, after many days of trying, the young man finds he cannot fulfill the princess's request. Finally, aided by the Great Spirit, he learns to play a wooden flute-like instrument—the *chirimia*—whose melodious music has not been heard before by the princess. This bilingual (English-Spanish) edition of the Guatemalan legend of the *chirimia* is illustrated in bold colors. *Notable 1990 Children's Trade Books in the Field of Social Studies.*

9.57 Wahl, Jan. **Little Eight John.** Illustrated by Wil Clay. Lodestar Books, 1992. ISBN 0-525-67367-9. 32p. 5–9.

Little Eight John was as mean as mean could be! Whatever his lovingly patient mother told him would bring misfortune to the family was exactly what he had to do. When her warnings proved prophetic, he would laugh himself silly. But one day his misbehavior leads to an encounter with Old Raw Head Bloody Bones, and the close call causes Little Eight John to consider the error of his ways. Wil Clay's realistic paintings reveal the southern rural setting of this cautionary tale drawn from African American folklore and used historically to warn children to be good. *Coretta Scott King Illustration Honor Book, 1993.*

9.58 Wahl, Jan, reteller. **Tailypo!** Illustrated by Wil Clay. Henry Holt, 1991. ISBN 0-8050-0687-7. 32p. 5–10.

One night after supper, a creature with a great big tail creeps through the cracks of an African American man's cabin. The old man grabs his hatchet. Wump! He cuts off the creature's tail and eats it up. But the creature wants its tail back, and how it goes about getting its tail makes a deliciously scary story for young readers. The finely detailed illustrations capture the suspense and the fright. The tale is good for reading aloud.

9.59 Wang, Rosalind C., reteller. **The Fourth Question: A Chinese Tale.** Illustrated by Ju-Hong Chen. Holiday House, 1991. ISBN 0-8234-0855-8. 32p. 6–10 (est).

In this retelling of a Chinese folktale, a young man who has always worked hard wonders why he has remained so poor. On his journey to seek an answer from the Wise Man in the mountains, he encounters three others who each have a question to ask. Since the Wise Man permits only three questions, the young man decides to give up his own. In the end his selflessness is rewarded, and his question, too, is answered.

9.60   Wisniewski, David. **Rain Player.** Illustrated by David Wisniewski. Clarion Books, 1991. ISBN 0-395-55112-9. 32p. 8–10.

In this original tale based on a Mayan legend, David Wisniewski relates the story of Pik, a young ballplayer who challenges the rain god to a game of *pok-a-tok,* a combination of present-day soccer and basketball. If Pik wins, the drought will end. If he loses, he will be turned into a frog. With the help of a jaguar, a quetzal, and a sacred *cenote,* or deep water-filled sinkhole, Pik meets the challenge. The special feature of this book is Wisniewski's cut-paper illustrations, which have a three-dimensional effect. An author's note provides useful background information.

9.61   Yacowitz, Caryn, adapter. **The Jade Stone: A Chinese Folktale.** Illustrated by Ju-Hong Chen. Holiday House, 1992. ISBN 0-8234-0919-8. 31p. 6–10 (est).

To follow the way of man or the way of nature? Such is the dilemma for Chan Lo, the village carver. From a perfect piece of jade, the emperor expects him to carve a dragon. But it is a carver's traditon to follow the stone's nature, and Chan Lo discovers that this stone wants to be something else. This Chinese tale is illustrated in ink and watercolor paintings and is further enhanced by the illustrator's technique of evoking the look of ancient woodblock prints with Chinese characters.

Realistic Tales

9.62   Ada, Alma Flor (translated by Bernice Randall). **The Gold Coin.** Illustrated by Neil Waldman. Atheneum, 1991. ISBN 0-689-31633-X. 32p. 7 and up (est).

"Juan had been a thief for many years." So begins this original tale, set in Central America, about the redemptive power of kindness and love. When Juan sees an old woman with a gold coin and hears her declare herself rich, he determines to steal all her gold. As he trails her on errands to help the sick and needy, he meets only kindness. By the time he finally comes face to face with Doña Josepha, Juan is already on his way to being a new person. *Notable 1991 Children's Trade Books in the Field of Social Studies.*

9.63   Alexander, Lloyd. **The Fortune-Tellers.** Illustrated by Trina Schart Hyman. Dutton Children's Books, 1992. ISBN 0-525-44849-7. 32p. 4–8.

A carpenter, dissatisfied with his trade, visits a fortune-teller. Will he be rich? famous? happy? Certainly—if he earns large sums of money, becomes well known, and avoids being miserable. How these and other predictions come true makes for an amusing original tale with a touch of slapstick added to the ironic plot. Trina Schart Hyman's illustrations play up the jewel-like colors of West African fabrics and reveal numerous details of daily life in a Cameroon village. *ALA Notable Children's Books, 1993; Boston Globe–Horn Book Honor Picture Book, 1993; Notable 1992 Children's Trade Books in the Field of Social Studies.*

9.64   Demi. **The Artist and the Architect.** Illustrated by Demi. Henry Holt, 1991. ISBN 0-8050-1685-6. 32p. 4–8 (est).

The emperor of China employs both an architect and an artist to serve him. The artist becomes jealous and devises a scheme to eliminate the architect, who plays along with this trickery. In the end, the architect manages to turn the tables on the artist. Demi's bright colors and minute detail capture the ornate style of ancient China.

9.65   Demi. **The Empty Pot.** Illustrated by Demi. Henry Holt, 1990. ISBN 0-8050-1217-6. 30p. 4–8 (est).

Virtue is rewarded in this tale from China. When it is time to choose his successor, the emperor gives each child a special seed. Whoever can show the emperor "their best in a year's time" shall become emperor. Ping can make anything grow, but try as he will, he cannot grow anything from the emperor's seeds. He must appear before the emperor with an empty pot. Humiliation turns to triumph when the emperor reveals the secret of the seeds. Demi's illustrations authentically reflect Chinese landscape and architecture. *Notable 1990 Children's Trade Books in the Field of Social Studies.*

9.66   Rohmer, Harriet, adapter. **Uncle Nacho's Hat/El Sombrero del Tío Nacho.** Illustrated by Veg Reisberg. Children's Book Press, 1989. ISBN 0-89239-043-0. 32p. 5–8 (est).

Change is difficult to accept at times, and Uncle Nacho demonstrates that to be the case. When his niece Ambrosia gives him a new hat, Uncle Nacho has a hard time getting rid of his old one. Several attempts to discard the old hat prove unsuccessful because he still thinks in the old ways. Finally, Ambrosia, a voice of change, provides her uncle with the solution to his problem. The text of this adapted Nicaraguan folktale is in both English and Spanish; the artwork is evocative of Central America.

9.67   Vá, Leong (translated by James Anderson). **A Letter to the King.** Illustrated by Leong Vá. HarperCollins, 1991. ISBN 0-06-020070-7. 32p. 4–8.

In ancient China, parents preferred sons because sons could care for them in their old age. A certain physician, the unhappy father of five girls, is unjustly imprisoned when a relative of the king's dies. If he only had a son, then he would be rescued! Ti Ying, his youngest daughter, accompanies him to the capital, and the father doctor learns the value of daughters when Ti Ying writes a poignant letter to the king on her father's behalf. The text is in both Chinese and English. Unique and colorful illustrations help tell the tale. *Notable 1991 Children's Trade Books in the Field of Social Studies.*

Collections

9.68   Belting, Natalia M. **Moon Was Tired of Walking on Air.** Illustrated by Will Hillenbrand. Houghton Mifflin, 1992. ISBN 0-395-53806-8. 48p. All ages.

These fourteen creation stories from various South American Indian tribes answer age-old questions about ourselves and our universe. They explain how the earth came to be, why the rainbow is bent, how rivers came into existence, and other natural phenomena. A handy map gives the location of the various tribal groups. Although the illustrations, which recall ancient times and artistic styles, are tastefully done and appropriate to the stories, some readers may be uncomfortable with the nudity or near-nudity shown in some scenes. *Notable 1992 Children's Trade Books in the Field of Social Studies.*

9.69   Bierhorst, John, editor. **Lightning inside You, and Other Native American Riddles.** Illustrated by Louise Brierley. William Morrow, 1992. ISBN 0-688-09582-8. 111p. All ages.

"What is there inside you like lightning?" This book is a well-researched collection of riddles from twenty different Indian tribal groups in North and South America. An introduction provides information about the tradition of riddling among native peoples, the various types of riddles, and their functions within the cultures. Helpful hints make it easier for readers to guess the answers, and editor John Bierhorst assures readers that their answers may be just as acceptable as the ones printed.

9.70   DeArmond, Dale, reteller. **The Boy Who Found the Light: Eskimo Folktales.** Illustrated by Dale DeArmond. Sierra Club Books/Little, Brown, 1990. ISBN 0-316-17787-3. 61p. 7 and up.

Woven through these three Eskimo folktales is respect for both humanity and nature. "The Boy Who Found the Light," in which an orphan boy named Tulugac is the light bringer, makes a useful comparison to stories in which Raven brings light to people. "The Raven and the Marmot" is a trickster tale in which Marmot outwits Raven. In "The Doll," Yuguk comes to life and brings precious gifts to his people. Black-and-white wood engravings capture the spirit of these tales from the North. *Notable 1990 Children's Trade Books in the Field of Social Studies.*

9.71   Fairman, Tony, reteller. **Bury My Bones but Keep My Words: African Tales for Retelling.** Illustrated by Meshack Asare. Henry Holt, 1992. ISBN 0-8050-2333-X. 196p. 10 and up.

In this collection, the title of which is a Luo proverb from Kenya, Tony Fairman presents thirteen traditional tales from various African peoples. Through varying typefaces, boxed asides, and onomatopoetic words, he attempts to represent a typical African oral context. Unfortunately, he tends to speak of Africa and "African spelling" (there is a pronunciation guide) in generic terms, and for story refrains he suggests some English melodies that may not be familiar to American readers. The specific source of each story is cited, and on the whole, the presentation is lively and inviting. *Notable 1992 Children's Trade Books in the Field of Social Studies.*

9.72   Hamilton, Virginia, reteller. **The Dark Way: Stories from the Spirit World.** Illustrated by Lambert Davis. Harcourt Brace Jovanovich, 1990. ISBN 0-15-222341-X. 154p. 9 and up.

These twenty-five stories from around the world are tales of the spirit world involving witches, fairies, and inhuman monsters. Some, such as the Medusa story, may be familiar; others will be less so. All are spine-tingling. Following each tale is an author's note giving the tale's origin(s) and adding important context. A bibliography is also included. Lambert Davis's color illustrations heighten the sense of dread. These tales are suitable for any audience that enjoys being safely scared.

9.73   Joseph, Lynn. **A Wave in Her Pocket: Stories from Trinidad.** Illustrated by Brian Pinkney. Clarion Books, 1991. ISBN 0-395-54432-7. 51p. 9 and up.

Amber's Tantie doesn't just tell a story: "She cause a big bacchanal and scare everybody." Six tales from Trinidad comprise this collection of authentic retellings of handed-down stories. Author Lynn Joseph smoothly blends family life with cultural lore using the flavorful cadences of island speech patterns. The stories are funny, frightening, tender, tricky, and thought-provoking. Brian Pinkney's black-and-white drawings add visual energy to the lively text. The book includes an afterword and glossary.

9.74   Lyons, Mary E., compiler. **Raw Head, Bloody Bones: African-American Tales of the Supernatural.** Charles Scribner's Sons, 1991. ISBN 0-684-19333-7. 88p. 10 and up.

"Raw Head was a man that was more'n a man. He was big and strong like Big Sixteen and he was two-headed. . . ." Raw Head is just one of the scary creatures found in these fifteen stories. They are stories, mostly of African origin, of goblins, ghosts, monsters, and superhumans, collected from sources in the United States and the Caribbean. Told in the dialects of the original tellers, these stories offer scary fun and a lesson or two as well. *Notable 1991 Children's Trade Books in the Field of Social Studies.*

9.75   Watkins, Yoko Kawashima. **Tales from the Bamboo Grove.** Illustrated by Jean and Mou-sien Tseng. Bradbury Press, 1992. ISBN 0-02-792525-0. 49p. 9–12.

Although author Yoko Kawashima Watkins is Japanese, as a child she lived in Korea, where her father was a diplomat. At dinnertime her father told stories, often to make a point. Guests and other family members also told stories. This collection of six tales reflects the Kawashima family's attempt to instill values and maintain their connections to their homeland. The author's introduction is informative, and the black-and-white illustrations reflect the moods of the stories.

9.76 Yep, Laurence. **Tongues of Jade.** Illustrated by David Wiesner. HarperCollins, 1991. ISBN 0-06-022471-1. 194p. 10 and up (est).

Laurence Yep introduces us to seventeen folktales passed down by Chinese immigrants who came to America seeking their fortune. These timeless tales, full of magical powers, eerie suspense, and moralistic messages, arouse the imagination. These stories connected the immigrants to their homeland and to their families, whom many would never see again. This is a companion volume to Yep's *The Rainbow People. Notable 1991 Children's Trade Books in the Field of Social Studies.*

10 Books for the Very Young

10.1 Calhoun, Mary. **While I Sleep.** Illustrated by Ed Young. Morrow Junior Books, 1990. ISBN 0-688-08201-7. 32p. 4–7. Fiction.

At bedtime a little girl asks, "Does everything go to sleep at night?" In reply, her parents affectionately describe how animals, trains, boats, planes, and even the sun rest in the night world. Each double-page spread has two parts: an insert showing the creature or thing asleep, and a large pastel drawing of the subject's daytime activity. Although the family looks Asian, the book has universal appeal.

10.2 Carlstrom, Nancy White. **Baby-O.** Illustrated by Suçie Stevenson. Little, Brown, 1992. ISBN 0-316-125851-1. 28p. 3–8. Fiction.

"Listen to the way our baby goes / Baby Baby Baby-O." Every member of this extended family has a sound to accompany his or her task: "tomatoma," "wusha wusha," "kongada," and more. Readers will want to join in as they follow three generations gathering and transporting their wares to market on a bus named Baby-O. At the end of the day, they reunite and ride Baby-O home. The colorful illustrations evoke the energy and vitality of the people of this unnamed Caribbean island and give young readers a picture of island life.

10.3 Greenfield, Eloise. **Big Friend, Little Friend.** Illustrated by Jan Spivey Gilchrist. Black Butterfly Children's Books, 1991. ISBN 0-86316-204-5. 12p. 1–5. Fiction.

One of a set of four board books with rhyming text by well-known African American writer Eloise Greenfield, this title can also be put to use in early literacy programs. The book focuses on comparative size, as the narrator shows that he is smaller than his big friend, but larger than his little friend, and that his role changes from learner to teacher, from smaller than to bigger than. Jan Spivey Gilchrist's watercolors are clear and uncluttered.

10.4   Greenfield, Eloise. **Daddy and I. . . .** Illustrated by Jan Spivey Gilchrist. Black Butterfly Children's Books, 1991. ISBN 0-86316-206-1. 12p. 1–5. Fiction.

This board book could easily find a place in a kindergarten or preschool. The rhyming text is about the things that an African American boy and his daddy do together. "We do the laundry, / my daddy and I. / He washes the socks, / I hang them to dry." Some big brothers or big sisters might enjoy reading this book to younger siblings.

10.5   Greenfield, Eloise. **I Make Music.** Illustrated by Jan Spivey Gilchrist. Black Butterfly Children's Books, 1991. ISBN 0-86316-205-3. 12p. 1–5. Fiction.

"I make good music / on my drums, / I make good music / with my thumbs." A little African American girl makes music on everything from the piano to her thigh to a trombone. Her parents think it is all good music. This is a rhythmic, rhyming, read-aloud book that invites everybody to join in with a clap or a pat of the foot. Another of Eloise Greenfield's board books for the very young, this one will also work in kindergarten or first grade.

10.6   Greenfield, Eloise. **My Doll, Keshia.** Illustrated by Jan Spivey Gilchrist. Black Butterfly Children's Books, 1991. ISBN 0-86316-203-7. 12p. 1–5. Fiction.

"My doll Keshia wants to play. / 'Okay, darling, jump!' I say." A little African American girl and her brother put her doll through its paces, "teaching" it to walk and dance and wave and talk. Then it is time for a rest; Keshia has been very busy. This board book, another of Eloise Greenfield's rhymed texts, makes a good read-aloud and predictable book for young listeners and new readers. Jan Spivey Gilchrist's watercolors make it easy to follow the action.

10.7   Horton, Barbara Savadge. **What Comes in Spring?** Illustrated by Ed Young. Alfred A. Knopf/Borzoi Books, 1992. ISBN 0-679-90268-6. 30p. 3–6. Fiction.

"Mama, what comes in spring?" Imagine a child snuggling in her mother's lap, asking inquisitive, personal questions about the changing seasons. Imagine the mother's melodic responses that tell a story about the child's own birth with each explanation. The rhythmic dialogue, punctuated by lively illustrations, renders inseparable the relationship between the child's growth and nature's own cycle of life. Ed Young's poignant and vivid drawings help to embody the seemingly universal theme into the experiences of an Asian family.

10.8   Joosse, Barbara M. **Mama, Do You Love Me?** Illustrated by Barbara Lavallee. Chronicle Books, 1991. ISBN 0-87701-759-X. 26p. 4–6. Fiction.

Mama's love is limitless and unconditional—even if the child were to throw water at the lamp, or put salmon in Mama's parka, or run away, or turn into a polar bear! Young children of all cultures will find this story reassuring. The illustrations show an Inuit mother and daughter living in the arctic region of northern Alaska as the Inuit lived long ago. Included is a glossary explaining terms and objects referred to in the story and offering further insight into Inuit life and culture.

10.9   Serfozo, Mary. **Rain Talk.** Illustrated by Keiko Narahashi. Margaret K. McElderry Books, 1990. ISBN 0-689-50496-9. 28p. 4–8. Fiction.

Splatt! Kerplunk! Click! These are some of the sounds that a little girl, who appears to be African American, hears as she frolics in the rain with her dog. After a while it is time to come in for supper, hear a story by the fire, and then go to bed to listen to the rain and wait for tomorrow. The watercolor illustrations reflect the gentle mood. The repetition of sounds and the use of onomatopoeia make this book excellent for reading aloud or creative drama.

10.10   Weiss, Nicki. **On a Hot, Hot Day.** Illustrated by Nicki Weiss. G. P. Putnam's Sons, 1992. ISBN 0-399-22119-0. 26p. 3–7. Fiction.

What fun Mama and Angel have cooling off in the spray from a water hydrant, sipping cocoa, reading quietly in the afternoon, frolicking with each other, and singing at bedtime! The story is set in a multiracial community. The name Angel and a sign for "El Bodegero" suggest the characters may be Hispanic. The repetitive rhyming text will appeal to young readers, as will the simple style of the illustrations.

10.11   Williams, Vera B. **"More More More," Said the Baby: Three Love Stories.** Illustrated by Vera B. Williams. Greenwillow Books, 1990. ISBN 0-688-09173-3. 33p. 4–6. Fiction.

Meet Little Guy, Little Pumpkin, and Little Bird. One is white; one is African American; one is Asian. Read and see how each of

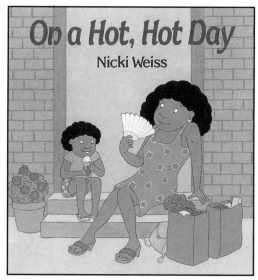

A.

B.

C.

D.

A. *On a Hot, Hot Day* written and illustrated by Nicki Weiss (see 10.10). **B.** *Mama, Do You Love Me?* by Barbara M. Joosse; illustrated by Barbara Lavallee (see 10.8). **C.** *What Comes in Spring?* by Barbara Savadge Horton; illustrated by Ed Young (see 10.7). **D.** *"More More More," Said the Baby: Three Love Stories* written and illustrated by Vera B. Williams (see 10.11).

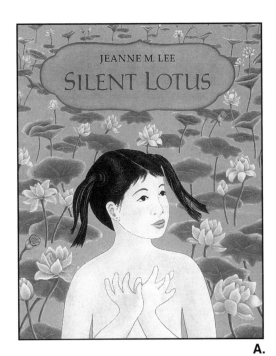

A.

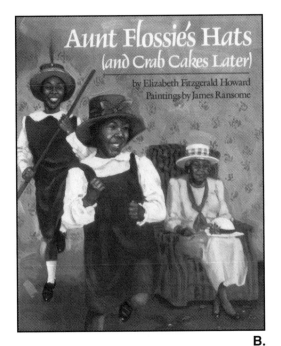

B.

C.

A. *Silent Lotus* written and illustrated by Jeanne M. Lee (see 11.47). **B.** *Aunt Flossie's Hats (and Crab Cakes Later)* by Elizabeth Fitzgerald Howard; illustrated by James Ransome (see 11.29). **C.** *Osa's Pride* written and illustrated by Ann Grifalconi (see 11.21).

these three babies is cared for, played with, and loved by the adults in their families. Vera Williams's rich watercolor illustrations and rhymthic text will leave you feeling warm and perhaps even slightly envious of the families in her three love stories. *ALA Notable Children's Books, 1991; Caldecott Honor Book, 1991.*

10.12 Young, Ruth. **Golden Bear.** Illustrated by Rachel Isadora. Viking Penguin, 1992. ISBN 0-670-82577-8. 32p. 2–6. Fiction.

A litttle African American child has a golden bear for a best friend. They do everything together—build a snowman, ice skate, make mud pies, and dream. The simple, rhyming text makes for good reading aloud. The large uncluttered illustrations leave the child's gender somewhat ambiguous, although there may be too much hair for a contemporary boy. The musical score on the end pages reveals that the text is a song lyric.

11 Picture Books: Primary and Beyond

11.1 Adoff, Arnold. **Hard to Be Six.** Illustrated by Cheryl Hanna. Lothrop, Lee and Shepard Books, 1991. ISBN 0-688-09579-8. 32p. 5–8. Fiction.

This is a poetic look at what it is like to be six—when your sister is ten. The six-year-old narrator cannot ride a ten-speed bike or pin the tail on the donkey, but he can make mud pies and dream himself big. The family is understanding, but it is Grandma who helps the boy understand the need to "take time slow, make life count, and pass love on." This is one of the rare books showing an interracial family.

11.2 Albert, Burton. **Where Does the Trail Lead?** Illustrated by Brian Pinkney. Simon and Schuster Books for Young Readers, 1991. ISBN 0-671-73409-1. 32p. 3–7. Fiction.

An African American boy runs along the rocks at the seashore, stopping here and there to look at periwinkles, explore deserted shanties, and wade in the pounding surf as he explores a trail. The trail leads back to his family, who prepare a meal of freshly caught fish. Lyrical language might remind some children of a poem. Brian Pinkney has drawn on childhood experiences at Cape Cod to lead readers along seashore paths.

11.3 Allen, Judy. **Tiger.** Illustrated by Tudor Humphries. Candlewick Press, 1992. ISBN 1-56402-083-5. 28p. 7–10 (est). Fiction.

There's a tiger out there! Desiring both the tiger's meat and its skin, the villagers plot the best way to kill it. Then a famous hunter arrives, and the villagers wish him luck—all except Lee, who wants the tiger to live. But there is more than one way to shoot a cat, and Lee is pleased with the outcome. Set in South China and illustrated with realistic watercolor paintings, this book aims to raise our consciousness about the endangered tiger.

11.4 Ashley, Bernard. **Cleversticks.** Illustrated by Derek Brazell. Crown, 1991. ISBN 0-517-58879-X. 32p. 3–6 (est). Fiction.

Ling Sung is a sensitive preschooler of Chinese descent who notices that other children are more capable than he at such tasks as tying their shoes and writing their names. However, one day when his cookie breaks, he picks up two paintbrushes and, without thinking, begins using them like chopsticks. His classmates are impressed by his dexterity, and all want to learn how to use chopsticks. The artist makes each child in this British multiracial classroom a distinct individual.

11.5   Axworthy, Anni. **Anni's India Diary.** Illustrated by Anni Axworthy. Whispering Coyote Press/Treld Bicknell Books, 1992. ISBN 1-879085-59-3. 32p. 7–10. Fiction.

This is a fictional diary of a two-and-a-half-month journey through India. Ten-year-old Anni and her parents begin in Delhi and travel by various means to many cities and to well-known tourist spots, such as the Taj Mahal. Busy color drawings and the brief text convey the sights, sounds, and tastes that Anni and her parents encounter. Included in the drawings are product labels, stamps, and other artifacts that give a flavor of India. The journey is traced on a map in the front of the book.

11.6   Bogart, Jo Ellen. **Daniel's Dog.** Illustrated by Janet Wilson. Scholastic Hardcover Books, 1990. ISBN 0-590-43402-0. 32p. 5–8. Fiction.

Daniel's mother is busy taking care of Carrie, the new baby in this African Canadian family, and Daniel plays alone until his friend Lucy, an imaginary dog, arrives. Mom understands that Daniel is feeling left out, and she lets him read a book to Carrie and hold her gently in his arms. When Daniel's real friend Norman expects to be alone for a while, Daniel knows just what to suggest.

11.7   Bond, Ruskin. **Cherry Tree.** Illustrated by Allan Eitzen. Boyds Mills Press/Caroline House, 1991. ISBN 1-878093-21-5. 32p. 6–8 (est). Fiction.

On the day when six-year-old Rakhi comes home from the bazaar eating cherries, her grandfather suggests that she plant one of the seeds. Although not many trees survive the soil and climate in her area of India, Rakhi's tree takes hold and grows over a few years until it is taller than she and produces lovely blossoms and sweet cherries. Grandfather reminds Rakhi that every living thing grows and changes, including herself.

11.8   Breckler, Rosemary K. **Hoang Breaks the Lucky Teapot.** Illustrated by Adrian Frankel. Houghton Mifflin, 1992. ISBN 0-395-57031-X. 14p. 5–8. Fiction.

When he left Vietnam for America, Hoang's grandmother gave him a lucky teapot. Now he has broken the pot, and it can no longer hold the *May Mun*, the good fortune to protect the family from evil spirits. How can they survive the first winter with bad luck looming? Young readers will empathize with Hoang and celebrate his achievement when he finds a solution. An informative introduction provides background and tells how to pronounce the Vietnamese words in the story.

11.9   Bunting, Eve. **The Wall.** Illustrated by Ronald Himler. Clarion Books, 1990. ISBN 0-395-51588-2. 32p. 4–8. Fiction.

A young Hispanic American boy and his father visit the Vietnam Veterans Memorial in Washington, D.C., to find the name of the boy's grandfather—George Munoz—on the long, shiny black wall. As his father scans the monument, the boy observes the visitors and mementos there. After finding the name, the father makes a special record of it, and the two leave behind a token of love and remembrance. Overall, this is a touching picture book for readers of all ages. *ALA Notable Children's Books, 1991; Notable 1990 Children's Trade Books in the Field of Social Studies.*

11.10 Cherry, Lynne. **The Great Kapok Tree: A Tale of the Amazon Rain Forest.** Illustrated by Lynne Cherry. Harcourt Brace Jovanovich/Gulliver Books, 1990. ISBN 0-15-200520-X. 33p. 8 and up (est). Fiction.

Conservation of the earth's natural resources is a topic of interest for children and adults alike. Hence, this compelling tale about the shrinking tropical rain forests of the world will appeal to readers young and old. Lynne Cherry's thought-provoking text and vivid paintings are bound to generate much classrooom discussion; the timely content will invite cross-curricular intructional connections, particularly across science and social studies. Interesting and informative insights can also be found on the inside cover and preface.

11.11 Clifton, Lucille. **Three Wishes.** Illustrated by Michael Hays. Doubleday Books for Young Readers, 1992. ISBN 0-385-30497-8. 32p. 5–8. Fiction.

On New Year's Day, while out playing with her best friend Victorius, an African American girl named Zenobia finds a penny with her birth year on it. This means that she can make three wishes and that they will come true. First, she wishes for warmer weather, and the sun comes out—right then. How should she "spend" the other two wishes? Before the day is over, Zenobia loses and regains a friend and learns what is really important. This is a newly illustrated version of Lucille Clifton's 1976 book.

11.12 Crews, Donald. **Shortcut.** Illustrated by Donald Crews. Greenwillow Books, 1992. ISBN 0-688-06437-X. 32p. 4–7 (est). Fiction.

In this sequel to *Bigmama's* (6.4), seven African American children take a shortcut home—along the railroad tracks surrounded by briers and water. After they pass the cutoff that leads back to the road, they hear the train! They realize that they should have taken the road. What do they do now? In his characteristic style, Donald Crews relates a terrifying experience from his childhood. As he states in the dedication, "All's well that ends well." His illustrations invite readers to join in making the "Klak-Klakity" and the "Whoo" sounds of the train.

11.13 Cummings, Pat. **Clean Your Room, Harvey Moon.** Illustrated by Pat Cummings. Bradbury Press, 1991. ISBN 0-02-725511-5. 32p. 4–7. Fiction.

It is Saturday morning and time for cartoons, but Harvey Moon's mother says that it is time to clean his room. His room does not seem messy to Harvey—just some dirty clothes and a few toys. But the illustrations and the rhyming text tell a different story. Harvey finds an amazing mess in his closet and under his bed. He puts everything away and announces that he has finished. But will it pass his mother's inspection? Young readers will enjoy the humorous presentation of this familiar situation. The illustrations reveal that this particular family is African American.

11.14 Cummings, Pat. **Petey Moroni's Camp Runamok Diary.** Illustrated by Pat Cummings. Bradbury Press, 1992. ISBN 0-02-725513-1. 30p. 5–9. Fiction.

Take a fourteen-day trip to Camp Runamok with Petey Moroni, a six-year-old African American boy. In his diary, Petey chronicles the camp mystery: the disappearance of hot dogs, gumdrop worms, and a host of other camp "contraband." The children set a trap for the thief, but it fails. Each page illustrates a clue to the mystery thief, and on day fourteen, as the bus pulls out of sight, the full-color illustration reveals the culprit lying in full view under a tree.

11.15   Curtis, Gavin. **Grandma's Baseball.** Illustrated by Gavin Curtis. Crown, 1990. ISBN 0-517-57390-3. 32p. 5–7 (est). Fiction.

Grandpa, who used to play baseball with a team in the old Negro leagues called the Monarchs, died last year. Now Grandma has come to live with the narrator's family. She is pretty grumpy, and when she catches the narrator playing with Grandpa's special baseball, he expects her to be angry. But her reaction surprises him. The baseball becomes the means for them to express their love and grief and come to a deeper understanding of each other. Here is a sympathetic look at a not uncommon family situation.

11.16   Dorros, Arthur. **Abuela.** Illustrated by Elisa Kleven. Dutton Children's Books, 1991. ISBN 0-525-44750-4. 40p. 8–10. Fiction.

Rosalba spends the day in the city with her grandmother, Abuela. A flock of birds stimulates Rosalba's imagination, and she and her grandmother take a fanciful flight over New York City. They visit Central Park, the New York harbor, the Statue of Liberty, JFK Airport, even their relatives' store. Spanish words are woven smoothly into the text, and a glossary is provided. The special feature of this book is the collage artwork, which makes New York sparkle. *ALA Notable Children's Books, 1992; Notable 1991 Children's Trade Books in the Field of Social Studies.*

11.17   Dragonwagon, Crescent. **Home Place.** Illustrated by Jerry Pinkney. Macmillan, 1990. ISBN 0-02-733190-3. 32p. 5–8. Fiction.

A white family on a Sunday hike come across an old homestead where daffodils come up each year to announce the coming of spring. A marble, a nail, a horseshoe, a piece of a plate, a yellow bottle, and a china doll's arm all conjure up a long-ago extended family of African Americans who might have lived and loved in this place. The poetic text and the luminous watercolors of this quiet book capture a sense of both change and continuity over time. *Notable 1990 Children's Trade Books in the Field of Social Studies.*

11.18   Eisenberg, Phyllis Rose. **You're My Nikki.** Illustrated by Jill Kastner. Dial Books for Young Readers, 1992. ISBN 0-8037-1129-8. 32p. 4–8. Fiction.

"But what if you forget me at your new job tomorrow?" Nikki needs to hear Mama say over and over again that she will not forget her daughter under any circumstances. Nikki dons several disguises and devises memory tests, but her mother always has the right answers. At the end of Mama's tiring first day at work, both Nikki and Mama need their reassuring bedtime conversation. The realistic illustrations show a middle-class African American family composed of a working mother and three children. *Notable 1992 Children's Trade Books in the Field of Social Studies.*

11.19 Gajadin, Chitra, reteller (adapted by Rabindranath Tagore). **Amal and the Letter from the King.** Illustrated by Helen Ong. Boyds Mills Press/Caroline House, 1992. ISBN 1-56397-120-8. 36p. 8 and up (est). Fiction.

Amal, who is too ill to go outdoors, sits by his window, dreaming and wishing that he could "go everywhere and see everything." One night a friend who is a fakir, or Hindu ascetic, tells Amal that the king will come and take him on a journey. Amal happily falls asleep, feeling no more pain. The allegorical story, adapted from the play *The Post Office* by Nobel Prize–winner Rabindranath Tagore, is illustrated with paintings that evoke India and capture the unyielding spirit of the boy Amal.

11.20 Greenfield, Eloise. **First Pink Light.** Illustrated by Jan Spivey Gilchrist. Black Butterfly Children's Books, 1991. ISBN 0-86316-207-X. 16p. 4–7. Fiction.

Daddy has been away for a month. Now he is coming home, and Tyree wants to sit up all night and wait. Mama lets him put on his pajamas and sit in the big chair. She tells him that when he sees the first pink light, it will be time to get ready to surprise Daddy. Tyree misses the first pink light, but he feels Daddy's love next morning when his father carries him off in his strong brown arms. Jan Spivey Gilchrist's watercolors capture the warmth of this loving African American home and family and give a new look to a story first published in 1976.

11.21 Grifalconi, Ann. **Osa's Pride.** Illustrated by Ann Grifalconi. Little, Brown, 1990. ISBN 0-316-32865-0. 32p. 5–8 (est). Fiction.

Osa is stubborn and full of pride. She brags about her father, who never returned from the war, but she refuses to listen to her friends' stories about their parents. When Osa's excessive pride interferes with her social life, Gran'ma Tika uses a story cloth to help Osa put things in perspective. The theme will connect with readers across cultures, as will the rich, warm illustrations. The story is set in the Cameroon, but only the village (Tos) is named, leaving readers to search for the specific African location. *Notable 1990 Children's Trade Books in the Field of Social Studies.*

11.22   Hamilton, Virginia. **Drylongso.** Illustrated by Jerry Pinkney. Harcourt Brace Jovanovich, 1992. ISBN 0-15-224241-4. 50p. 8 and up. Fiction.

When a big dust storm hits Lindy's midwestern farm, a young boy comes running before the wind-driven dust. His name is Drylongso. His own family is elsewhere, but he remembers what his mother said: "Where he goes, life will grow better." Drylongso helps Lindy's family for a while, but in time he must move on, leaving them with renewed hope. Virginia Hamilton has created a mythical African American character and a cautionary tale about the need to preserve the land.

11.23   Haskins, Francine. **Things I Like about Grandma.** Illustrated by Francine Haskins. Children's Book Press, 1992. ISBN 0-89239-107-3. 32p. 4–8 (est). Fiction.

What a lot of things there are to do with Grandma! She tells stories, makes quilts, bakes, goes to church, and visits the seniors' home. Best of all, her granddaughter gets to participate in all these activities—and more. Francine Haskins's simple text and somewhat stylized illustrations describe a warm and loving relationship between a young African American girl and her very active grandmother.

11.24   Havill, Juanita. **Treasure Nap.** Illustrated by Elivia Savadier. Houghton Mifflin, 1992. ISBN 0-395-57817-5. 32p. 4–8. Fiction.

It is too hot for a nap, so Alicia's mother tells a family story. The girl in the story takes a long trip to visit her grandfather, who teaches her to ride a burro, make wooden bird cages, and play the *pito* (flute). When it is time to leave, he gives her three gifts. That little girl was Alicia's great-great-grandmother. After her nap, Alicia takes Great-Great-Grandmother's treasures from the trunk and imagines herself in the mountains of Mexico, where her ancestors lived before coming to the United States.

11.25   Hayashi, Akiko. **Aki and the Fox.** Illustrated by Akiko Hayashi. Doubleday, 1991. ISBN 0-385-41947-3. 40p. 4–7. Fiction.

Kon is the stuffed fox that Grandma sent to look after Aki from the time she was born. Kon and Aki become inseparable, but after a few years Kon grows old. Together Aki and Kon set out for Grandma's so that she can mend Kon's seams. Their journey turns into an adventure, and the friends must take care of each other. But getting to Grandma's is worth the trip. This translated book retains its Japanese flavor in both text and illustrations.

11.26 Hill, Elizabeth Starr. **Evan's Corner.** Illustrated by Sandra Speidel. Viking Penguin, 1990. ISBN 0-670-82830-0. 32p. 3–8. Fiction.

There is little space for eight people in a two-room apartment, but Evan wants a place of his own. When Mama suggests that he choose one of the eight corners, Evan is delighted and sets about selecting and fixing up his corner. Somehow, though, just when his space should be right, something is missing. Evan discovers that his corner has room for one more. New illustrations help to update this classic tale of an African American family caring and sharing. *Notable 1991 Children's Trade Books in the Field of Social Studies.*

11.27 Hoffman, Mary. **Amazing Grace.** Illustrated by Caroline Binch. Dial Books for Young Readers, 1991. ISBN 0-8037-1040-2. 28p. 4–8. Fiction.

Grace loves to act out stories, so when the teacher of her British school announces that the class will perform the play *Peter Pan,* Grace naturally wants to be Peter. But her classmates say that she cannot be Peter—Peter is not a girl, and Peter is not Black. At home Grace sadly tells Ma and Nana what happened. Mama is angry, but it is Nana who convinces Grace that she can do anything she puts her mind to. The picture of Grace as Anansi is worth the price of the book. *ALA Notable Children's Books, 1992; Notable 1991 Children's Trade Books in the Field of Social Studies.*

11.28 Hort, Lenny. **How Many Stars in the Sky?** Illustrated by James E. Ransome. Tambourine Books, 1991. ISBN 0-688-10104-6. 32p. 5–8. Fiction.

A young African American boy, unable to sleep, decides to count the stars in the sky from his bedroom window, his backyard, and his tree house, but he still cannot see all of them. The boy and his daddy, who also cannot sleep, discover a great place for stargazing, but the stars are so close together they cannot be counted. After sleeping outside underneath the night sky, the boy and his father wake up to a special star that can be both seen and counted.

11.29   Howard, Elizabeth Fitzgerald. **Aunt Flossie's Hats (and Crab Cakes Later).** Illustrated by James Ransome. Clarion Books, 1991. ISBN 0-395-54682-6. 32p. 6–9. Fiction.

Playing dress-up in Aunt Flossie's hats makes Sarah and Susan's Sunday afternoons especially memorable because each hat evokes precious memories and exciting stories. Reminiscing becomes a sensory experience as Aunt Flossie passes down stories about the sights, sounds, and smells of early Baltimore. Later, the girls, their great-aunt, and their parents go out for delicious crab cakes. Full-color oil paintings depict an antique-filled house and energetic young girls, and convey the love and warmth found in this African American family. *Notable 1991 Children's Trade Books in the Field of Social Studies.*

11.30   Hudson, Wade. **Jamal's Busy Day.** Illustrated by George Ford. Just Us Books, 1991. ISBN 0-940975-21-1. 24p. 5–7 (est). Fiction.

Jamal's father, an architect, works hard. His mother, who is an accountant, works hard as well. Jamal goes to school, but he works hard, too. He is active all day—working with numbers, doing research, trying experiments, assisting his "supervisor" (teacher). He even brings work home. At dinnertime when his parents talk about their busy day at work, Jamal chimes in that he knows *exactly* what they mean. Grownups are not the only ones who have busy days. George Ford's realistic paintings bring out the humor of the story of this African American family. *Notable 1991 Children's Trade Books in the Field of Social Studies.*

11.31   Hughes, Shirley. **Wheels: A Tale of Trotter Street.** Illustrated by Shirley Hughes. Lothrop, Lee and Shepard Books. ISBN 0-688-09881-9. 28p. 5–8. Fiction.

Trotter street "blossoms" each spring with tricycles, roller skates, baby buggies, and a variety of wheels. Carlos and Billy, on their "old slow bikes," enjoy racing each other through familiar London neighborhoods and parks. When Billy gets a new racing bike and starts to win every race, Carlos is jealous and asks his mum for a new bike, too. On his birthday, he receives a number of parcels, but no bicycle. Carlos's surprise birthday wheels will make the final race of the holiday unforgettable.

11.32 Ichikawa, Satomi. **Nora's Duck.** Illustrated by Satomi Ichikawa. Philomel Books, 1991. ISBN 0-399-21805-X. 32p. 5–8 (est). Fiction.

Nora finds an injured duckling and takes it to Doctor John for help, even though he is not an animal doctor. At his farm the Japanese girl discovers a menagerie of animals that he is caring for, and she learns, among other things, why sheep do not graze on the pretty flowers, why abandoned hens need help, why turtles need a house, and what parrots eat. When the duck starts quacking at her, she must discover what it needs. Watercolor illustrations accompany her journey of discovery. An afterword provides information about the real Dr. John and his animal sanctuary in Kent, England.

11.33 Igus, Toyomi. **When I Was Little.** Illustrated by Higgins Bond. Just Us Books, 1992. ISBN 0-940975-32-7. 32p. 5–9 (est). Fiction.

Noel, a young African American boy, loves to go fishing every summer with Grandpa Will, who lives in the country. As they fish, Grandpa Will tells stories about what life was like for him as a young boy—no refrigerators, no jets, no indoor toilets, no TV. How did they ever get along? "Things are different now," says Grandpa Will, "but . . . the important things are just the same." Scenes from Grandpa's time are rendered in black and white, while the present time is shown in full color.

11.34 Ikeda, Daisaku (translated by Gearaldine McCaughrean). **The Cherry Tree.** Illustrated by Brian Wildsmith. Alfred A. Knopf/Borzoi Books, 1991. ISBN 0-679-92669-0. 28p. 5–8 (est). Fiction.

Left homeless and fatherless by the war, Taichi and Yumiko live in an abandoned farmhouse with their heartbroken mother. One day a stray cat leads the children to an old cherry tree that has not bloomed in many years. An old man is trying to protect the tree from winter in the hope that it will blossom again. The children help, and when spring comes, hope is reborn for them and for their entire village. Brian Wildsmith's characteristically colorful illustrations capture the spirit of hope. *Notable 1992 Children's Trade Books in the Field of Social Studies.*

11.35 Isadora, Rachel. **At the Crossroads.** Illustrated by Rachel Isadora. Greenwillow Books, 1991. ISBN 0-688-05271-1. 32p. 5–8. Fiction.

This simple story from South Africa offers a poignant look at life in the Black townships. The children are excited because their fathers are returning after ten long months away working in the mines. After school, the children go to the crossroads, where they are joined by friends and others in the community. They sing and dance in anticipation of the fathers' impending arrival, but it is dawn before the last six waiting children hear the rumble of the truck that brings their fathers home. *ALA Notable Children's Books, 1992; Notable 1991 Children's Trade Books in the Field of Social Studies.*

11.36   Isadora, Rachel. **Over the Green Hills.** Illustrated by Rachel Isadora. Greenwillow Books, 1992. ISBN 0-688-10510-6. 32p. 5–8 (est). Fiction.

Zolani and his mother travel on foot from the seashore, over the green hills, to visit Grandma Zindzi. Zolani's mother carries the baby on her back, a box of dried fish on her head, and a basket of corn on her arm. Zolani leads a goat carrying freshly gathered mussels. But Grandma Zindzi is not at home. As evening falls and they prepare to leave, Grandma finally appears, and the long journey seems worth every step. The present-tense text and vivid watercolor illustrations give a sense of everyday life in the Transkei, an independent Black state on the east coast of South Africa.

11.37   Johnson, Angela. **Do like Kyla.** Illustrated by James E. Ransome. Orchard Books/Richard Jackson Books, 1990. ISBN 0-531-08452-3. 32p. 3–7. Fiction.

A little sister adores her big sister Kyla. From morning to night she imitates her sister's every action, from pouring honey on oatmeal to crunching home from the store following their own footprints in the snow. Whatever Kyla does, the little sister says, "I do like Kyla." But at bedtime, when the day is ending just as it began—with birds gathering at the window—the little sister gets a chance to take the lead. A simple, somewhat repetitive text and strong watercolor paintings make this gentle story of an African American family a good read-aloud.

11.38   Johnson, Angela. **The Leaving Morning.** Illustrated by David Soman. Orchard Books/Richard Jackson Books, 1992. ISBN 0-531-08592-9. 32p. 4–7. Fiction.

Moving is difficult at any age, but especially for this young African American boy who leaves behind relatives, friends, and neighbors. The family has completed all of its packing, and the only thing remaining is saying good-bye to all the special people whom they are leaving behind. The young boy leaves his "lips" and kisses on the windows of his old home as a fond remembrance. David Soman's watercolors enhance the gentle tone of the text.

11.39   Johnson, Angela. **One of Three.** Illustrated by David Soman. Orchard Books, 1991. ISBN 0-531-08555-4. 32p. 4–7 (est). Fiction.

"Since I can remember I've been one of three—Eva, Nikki, and me." The three sisters do many things together: walk to school, play dress-up, ride the subway, shop. But every once in a while, Eva and Nikki will not allow their little sister to tag along. Then Mama and Daddy and Sister make their own special times together—a different set of three. Many "youngest-in-the-family" children will recognize themselves in this warm story about an African American family.

11.40   Johnson, Angela. **When I Am Old with You.** Illustrated by David Soman. Orchard Books/Richard Jackson Books, 1990. ISBN 0-531-08484-1. 32p. 4–7. Fiction.

A young African American boy spends time with his Grandaddy. They sit on the porch, go fishing, play cards, ride a tractor, peruse old family clothing and pictures stored in the attic, and enjoy a corn roast with family and friends. Throughout, the boy tells the Grandaddy that "when I am old with you," the two of them will do all their favorite things together—exactly what they are doing now. The dreadlocked little boy is a happy surprise in this universal story of love between a grandfather and his grandson. *ALA Notable Children's Books, 1991; Coretta Scott King Writing Honor Book, 1991; Notable 1990 Children's Trade Books in the Field of Social Studies.*

11.41   Johnson, Dolores. **The Best Bug to Be.** Illustrated by Dolores Johnson. Macmillan, 1992. ISBN 0-02-747842-4. 32p. 4–8. Fiction.

Kelly is disappointed when she is cast as a "good-for-nuthin' bumblebee" in the school play. Megan will be the cutest ladybug; Robert the only toad in the froggy pond; and Sharon the Queen of the butterflies. But all bees do is buzz! When Kelly's parents let her know that they expect her to do her best in the role, Kelly works hard at being a good bumblebee. On the night of the play, the hard work of this African American girl pays off.

The watercolor illustrations portray a delightful multiracial cast of expressive characters.

11.42   Johnson, Dolores. **What Kind of Baby-sitter Is This?** Illustrated by Dolores Johnson. Macmillan, 1991. ISBN 0-02-747846-7. 32p. 5–8. Fiction.

Kevin's mother takes classes in the evenings, but he does not want to have a sitter. Baby-sitters just talk on the phone, eat all the snacks, and watch soap operas. Not this sitter—boy, is she different! She wears a baseball cap with the logo of Kevin's favorite team; she waves a pennant while she watches the game; and she actually knows the rules of the game. And there are more surprises to come in this appealing and amusing story of an intergenerational friendship between an African American boy and a baseball-loving baby-sitter.

11.43   Johnson, Dolores. **What Will Mommy Do When I'm at School?** Illustrated by Dolores Johnson. Macmillan, 1990. ISBN 0-02-747845-9. 32p. 4–6. Fiction.

A little African American girl is starting school tomorrow. How will her mother ever manage without her? When she goes to school, there will not be time to make muffins together, or watch cartoons, or comb Mom's hair. And who will help with the groceries? Dad tries to be reassuring, but not until Mom announces that she is about to begin her own new adventure does the little girl know that she will not need to worry about her mother. This story will connect with any young child who has had to face a new challenge.

11.44   Johnson, Ryerson. **Kenji and the Magic Geese.** Illustrated by Jean and Mou-sien Tseng. Simon and Schuster Books for Young Readers, 1992. ISBN 0-671-75974-4. 32p. 7 and up. Fiction.

Kenji loves the family's valuable painting of five geese in flight. When a flood destroys the family's rice crop, his father must sell the painting. Kenji gives his beloved geese a going-away gift of a ride on his kite, but when it returns, there are only four geese in the painting! The magic continues in this story set in Japan. Eventually Kenji's father finds a way to keep the picture and share the art with others. The color illustrations capture the emotions of the people and the spirit of the theme.

11.45   Johnston, Tony. **Lorenzo, the Naughty Parrot.** Illustrated by Leo Politi. Harcourt Brace Jovanovich, 1992. ISBN 0-15-249350-6. 32p. 5–8. Fiction.

Lorenzo the parrot thinks that he is the family protector. He lives in the garden and squawks a warning at everyone who enters. He gets into all sorts of mischief as he "participates" in all the family activities, including Ana's birthday party and San Nicolás's Christmas Eve visit. But more than anything, Lorenzo loves cookies. How this love of cookies helps find Papa's missing wedding ring makes an amusing family story. The illustrations show a contemporary family living in Mexico.

11.46 Keller, Holly. **Island Baby.** Illustrated by Holly Keller. Greenwillow Books, 1992. ISBN 0-688-10580-7. 32p. 4–7. Fiction.

Set on an unnamed Caribbean island, this is the story of friendship between a young boy and an elderly man who keeps a bird hospital. Simon comes by every morning to help Pops with his birds. One day Simon finds an injured flamingo whom he names Baby. Simon nurses Baby back to health, and the two become attached. Then the time comes for Simon to set the bird free. He must handle that difficult task and take a step toward his own growth as well.

11.47 Lee, Jeanne M. **Silent Lotus.** Illustrated by Jeanne M. Lee. Farrar, Straus and Giroux, 1991. ISBN 0-8050-0169-7. 30p. 7–10 (est). Fiction.

Lotus is deaf and cannot speak, but she loves to imitate the graceful walk of the cranes and herons that she observes around her in Kampuchea. Seeking a way to help their unhappy child, her parents take her from her village to the king's palace in the city. There she sees the court dancers and "hears" the vibrations of their music. She has, her parents think, found her calling. How Lotus triumphs over silence and enchants the royal court makes an inspiring story. Jeanne Lee's vibrant illustrations bring this Cambodian tale to life.

11.48 Martin, Ann. **Rachel Parker, Kindergarten Show-off.** Illustrated by Nancy Poydar. Holiday House, 1992. ISBN 0-8234-0935-X. 40p. 5–8. Fiction.

Five-year-old Olivia, an only child, is quite satisfied with her accomplishments. She is the only one in her kindergarten class who can read or write. Then Rachel Elizabeth Parker moves in next door. Not only can she read and write, but she has a granddaddy and a baby sister and two first names! She can do everything Olivia can do. Who could be friends with this kindergarten show-off? How the girls resolve their differences and develop an interracial friendship makes a satisfying story for young readers. *Notable 1992 Children's Trade Books in the Field of Social Studies.*

11.49 McKissack, Patricia C. **A Million Fish . . . More or Less.** Illustrated by Dena Schutzer. Alfred A. Knopf/Borzoi Books, 1992. ISBN 0-679-90692-4. 32p. All ages. Fiction.

Hugh Thomas encounters Pappa-Daddy and Elder Abbajon while fishing early one morning on the Bayou Clapateaux. He listens as they trade tall tales of strange happenings around the bayou. Later, Hugh becomes involved in his own strange happenings while he catches a million fish . . . more or less. Patricia McKissack's skillfully woven tale of an African American boy is strongly supported by Dena Schutzer's bright acrylic illustrations. *Notable 1992 Children's Trade Books in the Field of Social Studies.*

11.50 Medearis, Angela Shelf. **Dancing with the Indians.** Illustrated by Samuel Byrd. Holiday House, 1991. ISBN 0-8234-0893-0. 32p. 5–8. Fiction.

In a rhyming text, Angela Shelf Medearis celebrates the connection between people of two cultures. Her great-grandfather, "Papa John," escaped from slavery and was rescued by Seminole Indians. For generations, his family has kept up the tradition of taking part in the semi-annual Seminole powwow in Oklahoma. This story is told from the perspectve of a young girl of the 1930s who joins her family in respectfully watching the Indian dances and then being invited to join in. *Notable 1991 Children's Trade Books in the Field of Social Studies.*

11.51 Merrill, Jean, adapter. **The Girl Who Loved Caterpillars: A Twelfth-Century Tale from Japan.** Illustrated by Floyd Cooper. Philomel Books, 1992. ISBN 0-399-21871-8. 32p. 5–8. Fiction.

In this story, taken from a twelfth-century Japanese scroll, the unconventional Izumi has no interest in the ladylike fashion of the Japanese court. She prefers studying and playing with caterpillars to plucking her eyebrows and blackening her teeth, as is the fashion for women. Izumi's reputation captures the attention of the captain of the stables. Although the story ends abruptly, it leaves readers to ponder what happens after Izumi and the captain correspond. Floyd Cooper's luminous oil-wash paintings are striking and capture the drama of the story.

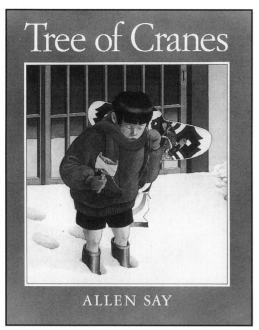

A.

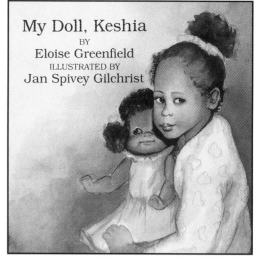

B.

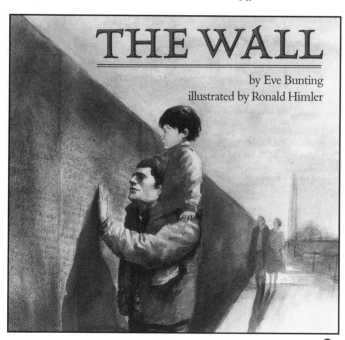

C.

A. *Tree of Cranes* written and illustrated by Allen Say (see 11.66). **B.** *My Doll, Keshia* by Eloise Greenfield; illustrated by Jan Spivey Gilchrist (see 10.6). **C.** *The Wall* by Eve Bunting; illustrated by Ronald Himler (see 11.9).

A. *When I Am Old with You* by Angela Johnson; illustrated by David Soman (see 11.40).
B. *Jonathan and His Mommy* by Irene Smalls-Hector; illustrated by Michael Hays (see 11.71). **C.** *When Africa Was Home* by Karen Lynn Williams; illustrated by Floyd Cooper (see 11.76). **D.** *The Girl Who Loved Caterpillars: A Twelfth-Century Tale from Japan* adapted by Jean Merrill; illustrated by Floyd Cooper (see 11.51).

11.52 Mills, Claudia. **A Visit to Amy-Claire.** Illustrated by Sheila Hamanaka. Macmillan, 1992. ISBN 0-02-766991-2. 32p. 5–8 (est). Fiction.

Five-year-old Rachel looks forward to visiting her cousin Amy-Claire and doing all the things that they did together on the last visit—making report cards, taking bubble baths, swinging on the tire. But all Amy-Claire wants to do is play with Rachel's two-year-old sister, Jessie. Rachel eventually finds a way to solve her problem. Sheila Hamanaka's vibrant paintings give life to this tale of sibling rivalry. The families appear to be biracial and Asian, but no more specific information is given.

11.53 Mora, Pat. **A Birthday Basket for Tía.** Illustrated by Cecily Lang. Macmillan, 1992. ISBN 0-02-767400-2. 29p. 4–8 (est). Fiction.

Young Cecilia wants to do something special for her great-aunt's ninetieth birthday. With the aid of her new cat, Chica, she prepares a birthday basket that reminds Tía of their special times together. Tía is both surprised and pleased. The cumulative story will appeal to young readers, as will the vibrant illustrations of this Mexican American family. Appropriately placed Spanish words add just the right touch.

11.54 Nodar, Carmen Santiago. **Abuelita's Paradise/El Paraíso de Abuelita.** Illustrated by Diane Paterson. Albert Whitman, 1992. ISBN 0-8075-0129-8 (0-8075-6346-3, Spanish ed.). 32p. 5–8. Fiction.

When Marita's grandmother dies, Marita inherits her old rocking chair. As Marita rocks and leans on Abuelita's old faded blanket with the word *paraíso* ("paradise") on it, she recalls the wonderful stories that her grandmother used to tell of her youth in Puerto Rico. The evocative illustrations add to the poignancy of the story.

11.55 Orr, Katherine. **My Grandpa and the Sea.** Illustrated by Katherine Orr. Carolrhoda Books, 1990. ISBN 0-87614-409-1. 32p. 5–9. Fiction.

Lila's grandfather is a fisherman who loves the sea. He and Grammy live on the Caribbean island of St. Lucia, and when Lila spends time with them, Grandpa passes on his wisdom about nature and life. When technologically advanced fishing methods deplete the supply of fish, Grandpa must find a new way to make a living. He tries several occupations, but ultimately he is happy to return to the sea. The color illustrations give a sense of the beauty of the island and the sea.

11.56 Pinkney, Gloria Jean. **Back Home.** Illustrated by Jerry Pinkney. Dial Books for Young Readers, 1992. ISBN 0-8037-1169-7. 40p. 5–9 (est). Fiction.

Ernestine spends part of the summer with her North Carolina kinfolk: Uncle June, Aunt Beula, and Cousin Jack. Life on the farm is not at all like life in the city, but Ernestine feels right at home—when Jack is not teasing her about her "citified" clothes and her "citified" ways. Can they ever be friends? The Pinkneys capture in words and illustrations an experience familiar to generations of northern urban African Americans—maintaining their roots "back home" in the South. *ALA Notable Children's Books, 1993; Notable 1992 Children's Trade Books in the Field of Social Studies.*

11.57 Polacco, Patricia. **Chicken Sunday.** Illustrated by Patricia Polacco. Philomel Books, 1992. ISBN 0-399-22133-6. 32p. 5–9. Fiction.

Winston, Stewart, and their white "sister friend" love Miss Eula and her voice that sounds "like slow thunder and sweet rain." They also love her soul food dinners after church on "chicken Sundays." They want to buy her a special gift for Easter, but just when they go to ask Mr. Kodinski to give them work, he falsely accuses them of throwing eggs at him. How they convince him of the truth and earn the gift makes an appealing story of interracial, intercultural friendship and creativity. *ALA Notable Children's Books, 1993; Notable 1992 Children's Trade Books in the Field of Social Studies.*

11.58 Polacco, Patricia. **Mrs. Katz and Tush.** Illustrated by Patricia Polacco. Bantam Little Rooster Books, 1992. ISBN 0-553-08122-5. 32p. 5–8. Fiction.

Larnel convinces his neighbor, Mrs. Katz, to adopt a scrawny, tailless kitten—ugly and unwanted. As the kitten grows, so does the relationship between the lonely Jewish widow and the African American boy. The friends discover that they have much in common when Mrs. Katz invites Larnel to celebrate a passover seder with her. Lively illustrations flesh out the story with details of interiors, neighborhood surroundings, and real people. *Notable 1992 Children's Trade Books in the Field of Social Studies.*

11.59 Reddix, Valerie. **Dragon Kite of the Autumn Moon.** Illustrated by Jean and Mou-sien Tseng. Lothrop, Lee and Shepard Books, 1991. ISBN 0-688-11031-2. 32p. 5–10. Fiction.

There is an old Chinese belief that if you set your kite free, it will take whatever misfortune you have with it. Young Tad Tin's grandfather becomes gravely ill. He had been a kite maker and had made a beautiful big dragon kite for Tad Tin when he was born. Seeing his grandfather so sick, Tad Tin knows that he must fly his dragon kite and set it free in order to make his grandfather well again in this story set in Taiwan.

11.60 Ringgold, Faith. **Aunt Harriet's Underground Railroad in the Sky.** Illustrated by Faith Ringgold. Crown, 1992. ISBN 0-517-58768-8. 32p. 7 and up (est). Fiction.

In this sequel to *Tar Beach* (11.61), Cassie Louise Lightfoot and her brother Be Be fly up to the sky, where they encounter the Underground Railroad train and its conductor, Aunt Harriet Tubman. While Be Be rides on the train, Aunt Harriet guides Cassie on a journey from the hardships of slavery to the jubilation of freedom and a reunion with her brother. The color illustrations are in much the same style as those in *Tar Beach*. A biographical sketch of Harriet Tubman, accompanied by a map and a brief bibliography, is included.

11.61 Ringgold, Faith. **Tar Beach.** Illustrated by Faith Ringgold. Crown Publishers, 1991. ISBN 0-517-58031-4. 32p. 7 and up (est). Fiction.

Cassie Louise Lightfoot, eight years old, enjoys family outings on tar beach, the rooftop of her Harlem apartment building. From there, while her parents play cards with Mr. and Mrs. Honey, Cassie imagines that she can fly over the city, claiming all that she surveys and righting wrongs along the way. Based on a story quilt that hangs in the Guggenheim Museum, the illustrations, bordered by reproductions from the original quilt, are the exciting feature of this book by an established African American artist. See also *Aunt Harriet's Underground Railroad in the Sky* by Faith Ringgold (11.60). *ALA Notable Children's Books, 1992; Caldecott Honor Book, 1992; Coretta Scott King Illustration Award, 1992.*

11.62 Roe, Eileen. **Con Mi Hermano/With My Brother.** Illustrated by Robert Casilla. Bradbury Press, 1991. ISBN 0-02-777373-6. 32p. 4–7. Fiction.

In both English and Spanish, this story is told in the words of a young boy who wants to be just like his older brother. He admires the way his brother can ride a bus to school, deliver newspapers, and play ball on Saturdays. The older brother affectionately makes time for the little one, making their ties especially close. The evocative illustrations of the boys playing baseball, wrestling, and reading together capture the warm and loving relationship of two Hispanic American brothers.

11.63 Sage, James. **The Little Band.** Illustrated by Keiko Narahashi. Margaret K. McElderry Books, 1991. ISBN 0-689-50516-7. 28p. 4–8. Fiction.

A little band weaves its way through a town, delighting all the people who hear its music. Long after it has gone, the townspeople remember its music, "and nothing was ever the same again." The lyrical text and the gentle illustrations combine for a soothing effect. The band is racially integrated, as are the townspeople. The book offers a vision of a harmonious multicultural world.

11.64 Sakai, Kimiko. **Sachiko Means Happiness.** Illustrated by Tomie Arai. Children's Book Press, 1990. ISBN 0-89239-065-4. 30p. 6–10 (est). Fiction.

In this story about a Japanese American family, Sachiko's grandmother sometimes does not recognize her own family or know where she is. Sachiko is upset with this change in the loving grandmother who gave her her name. When Grandmother starts to weep while trying to find "home," Sachiko looks into her eyes and recognizes that in her mind she is a frightened five-year-old child. Her new understanding gives her the patience to treat her grandmother with kindness and love. Full-color illustrations have a Japanese flavor.

11.65 Samton, Sheila White. **Jenny's Journey.** Illustrated by Sheila White Samton. Viking Penguin, 1991. ISBN 0-670-83490-4. 32p. 3–8. Fiction.

When Maria moves away and writes of her loneliness to Jenny, her best friend, Jenny finds a creative way to make her friend feel better. Jenny's exciting sea journey owes a great deal to imagination. The book, with its lively illustrations full of details that extend the text, is a celebration of a friendship that happens to be interracial.

11.66 Say, Allen. **Tree of Cranes.** Illustrated by Allen Say. Houghton Mifflin, 1991. ISBN 0-395-52024-X. 32p. 4–8. Fiction.

Having taken a chill playing at a forbidden pond, a young Japanese boy understands why he must take a hot bath, eat a hot meal, and go to bed. But he is puzzled by his mother's behavior—folding paper cranes and digging up his birth tree. It is the seventh day before the New Year, and his mother, who was born in California, introduces him to the spirit and customs of Christmas. Allen Say's autobiographical depiction of his first Christmas is illustrated in luminous watercolors. *ALA Notable Children's Books, 1991; Notable 1991 Children's Trade Books in the Field of Social Studies.*

11.67 Schoberle, Cecile. **Esmeralda and the Pet Parade.** Illustrated by Cecile Schoberle. Simon and Schuster Books for Young Readers, 1990. ISBN 0-671-67958-9. 32p. 5–8. Fiction.

Esmeralda, Juan's goat, is always in trouble. She was a gift from Grandfather, who calls her an explorer and insists that one day she will be famous. The Garcia Street children only hope that Essie will not spoil their chances at the Santa Fe pet parade. Esmeralda is irrepressible, and in the end the Garcia Street youngsters have a pleasant surprise. The linoleum-block print illustrations are in the colors of the Southwest in this story about a Mexican American family.

11.68 Scott, Ann Herbert. **On Mother's Lap.** Illustrated by Glo Coalson. Clarion Books, 1992. ISBN 0-395-58920-7. 32p. 5–7. Fiction.

Michael was rocking on Mother's lap. Soon Dolly, boat, and puppy are all cuddled under the reindeer blanket and rocking on Mother's lap, too. Then Baby starts to cry, and Mother thinks she wants to rock, too. "There isn't room," says Michael. "Let's see," says Mother, and soon Michael sees how big Mother's lap—and Mother's love—can be. The drawings in this full-color new edition reveal that this universal story takes place in the home of an Eskimo family living in an Alaskan village.

11.69 Shelby, Anne. **We Keep a Store.** Illustrated by John Ward. Orchard Books, 1990. ISBN 0-531-08456-6. 32p. 5–8. Fiction.

A small girl relates the good things about keeping a country store: her family working together, not paying yourself for items from the shelves, sneaking a piece of candy, and neighbors gathering around the stove, on the porch, and in the yard. This brief portrait of an African American family at work conveys the small pleasures and warmth of sharing with those who care. Realistic paintings by John Ward bring the people and details to life. *Notable 1990 Children's Trade Books in the Field of Social Studies.*

11.70   Smalls-Hector, Irene. **Irene and the Big, Fine Nickel.** Illustrated by Tyrone Geter. Little, Brown, 1991. ISBN 0-316-79871-1. 32p. 5–8. Fiction.

In this autobiographical story set in the 1950s, free-spirited seven-year-old Irene begins the day exploring her Harlem neighborhood. She enjoys a biscuit at Miss Sally's house, has a disagreement with Charlene on the sidewalk, and plays adventurous games with Lulabelle and Lulamae. A nickel found in the gutter buys a raisin bun plus some crumbs put in the bag by Miss Susie. While the friends sit on the curb and relish the good taste, Irene silently anticipates Miss Sally's banana pudding to end this special day for her.

11.71   Smalls-Hector, Irene. **Jonathan and His Mommy.** Illustrated by Michael Hays. Little, Brown, 1992. ISBN 0-136-79870-3. 32p. 4–7. Fiction.

Five-year-old Jonathan and his mother do more than walk through their urban neighborhood. They race, take giant steps and little steps, do ballet steps, and stop to dance to reggae music. The rhythmic text and vibrant illustrations portray an African American mother and son having fun together and enjoying each other's company.

11.72   Tan, Amy. **The Moon Lady.** Illustrated by Gretchen Schields. Macmillan, 1992. ISBN 0-02-788830-4. 32p. 9–12. Fiction.

One rainy afternoon, Maggie, Lily, and June are bored. Grandmother (Nai-nai) tells them a story from her childhood in China. On one Chinese Moon Festival, her family had gone on a boat to Tai Lake for a great feast and celebration. On the trip, Nai-nai learned what secret wishes mean and how they can be fulfilled. A description of a traditional holiday celebration is craftily woven into this story, adapted from Amy Tan's *The Joy Luck Club.* *Notable 1992 Children's Trade Books in the Field of Social Studies.*

11.73   Walker, Alice. **Finding the Green Stone.** Illustrated by Catherine Deeter. Harcourt Brace Jovanovich, 1991. ISBN 0-15-227538-X. 38p. 7–10. Fiction.

In this moralistic tale by Alice Walker, one of America's best-known writers, Johnny learns of the destructive powers of negative emotions and the healing power of love. Everyone in his multiracial community has a shining green stone. When Johnny is unkind to friends and family, he loses his stone, and everyone tries to help him find it. But Johnny must find his green stone himself. The long text calls for reading aloud to younger students, but middle readers can read the book themselves.

11.74 Walter, Mildred Pitts. **Two and Too Much.** Illustrated by Pat Cummings. Bradbury Press, 1990. ISBN 0-02-792290-1. 32p. 4–7. Fiction.

Two-year-old Gina is always into something. When seven-year-old Brandon volunteers to help Mama get ready for company, Mama asks him to baby-sit Gina. He tries his best, but Gina is always one step ahead of him. Just when he is about to play his records for her, Gina disappears. The youngster turns up, but Brandon thinks Gina is "two and too much!" Children with younger siblings will recognize themselves in this realistically drawn African American family.

11.75 Williams, Karen Lynn. **Galimoto.** Illustrated by Catherine Stock. Lothrop, Lee and Shepard Books/Mulberry Books, 1990. ISBN 0-688-10991-8. 27p. 5–8. Fiction.

Kondi wants to make a *galimoto,* a Chichewa word for a toy vehicle made from old wires, but he does not have enough wire. His determination and ingenuity spur him in a village-wide search for what he needs. By nightfall the village children can all play with the fruit of his labors. As Kondi scours his Malawi village, the reader also encounters the sights, sounds, smells, and busy life of the people. The full-color paintings accompanying this inspiring story add reality and immediacy. *Notable 1990 Children's Trade Books in the Field of Social Studies.*

11.76 Williams, Karen Lynn. **When Africa Was Home.** Illustrated by Floyd Cooper. Orchard Books/Richard Jackson Books, 1991. ISBN 0-531-08525-2. 32p. 4–8. Fiction.

Barefoot, hatless Peter and his parents live in an African village. Peter, a blond, white American, and Yekha, a Black village child, are inseparable. Together they slide down anthills, eat fish sauce—eyes and all—and relish sugar cane treats. When it is time to return "home" to America, not even popsicles seem inviting to Peter. After months in America, the family happily returns to Africa. This sensitively told story is flawed by its failure to specify its setting, thereby feeding the myth of a generic "Africa." Chichewa words are used in the text, indicating that the setting is Malawi. *Notable 1991 Children's Trade Books in the Field of Social Studies.*

11.77   Williams, Sherley Anne. **Working Cotton.** Illustrated by Carole Byard. Harcourt Brace Jovanovich, 1992. ISBN 0-15-299624-9. 32p. 5–9. Fiction.

Shelan's family and other workers arrive at the cotton fields of central California before it is light, pick cotton all day, and leave when it is dark again. Shelan piles cotton in the middle of the row for Mamma. She is proud of Daddy's speed and skill, and imagines how much she can pick when she is older. The poetic text and dramatic illustrations give a sense of how these African American migrant farm hands maintain their dignity while performing backbreaking work for minimal compensation. *ALA Notable Children's Books, 1993; Caldecott Honor Book, 1993; Coretta Scott King Illustration Honor Book, 1993; Notable 1992 Children's Trade Books in the Field of Social Studies.*

11.78   Wilson, Beth P. **Jenny.** Illustrated by Dolores Johnson. Macmillan, 1990. ISBN 0-02-793120-X. 30p. 6–8. Fiction.

This is a collection of vignettes in the voice of Jenny, a pensive seven-year-old girl. She talks, among other things, about her teacher, her grandma and grandpa, chocolate cookies, and what seems spooky. Readers will notice her expression of disgust when she says, "When I go visiting with Grandma she likes to show people my baby pictures...." The illustrations offer a realistic picture of an African American girl, her family, and the multiracial group of people who are a part of her world. *Notable 1990 Children's Trade Books in the Field of Social Studies.*

11.79   Yolen, Jane. **Encounter.** Illustrated by David Shannon. Harcourt Brace Jovanovich, 1992. ISBN 0-15-225962-7. 32p. 8 and up. Fiction.

In an interesting reversal, the landing of Columbus on the Bahamian island of San Salvador in 1492 is recounted through the eyes of a Taino Indian boy who has dreams and premonitions about the disasters that will befall his people because of the Spaniards' greed for gold. Nobody heeds his warning, and the story concludes with the boy as an old man, robbed of his dreams and his land. See also *The Tainos: The People Who Welcomed Columbus* by Francine Jacobs (7.9) and *Morning Girl* by Michael Dorris (13.10).

11.80 Zimelman, Nathan. **The Great Adventure of Wo Ti.** Illustrated by Julie Downing. Macmillan, 1992. ISBN 0-02-793731-3. 32p. 5–8. Fiction.

Wo Ti the carp lives a safe and comfortable life in the pond at the emperor's Summer Palace in Beijing, but he feels that something is missing. Then Kitti Ho the alley cat leaps over the palace walls, and the birds and fish are no longer safe. Wo Ti devises a clever plan to rid them of the menace, and through this undertaking his life becomes fulfilled. The carp's adventure is brought to life by artist Julie Downing's evocative watercolors.

12 Fiction for Middle Readers

12.1   Bunting, Eve. **Summer Wheels.** Illustrated by Thomas B. Allen. Harcourt Brace Jovanovich, 1992. ISBN 0-15-207000-1. 48p. 6–10. Fiction.

The bicycle man repairs bikes and lends them to the neighborhood children. Two rules prevail—bikes must be returned by 4:00 P.M.; and if a bike breaks while you are riding it, you repair it. One day a new boy, Leon, shows up and borrows the favorite bike of Lawrence. Then Leon fails to return the bike on time. Lawrence and his friend Brady go after him to see that justice is done. What happens to the rule breaker in this interracial story makes a strong statement about the power of kindness and trust. *Notable 1992 Children's Trade Books in the Field of Social Studies.*

12.2   Gogol, Sara. **Vatsana's Lucky New Year.** Lerner, 1992. ISBN 0-8225-0734-X. 156p. 9–12. Fiction.

Born in America to Laotian parents, Vatsana considers herself an American. Why does she need to know Laotian customs? Vatsana must learn to cope with a racist bully and to help her newly arrived cousin adjust to America. In doing so, she comes to accept being part of two cultures and to appreciate her own dual heritage. Although the theme is a bit too obvious, the book can help readers sympathize with the plight of recent immigrants from Southeast Asia and other regions of the world.

12.3   Gordon, Sheila. **The Middle of Somewhere: A Story of South Africa.** Orchard Books/Richard Jackson Books, 1990. ISBN 0-531-08508-2. 154p. 8–12. Fiction.

Nine-year-old Rebecca's family and the rest of the Black villagers have been told that they must move because the area is to be used for a new white suburb. The bulldozers may come any day. This is South Africa, where apartheid rules. But this time the community decides to protest. Resistance will bring attention to their plight, but it also brings risk. Ultimately, the focus is on both the strength of the family and community and the hope that sustains a people. *Jane Addams Honor Book, 1991.*

12.4　　Greenfield, Eloise. **Koya DeLaney and the Good Girl Blues.** Scholastic Hardcover Books, 1992. ISBN 0-590-43300-8. 128p. 8–10. Fiction.

Koya is a sixth-grade African American girl who uses humor to approach and often avoid difficult situations. She refuses to get angry because she fears it will permanently mar her character. It is only after her sister Loritha is treated unfairly and the singing of her rock-star cousin Delbert is interrupted by rude fans that Koya comes to terms with the appropriateness of angry feelings. This book is good for promoting classroom discussions on emotions and family activities.

12.5　　Hamilton, Virginia. **The All Jahdu Storybook.** Illustrated by Barry Moser. Harcourt Brace Jovanovich, 1991. ISBN 0-15-239498-2. 108p. 7–10. Fiction.

Virginia Hamilton remodeled the original tales about the magical trickster Jahdu and added four lively new adventures for this complete collection. Mama Luka, the baby-sitter, is missing from the stories, but her absence brings the reader closer to the endearing African American hero. Paintings by Barry Moser add to the flavor of mystery and magic. This is an excellent read-aloud choice.

12.6　　Hamilton, Virginia. **Cousins.** Illustrated by Jerry Pinkney. Philomel Books, 1990. ISBN 0-399-22164-6. 125p. 9–12. Fiction.

Cammy misses her beloved Gran and sneaks into the nursing home to visit Gran, but she cannot resolve her other problem, goody-goody cousin Patricia Ann. If only Patty would vaporize! All the anger, hurt, and rivalry between these two cousins come together one fateful afternoon. The tragedy of Patty's death is nearly doubled when Cammy tries to give in to despair, but strong family ties pull her through. This novel explores complex relationships within a believable African American family of strong and unique individuals. *ALA Notable Children's Books, 1991; Best Books for Young Adults, 1991.*

12.7　　Hurwitz, Johanna. **Class President.** Illustrations by Sheila Hamanaka. Scholastic/Apple Paperbacks, 1991. ISBN 0-590-44064-0. 85p. 10 and up. Fiction.

Julio Sanchez realizes that the new school year may be different from what he expected once he discovers that the new fifth-grade teacher is a man, Ernesto Flores. Julio's first lesson is to take pride in his Puerto Rican name and the heritage it symbolizes.

He also learns how to be a true leader, how to help a friend, and how to make brownies—lessons different from the subjects that he was prepared to study. Readers will enjoy the familiarity of the joys and trials of school life.

12.8   Kidd, Diana. **Onion Tears.** Illustrated by Lucy Montgomery. Orchard Books, 1991. ISBN 0-531-08470-1. 62p. 7–10. Fiction.

Nam Huong is a Vietnamese girl living in Australia. She has lost her entire family and is having difficulty adjusting to life in this new place. Nam Huong cries onion tears while helping in Auntie's restaurant, although she wishes she could cry real tears. But she can trust no one—until she gets to know Miss Lily, an eccentric teacher living nearby. This wistful journey of self-discovery is guided by Nam Huong's personal view. *Notable 1991 Children's Trade Books in the Field of Social Studies.*

12.9   Kraus, Joanna Halpert. **Tall Boy's Journey.** Illustrated by Karen Ritz. Carolrhoda Books, 1992. ISBN 0-87614-746-5. 48p. 6–9. Fiction.

When his grandmother dies, eight-year-old Kim Moo Yong is adopted by an American couple. Torn away from Korea and everything that he knows, he finds America confusing and frightening. He has promised his uncle to be a "tall boy," but the situation is overwhelming. Then he meets Mr. Cho, a Korean friend of his new father's. Mr. Cho becomes a source of information and comfort to Kim Moo Yong and helps him learn to adjust. One illustration does not match the text, but overall this is a sympathetic view of an increasingly common event.

12.10   Myers, Walter Dean. **Mop, Moondance, and the Nagasaki Knights.** Delacorte Press, 1992. ISBN 0-385-30687-3. 150p. 8–12. Fiction.

In this sequel to *Me, Mop and the Moondance Kid*, T.J., his younger brother Moondance, their friend Mop, and their Elks teammates try to earn a trip to Japan by winning a special international baseball tournament. But the Eagles and their coach are big obstacles. Then there are the teams from Mexico, France, and Japan—the Elks don't speak their languages. The kids nevertheless find a way to make friends—and temporary enemies. In the end, the kids' concern for one another, coupled with their athletic skills, saves the day.

12.11   Namioka, Lensey. **Yang the Youngest and His Terrible Ear.** Illustrated by Kees de Kiefte. Little, Brown/Joy Street Books, 1992. ISBN 0-316-59701-5. 134p. 9–11 (est). Fiction.

The Yangs have recently moved to Seattle from China. Yingtao, the youngest, has the misfortune of having been born into a musically talented family. Despite his inability to play in tune, his parents expect his musical talent to emerge. Yingtao's talents are in baseball, but he has a difficult time convincing his parents that he should quit the violin. Yingtao and his friend Matthew devise a scheme to prove that he is different from his musical siblings. Humorously told in the first person, this is an excellent read-aloud book.

12.12   Pinkwater, Jill. **Tails of the Bronx: A Tale of the Bronx.** Macmillan, 1991. ISBN 0-02-774652-6. 208p. 8–12. Fiction.

All the cats on Burnbridge Avenue are missing. Ten-year-old Loretta Berstein and her multicultural group of friends in a largely working-class community in the Bronx decide to search for them. They soon solve the mystery of the missing cats, but in the process the friends learn firsthand about the far more difficult problem of homelessness. Although the plot sometimes borders on the improbable, the story is one of the few children's books to broach this societal issue.

12.13   Regan, Dian Curtis. **The Curse of the Trouble Dolls.** Illustrated by Michael Chesworth. Henry Holt/Red Feather Books, 1992. ISBN 0-8050-1944-8. 58p. 7–10. Fiction.

In a hilarious depiction of a fourth-grade classroom, Chinese American Angie Wu becomes popular when she shares her six trouble dolls from Guatemala with her friends. The dolls are supposed to dispel trouble, but when Angie lends the dolls one by one to her classmates, the blessing of the trouble dolls turns out to be a curse. Some customs and beliefs of the Mayas are superficially interlaced into the plot.

12.14   Roop, Peter, and Connie Roop. **Ahyoka and the Talking Leaves.** Illustrated by Yoshi Miyake. Lothrop, Lee and Shepard Books, 1992. ISBN 0-688-10697-8. 64p. 6 and up. Fiction.

Sequoyah and his daughter, Ahyoka, are the only individuals known to have created a written language. This fictionalized account of the Cherokee visionary places his daughter at the center of the story. It describes their hardships, from being accused of doing evil magic to having their cabin burned. It also makes clear Sequoyah's commitment to the project and the enormity of their achievements. One wishes for more information about the accuracy of the illustrations, but the story is worth reading. *Notable 1992 Children's Trade Books in the Field of Social Studies.*

12.15 Stolz, Mary. **Go Fish.** Illustrated by Pat Cummings. HarperCollins, 1991. ISBN 0-06-025822-5. 73p. 7–11. Fiction.

Grandfather agrees to take Thomas fishing, one of their favorite pastimes. At the end of the day, Thomas is once again eager to hear Grandfather's stories, which have been passed down through the centuries from West Africa. In this sequel to *Storm in the Night,* characterization is strong, there is obvious affection between Thomas and his grandfather, and their love of reading and storytelling are skillfully woven into the story. See also *Stealing Home* by Mary Stolz (12.16). *Notable 1991 Children's Trade Books in the Field of Social Studies.*

12.16 Stolz, Mary. **Stealing Home.** HarperCollins, 1992. ISBN 0-06-021157-1. 154p. 8–11. Fiction.

Just when Thomas thinks that life is at its coziest, Aunt Linzy arrives for an extended visit. She does not like baseball and disapproves of fishing. She *does* like to clean up. Adjusting to the changes that she brings to their lives is not easy for Thomas or his grandfather. This sequel to *Storm in the Night* and *Go Fish* (12.15) includes the humor and strong characterization that readers have come to expect from Mary Stolz's stories about an orphaned African American boy being raised in Florida by his wise and loving grandfather.

12.17 Tate, Eleanora E. **Thank You, Dr. Martin Luther King, Jr.!** Franklin Watts, 1990. ISBN 0-531-10904-6. 237p. 8–10. Fiction.

Mary Elouise is dark-skinned and unhappy about it. She hates the Black dolls that Big Mama gives her for Christmas. She is willing to give up her good friend if she can be friends with Brandy, a light-skinned girl whose family is well-off. But when a storyteller who calls herself Imani Afrika comes into her classroom and into her life, Mary Elouise begins her journey toward self-acceptance, supported by her true friends and by her loving and wise grandmother. *Notable 1990 Children's Trade Books in the Field of Social Studies.*

12.18 Taylor, Mildred D. **Mississippi Bridge.** Illustrated by Max Ginsburg. Dial Books for Young Readers, 1990. ISBN 0-8037-0427-5. 62p. 8 and up. Fiction.

Jeremy Simms, a white boy, relates the events that unfold as the weekly bus arrives at his family's store one rainy day in the 1930s, a time of blatant racism in rural Mississippi. Before crossing the raging creek, the bus driver makes the Black passengers, including the Logan children's grandmother, get off the bus to make room for some whites, which proves to be a fateful decision. This hard-hitting tale expands the story of the Logans from *Roll of Thunder, Hear My Cry. Notable 1990 Children's Trade Books in the Field of Social Studies.*

12.19 Yee, Paul. **Roses Sing on New Snow: A Delicious Tale.** Illustrated by Harvey Chan. Macmillan, 1991. ISBN 0-02-793622-8. 32p. 6–11 (est). Fiction.

In this humorous and moral tale by Canadian author Paul Yee, a father falsely boasts that his two sons, rather than his daughter, are the best cooks in town. An inevitable predicament arises when the visiting governor of China requests the recipe for the daughter's exquisite dish called "Roses Sing on New Snow." The artist accurately depicts the New World setting of the early Chinese immigrants and particularly captures the emotions of the rotund protagonists. This is a good accompaniment to Paul Yee's *Tales from Gold Mountain.*

13 Novels for Older Readers

13.1   Alexander, Lloyd. **The Remarkable Journey of Prince Jen.** Dutton Children's Books, 1991. ISBN 0-525-44826-8. 274p. 11 and up (est). Fiction.

Young Prince Jen, with the aid of his loyal manservant Mafoo, seeks the legendary kingdom of Tien Kuo in order to learn from its wise ruler, Yuan Ming. An old sage chooses six simple gifts for Prince Jen to bear in homage, and unbeknown to him, the gifts have magical powers. The numerous obstacles overcome serve as rites of passage into manhood. Author Lloyd Alexander weaves an intricate tale not unlike Chinese legends of old.

13.2   Armstrong, Jennifer. **Steal Away.** Orchard Books/Richard Jackson Books, 1992. ISBN 0-531-08583-X. 210p. 10 and up. Fiction.

It is 1855. Orphaned Susannah has come from Vermont to live with her slaveholding Virginia relatives. Bethlehem is a "gift" to Susannah from the family. Both girls are desperate to escape, and together this unlikely interracial pair of thirteen year olds runs away. On the girls' journey north, their courage, their friendship, and their values are all tested. Forty years later, they tell the story of their adventure to their thirteen-year-old granddaughters. Readers will find much food for thought in this story of two strong and honest women. *ALA Notable Children's Books, 1993; Best Books for Young Adults, 1993.*

13.3   Berry, James. **Ajeemah and His Son.** HarperCollins/Willa Perlman Books, 1992. ISBN 0-06-021044-3. 83p. 11 and up. Fiction.

In an unnamed African nation in the early 1800s, Ajeemah and his eighteen-year-old son, Atu, are walking to a neighboring village with a dowry for Atu's chosen bride when they are kidnapped and sold into slavery. They survive the six-week voyage and land in Jamaica, where they are sold to separate sugar plantations, never to meet again. James Berry tells their parallel stories in this hard-hitting exploration of the effects of slavery on the lives of the enslaved and their descendants. This book is for mature readers. *ALA Notable Children's Books, 1993; Best Books for Young Adults, 1993; Boston Globe–Horn Book Fiction*

Award, 1993; Notable 1992 Children's Trade Books in the Field of Social Studies.

13.4 Blair, David Nelson. **Fear the Condor.** Lodestar Books, 1992. ISBN 0-525-67381-4. 137p. 10 and up (est). Fiction.

Bartolina Ch'oke and her Aymara Indian family work for the patrón of a large farm in Bolivia in the 1930s. Bartolina learns the cruelties of the subservient life that she and her family are forced to live when she is given added housekeeping duties and when her father is conscripted into the Bolivian army to fight in a war in which he has no investment. Bartolina is determined to learn how to read, and her literacy provides the catalyst for trying to bring about change in her people's way of life.

13.5 Booth, Coleen E. **Going Live.** Charles Scribner's Sons, 1992. ISBN 0-684-19392-2. 181p. 10 and up. Fiction.

Assuming the responsibility of being one of the three hosts on a TV talk show is a great challenge for an eleven-year-old African American girl named Delaney Crawford. She soon learns that cooperation, making choices, and decision making are central to fulfilling this challenge. Delaney misses her friends, has no time for fun, and cannot keep up with her homework. Adding to her anguish is the decision of her widowed mother to date a fellow dentist. This first novel will connect with many modern teenagers.

13.6 Buss, Fran Leeper (with Daisy Cubias). **Journey of the Sparrows.** Lodestar Books, 1991. ISBN 0-525-67362-8. 155p. 12 and up. Fiction.

Fifteen-year-old María, two siblings, and another teenager are smuggled into the United States from Mexico in a crate in order to escape murder in their home country of El Salvador. In Chicago, they suffer starvation and cruel working conditions. María's sense of hope and her determination to reunite with her mother and baby sister, still in Mexico, make the story ultimately affirming. The author's frankness about the terror that illegal aliens face makes for mature reading. This is a topic not well represented in young adult literature. *Jane Addams Award, 1992; Notable 1991 Children's Trade Books in the Field of Social Studies.*

13.7 Case, Dianne. **Love, David.** Illustrated by Dan Andreasen. Lodestar Books, 1991. ISBN 0-525-67350-4. 128p. 10–12. Fiction.

Although she loves her parents and the baby sister for whom she cares daily, for Anna Jantjies, a "colored" South African, life centers on her beloved half-brother, David. David loves her, too, but he wants to escape their unyielding poverty and his abusive stepfather. In this first-person narrative, Anna relates her own hopes and fears, and what happens when, inevitably, her father abuses the dog that David had rescued from drowning and had grown to love. The novel gives human faces to South Africa's racial oppression.

13.8   Choi, Sook Nyul. **Year of Impossible Goodbyes.** Houghton Mifflin, 1991. ISBN 0-395-57419-6. 171p. 10 and up. Fiction.

Ten-year-old Sookan lives in Japanese-occupied North Korea. Her brothers and father are off fighting in the resistance. When her grandfather dies, his spirit broken by the cruelty of the Japanese soldiers, Sookan, her mother, and her brother plan their escape to American-occupied South Korea. The harsh realities of war as seen through this young girl's year of impossible goodbyes provide a heart-wrenching perspective on an aspect of World War II that is probably not familiar to U.S. readers. *ALA Notable Children's Books, 1992; Best Books for Young Adults, 1992.*

13.9   Davis, Ossie. **Just like Martin.** Simon and Schuster Books for Young Readers, 1992. ISBN 0-671-73202-1. 215p. 10 and up (est). Fiction.

It is 1963 in Alabama. Through his pastor, Stone has met Dr. Martin Luther King Jr. and wants to be a preacher, "just like Martin." But Stone's father, embittered by his Korean War experience, sees nonviolence as cowardly and refuses to embrace it. Stone finds himself pulled between his love for his father, who carries a gun in his truck, and his own ideals. This is a vivid, albeit sometimes humorous, re-creation of an eventful period in the African American struggle for freedom. *Notable 1992 Children's Trade Books in the Field of Social Studies.*

13.10   Dorris, Michael. **Morning Girl.** Hyperion Books for Children, 1992. ISBN 1-56282-285-3. 74p. 10 and up. Fiction.

Growing up on one of the Bahama Islands in the late fifteenth century, twelve-year-old Morning Girl likes being out to greet the morning, but her younger brother Star Boy wants to be an expert on the night. Alternating chapters from the perspectives of these two very different children re-create the everyday lives and culture of a Taino family and community. Their lives seem

A.

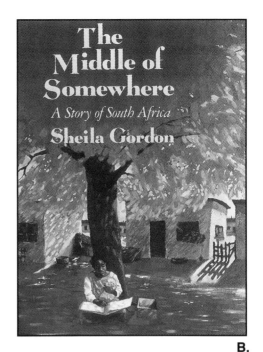

B.

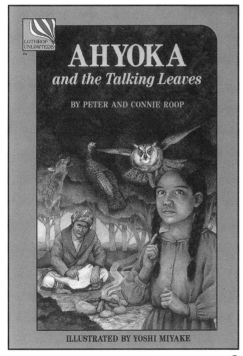

C.

D.

A. *Class President* by Johanna Hurwitz; illustrated by Sheila Hamanaka (see 12.7). **B.** *The Middle of Somewhere: A Story of South Africa* by Sheila Gordon (see 12.3). **C.** *Ahyoka and the Talking Leaves* by Peter and Connie Roop; illustrated by Yoshi Miyake (see 12.14). **D.** *The Dark Thirty: Southern Tales of the Supernatural* by Patricia C. McKissack; illustrated by Brian Pinkney (see 14.6).

A.

B.

C.

D.

A. *Morning Girl* by Michael Dorris (see 13.10). **B.** *Year of Impossible Goodbyes* by Sook Nyul Choi (see 13.8). **C.** *Taste of Salt: A Story of Modern Haiti* by Frances Temple (see 13.30). **D.** *Goodbye, Vietnam* by Gloria Whelan (see 13.32).

ordinary and comfortable. Then one day in 1492 Morning Girl, out for a swim, meets a group of strangers in a fat canoe. See also *The Tainos: The People Who Welcomed Columbus* by Francine Jacobs (7.9) and *Encounter* by Jane Yolen (11.79). *Scott O'Dell Award for Historical Fiction, 1993.*

13.11   Girion, Barbara. **Indian Summer.** Scholastic Hardcover Books, 1990. ISBN 0-590-42636-2. 183p. 10–12. Fiction.

Joni McCord and Sarah Birdsong are forced to share Sarah's bedroom when Joni's father becomes the summer resident physician on the Iroquois reservation. Joni, resentful that she had to come, and Sarah, distrustful of this interloper in her home and community, struggle to lay aside their misconceptions and hurts so that they may become friends. Ghostly faces in a tree, missing possessions, and barbed words lie between them and threaten to ruin the summer until one impulsive act during the annual powwow.

13.12   Haugaard, Erik Christian. **The Boy and the Samurai.** Houghton Mifflin, 1991. ISBN 0-395-56398-4. 221p. 10 and up. Fiction.

Saru is orphaned when his mother dies in childbirth and his father dies fighting in the civil war in sixteenth-century Japan. Eventually Saru finds himself alone on the streets. Comparing himself to the "monkey who does not speak," he survives by carefully observing the world around him. When he agrees to help rescue a samurai's imprisoned wife, Saru's survival skills come into play. This is an absorbing tale that accurately reflects this period in Japanese history.

13.13   Higginsen, Vy (with Tonya Bolden). **Mama, I Want to Sing.** Scholastic Hardcover Books, 1992. ISBN 0-590-44201-5. 183p. 11 and up. Fiction.

This novel is based on the off-Broadway musical of the same title. It tells the story of Doris Winter, an African American girl who grows up singing in the choir of her father's church in the 1940s. But Doris is also attracted to the popular music that her mother calls "wordly." Working at the Apollo Theatre without her mother's knowledge helps to keep her dream alive. Doris must find a way to convince her mother to let her follow her dream.

13.14   Hill, Kirkpatrick. **Toughboy and Sister.** Margaret K. McElderry Books, 1990. ISBN 0-689-50506-X. 121p. 8–12. Fiction.

"Mama died in October, just before the Yukon froze up for the winter." Now eleven-year-old John (Toughboy) and his younger sister Laurie are left with their father. When summer comes, Daddy takes them as usual to the fishing camp in the Yukon. Then, after a drinking binge, the father dies, leaving the children stranded in the camp. There they must learn to feed themselves and ward off danger. This is a compelling survival story about two Athabascan children in whom children everywhere can see something of themselves.

13.15   Houston, James. **Drifting Snow: An Arctic Search.** Illustrated by James Houston. Margaret K. McElderry Books, 1992. ISBN 0-689-50563-9. 150p. 10 and up. Fiction.

Because of the threat of tuberculosis, Apoutee, now named Elizabeth Queen, was separated from her parents along with other young Inuit children on Nisek Island. Her life was spared, but all records and identification of her family were lost. Now, at age fourteen, Elizabeth returns to the Arctic to search for her parents and to learn the language and lifestyle of her family. One Inuit family takes her in, and soon Elizabeth is faced with starvation and the struggle to survive in her new nomadic life. When she finds her family, Elizabeth must make a difficult decision. *Notable 1992 Children's Trade Books in the Field of Social Studies.*

13.16   Lyons, Mary E. **Letters from a Slave Girl: The Story of Harriet Jacobs.** Charles Scribner's Sons, 1992. ISBN 0-684-19446-5. 146p. 12 and up. Fiction.

Harriet Jacobs is attractive and intelligent, a dangerous combination for a female slave in the mid-1800s. Her "owner" tries to subjugate her sexually; but Harriet avoids his advances and chooses another, seemingly kinder white man, hoping to be freed. They have two children, who are eventually freed. Harriet, however, is pursued by her "owner" and spends seven years hiding in the attic of her grandmother's house before she can escape to the North. This account of Harriet's life, told through fictional letters that Harriet writes to various family members, reveals the ways in which enslaved women were exploited. Readers may want to read the actual autobiography of Harriet Jacobs (1813–97). *ALA Notable Children's Books, 1992; Best Books for Young Adults, 1993.*

13.17   Mazzio, Joan. **The One Who Came Back.** Houghton Mifflin, 1992. ISBN 0-395-59506-1. 178p. 11 and up. Fiction.

Alex and Eddie are good friends who share their dreams and adventures in the mountains of New Mexico. When Eddie disappears after spending the day with Alex, no one believes Alex's version of what may have happened to the Mexican American boy. This story of two teenage boys deals with interracial friendship and familial relationships. An underlying theme of prejudice and fear ties the story together, linking adults' suspicions of children and blatant prejudice directed toward Mexican Americans. The story is a gripping adventure and coming-of-age story. *Recommended Books for Reluctant Young Adult Readers, 1993.*

13.18 Moore, Yvette. **Freedom Songs.** Orchard Books, 1991. ISBN 0-531-08412-4. 168p. 12 and up. Fiction.

It is 1963. Fourteen-year-old Sheryl, who has always lived in Brooklyn, goes with her family to visit relatives in North Carolina. Sheryl is surprised at the overt racism that she encounters in the South. She admires her young Uncle Pete, who is a Freedom Rider involved in voter registration. Back in Brooklyn, Sheryl realizes that northerners are part of the struggle, too. Inspired by her uncle's courage and undaunted by family tragedy, Sheryl and her friends find a way to participate. *Notable 1991 Children's Trade Books in the Field of Social Studies.*

13.19 Myers, Walter Dean. **The Mouse Rap.** Harper and Row, 1990. ISBN 0-06-024344-9. 186p. 10 and up. Fiction.

"Ka-phoomp! Ka-phoomp! Da Doom Da Dooom!" Each chapter in this humorous novel opens with an introductory rap by Mouse, the fourteen-year-old narrator of a tale of summer adventure in Harlem. Girls, a father trying to drop back *into* his family, and rumors of large sums of money left in an abandoned building all complicate Mouse's life and make for a memorable summer. Walter Dean Myers's playful handling of the vernacular of urban Black adolescents adds to the book's appeal to preteen and teen readers. *Best Books for Young Adults, 1991.*

13.20 Myers, Walter Dean. **The Righteous Revenge of Artemis Bonner.** HarperCollins, 1992. ISBN 0-06-020846-5. 140p. 10 and up. Fiction.

In this funny Western spoof set in 1882, Artemis Bonner, an African American teenager, travels from New York to Arizona to avenge the murder of his Uncle Ugly. Out West, Artemis teams up with a Cherokee boy named Frolic, and the two of them pursue villain Catfish Grimes and his woman, Lucy Featherdip, from Tombstone to Alaska and back. Can Truth and Honest Determination win out over evildoers? Will Artemis find Uncle Ugly's hidden treasure? The outcome does not matter; readers should go along for the fun and adventure! *Best Books for Young Adults, 1993.*

13.21 Myers, Walter Dean. **Somewhere in the Darkness.** Scholastic Hardcover Books, 1992. ISBN 0-590-42411-4. 168p. 12 and up. Fiction.

Tenth-grader Jimmy leaves Harlem and his loving foster mother, Mama Jean, to make an odyssey across the country with Crab, the father whom he barely remembers. Crab, who has recently escaped from prison, has something he needs to do, and Jimmy has questions that need to be answered. As they journey back to Crab's old haunts, both father and son learn painful lessons about family and trust, and the requirements of fatherhood. Here is a poignant story that will strike a familiar chord with many readers. *ALA Notable Children's Books, 1993; Best Books for Young Adults, 1993; Boston Globe–Horn Book Fiction Honor Book, 1992; Coretta Scott King Writing Honor Book, 1993; Newbery Honor Book, 1993; Recommended Books for Reluctant Young Adult Readers, 1993.*

13.22 Naidoo, Beverley. **Chain of Fire.** Illustrated by Eric Velasquez. HarperCollins, 1990. ISBN 0-397-32427-8. 242p. 11 and up. Fiction.

In South Africa, Black and white people live separately by law. When fifteen-year-old Naledi, her friend Taolo, and their neighbors discover large numerals painted on their homes, they are upset. The numbers mean that they must leave their homes and move to a barren "homeland." When Naledi and her friends form an "anti-removal" committee, they discover how cruel apartheid can be. This sequel to *Journey to Jo'burg* will help students understand one of the most important human rights issues of the day. *Best Books for Young Adults, 1991; Notable 1990 Children's Trade Books in the Field of Social Studies.*

13.23 Namioka, Lensey. **The Coming of the Bear.** HarperCollins, 1992. ISBN 0-06-020289-0. 230p. 11 and up. Fiction.

Zenta and Matsuzo, two disgraced samurai from feudal Japan, are shipwrecked on a strange island after escaping from sure death in Japan. They are rescued by aboriginal tribal people, the Ainus, who live on Yezo (now Hokkaido), and are taught some of the Ainu customs. Horrified by the brutal Bear Festival, the two young warriors resolve to escape to a nearby Japanese settlement. However, the Japanese settlement is not what they expect, and they find themselves in the middle of a war between their people and their Ainu rescuers.

13.24 Prather, Ray. **Fish and Bones.** HarperCollins, 1992. ISBN 0-06-025122-0. 255p. 10 and up. Fiction.

It is August 1971. The Sun City, Florida, bank has been robbed, and thirteen-year-old Bones wants to collect the reward for solving the crime. Many of the town's best-known citizens, Black and white, become suspects as portions of the stolen money turn up in unexpected places. As Bones makes his rounds in town and on the river, what he uncovers is some of the town's disturbing history. In spite of the many touches of humor, the book is for mature readers.

13.25 Robinson, Margaret A. **A Woman of Her Tribe.** Charles Scribner's Sons, 1990. ISBN 0-684-19223-3. 131p. 12 and up. Fiction.

Fifteen-year-old Annette has won a scholarship to St. John's Academy in Victoria, British Columbia. Acceptance means leaving the Nootka village where she grew up with her father's people. Her mother, who is not a Nootka Indian, thinks Annette needs to expand her horizons. At school Annette faces racism, but with the help of two special teachers and a friend, she begins to adjust. Then at holiday time, she returns to the Nootka village and wrestles with the choices inherent in dealing with her dual cultural inheritance. This book has mature content.

13.26 Salisbury, Graham. **Blue Skin of the Sea: A Novel in Stories.** Delacorte Press, 1992. ISBN 0-385-30596-6. 215p. 10 and up. Fiction.

Since his mother's death, seven-year-old Sonny Mendoza has lived with his aunt. Then he goes to live on the Big Island of Hawaii with his father. Though he comes from a family of fishermen, Sonny is secretly afraid of the sea. In eleven stories, covering the thirteen years from 1953 to 1966, Graham Salisbury shows how Sonny faces his fears and comes to know and love his father. This is an engaging story about a family whose lives are intertwined with the sea. *Best Books for Young Adults, 1992; Notable 1992 Children's Trade Books in the Field of Social Studies.*

13.27 Soto, Gary. **Pacific Crossing.** Harcourt Brace Jovanovich, 1992. ISBN 0-15-259187-7. 134p. 10 and up (est). Fiction.

Lincoln Mendoza and his barrio brother Tony take part in a six-week student exchange program with host families in Japan. Lincoln, who is Mexican American, becomes a "son" to Mr. and Mrs. Ono and a brother to Mitsuo—working on their farm, studying *kempo* (a type of Japanese martial arts), and learning something about Japanese culture. Lincoln and his new family must learn to understand their differences and discover the similarities between their lives. The book includes a glossary of Spanish and Japanese phrases.

13.28 Soto, Gary. **Taking Sides.** Harcourt Brace Jovanovich, 1991. ISBN 0-15-284076-1. 138p. 10 and up. Fiction.

When eighth-grader Lincoln Mendoza and his mother move from an urban barrio to a white suburb, Lincoln must contend with being a minority in school and on the basketball team. Decisions about old and new friends and his mother's new boyfriend occur in a realistic fashion. Conversations include several Spanish words, which appear in the glossary. Gary Soto dramatically weaves the pressures of growing up with Lincoln's need and desire to maintain his Mexican American cultural identity.

13.29 Spinelli, Jerry. **Maniac Magee.** Little, Brown, 1990. ISBN 0-316-80722-2. 184p. 9 and up. Fiction.

When Jeffrey Lionel "Maniac" Magee's parents die in a tragic railroad accident, the three-year-old boy is placed in the custody of his dour, feuding, and distant aunt and uncle. By age eleven, he can no longer tolerate the tension and anger, so he runs away to another town, where he meets Amanda, an African American girl who forges a friendship with him. Jeffrey amazes adults and children with his athletic prowess and ability to face all challenges, but he increasingly comes to feel like an outsider. Jeffrey begins a journey to find a place where he is loved, accepted, and made a part of a family. *Boston Globe–Horn Book Fiction Award, 1990; Newbery Medal, 1991.*

13.30 Temple, Frances. **Taste of Salt: A Story of Modern Haiti.** Orchard Books/Richard Jackson Books, 1992. ISBN 0-531-08609-7. 179p. 11 and up. Fiction.

Authentic voices tell the story of two Haitian teens who are working with social reformer Jean-Bertrand Aristide before and after his presidential election. After Djo is beaten by the Tonton Macoute (the private army of repressive president François

Duvalier), Aristide asks Jeremie to record Djo's life story. As she listens, Jeremie is drawn to Djo and feels compelled to share her own very different story. The engrossing first-person narration reveals parallels between the coming of age of the two teenagers and Haiti's changing sociopolitical situation. This is an impressive first novel that mature readers will find accessible.

13.31 Thomas, Joyce Carol. **When the Nightingale Sings.** HarperCollins, 1992. ISBN 0-06-020295-5. 148p. 12 and up. Fiction.

This is a gospel version of the Cinderella story. Fourteen-year-old Marigold, an African American orphan of mysterious origins, has been raised by mean Ruby and her no-singing twin daughters, who treat Marigold like a servant. When the young Minister of Music hears Marigold's nightingale voice, he is so enchanted that he sets up a Great Gospel Convention to find a new lead gospel singer, with predictable results. Full of lyricism and sly church humor, this modern fairy tale speaks of love, of family, and of self-respect.

13.32 Whelan, Gloria. **Goodbye, Vietnam.** Alfred A. Knopf/Borzoi Books, 1992. ISBN 0-679-92263-6. 136p. 12 and up. Fiction.

Thirteen-year-old Mai and her family escape from Vietnam through a dangerous sea voyage, only to find themselves in a refugee camp in Hong Kong. Their courage bolstered by the threat of imprisonment for the father and grandmother should they return to Vietnam, Mai and her family quietly endure many hardships as they wait to see if they will be able to find a home outside Vietnam. Acknowledging the people and the refugee agency who helped her work, author Gloria Whelan presents a timely story.

13.33 Woodson, Jacqueline. **The Dear One.** Delacorte Press, 1991. ISBN 0-385-30416-1. 145p. 12 and up. Fiction.

When her mother agrees to care for a friend's pregnant daughter, Feni is furious. A teenager from Harlem will surely disrupt their upper-middle-class home. Rebecca, the mother-to-be, is none too happy with the arrangement either, but everyone tries to make the best of it. Mama, Feni, and their friends encircle Rebecca in their warmth as they help both her and themselves. The novel deals with such contemporary issues as alcoholism and homosexuality, but without sensationalism or moralizing.

13.34 Woodson, Jacqueline. **Last Summer with Maizon.** Delacorte Press, 1990. ISBN 0-385-30045-X. 105p. 10 and up. Fiction.

The summer brings major changes to Margaret's life. Her father dies, and to add to her sense of loss, her best friend Maizon is offered a scholarship to a New England boarding school. The girls have different temperaments; the out-going Maizon tends to overshadow Margaret's quieter gifts. In the fall, while Maizon tries to meet the challenges of being Black and lacking in material wealth in a predominantly white private school, Margaret remains in Brooklyn and discovers her own talents. For a time, it looks as if the friendship may not survive, but the ties between the girls are binding.

13.35 Woodson, Jacqueline. **Maizon at Blue Hill.** Delacorte Press, 1992. ISBN 0-385-30796-9. 131p. 10 and up. Fiction.

In this sequel to *Last Summer with Maizon* (13.34), Maizon leaves Brooklyn to go to Blue Hill, a private boarding school in Connecticut. Although Blue Hill offers many advantages and Maizon does well academically, she misses her grandmother and her best friend Margaret. Being one of five or six Black girls in this elite setting forces Maizon to wrestle with issues of race and class, and to wonder not only whether she belongs at Blue Hill but whether she can ever belong anywhere. *Best Books for Young Adults, 1993; Notable 1992 Children's Trade Books in the Field of Social Studies.*

13.36 Wunderli, Stephen. **The Blue between the Clouds.** Henry Holt, 1992. ISBN 0-8050-1772-0. 114p. 10–12. Fiction.

Two Moons is named for the two halves of the world, white and Indian, in which he lives. Matt is given the name Blue between the Clouds after the hope that clouds will bring rain to the crops, but pass before it floods. Together these two boys, one white, one Navajo, share adventures and dreams of flying. Set in Thistle, Utah, in the early 1940s, this book is rich in descriptions of Navajo life and culture, although the story is told from Matt's perspective.

14 Anthologies: Gatherings of Poems and Stories

14.1 Carlson, Lori M., and Cynthia L. Ventura, editors. **Where Angels Glide at Dawn: New Stories from Latin America.** Illustrated by José Ortega. J. B. Lippincott, 1990. ISBN 0-397-32425-1. 114p. 10 and up. Fiction.

Introduced by Isabel Allende, these ten stories evoke the geography of Latin America and the spirit of its people yet demonstrate the diversity of cultures, politics, and living conditions. Some stories are realistic, others are fanciful. We learn, for instance, of the bear in the pipes of a house, the rebellion of the magical rabbits, and a Holy Week celebration in the town of Tarma, Peru. Each story is followed by a brief note about its source. A glossary of unfamiliar words and phrases and additional information about the authors and editors is provided.

14.2 Carlstrom, Nancy White. **Light: Stories of a Small Kindness.** Illustrated by Lisa Desimini. Little, Brown, 1990. ISBN 0-316-12857-0. 42p. 9–12. Fiction.

These seven original short stories are set in the diverse settings of Mexico, Guatemala, Haiti, and New York City. Each story involves a "small kindness," an event that is or seems miraculous. A young boy braves a dark cave. Another has his achievement celebrated by his classmates. Students on a school trip narrowly escape danger. Every story speaks of the triumph of the human spirit. An author's note reveals the way in which the stories relate to her own experiences.

14.3 Durell, Ann, and Marilyn Sachs, editors. **The Big Book for Peace.** Dutton Children's Books, 1990. ISBN 0-525-44605-2. 120p. 6–12 (est). Fiction.

Seventeen stories and poems and accompanying illustrations by more than thirty well-known writers and artists make up this anthology designed to promote peace and harmony among the people of the earth. A letter from a Japanese American World War II internment camp, an adaptation of the Iroquois Book of the Great Law, and a story about the Mississippi Democratic Freedom Party are a few of the features—some humorous, some sad—of this book that celebrates the idea of peace. *Jane Addams Award, 1991; ALA Notable Children's Books, 1991; Notable 1990 Children's Trade Books in the Field of Social Studies.*

14.4   Hirschfelder, Arlene B., and Beverly R. Singer, compilers. **Rising Voices: Writings of Young Native Americans.** Charles Scribner's Sons, 1992. ISBN 0-684-19207-1. 115p. 12 and up. Nonfiction.

"A voice made of many voices of proud men and women with a hope and a question. . . . Will we make it? Listen!" In this collection of poems and testimonies, contemporary young Native Americans speak of their identity, families, homelands, rituals and ceremonies, education, and the harsh realities of their lives. This work provides insight into the feelings of the young writers, who are forced to live in two worlds and who are trying to be in harmony with both. *Notable 1992 Children's Trade Books in the Field of Social Studies.*

14.5   Larrick, Nancy, and Wendy Lamb, editors. **To Ride a Butterfly: Original Stories, Poems, and Songs for Children by Fifty-two Distinguished Authors and Illustrators.** Bantam Doubleday Dell, 1991. ISBN 0-440-50402-3. 96p. 5–10. Fiction.

Fifty-two well-known authors and illustrators, from Verna Aardema to Charlotte Zolotow, have contributed to this anthology of illustrations, stories, folktales, fables, poems, songs, and nonfiction writings. Produced for the twenty-fifth anniversary of Reading Is Fundamental (RIF), it contains pieces created or adapted for this volume. Contributors include Lucille Clifton, John Steptoe, Brian Pinkney, and Patricia McKissack. The pieces are appealing. Sadly, however, Native peoples, Latinos, and Asians (except for one Yashima painting) are not to be found. It's a collection in Black and white.

14.6   McKissack, Patricia C. **The Dark Thirty: Southern Tales of the Supernatural.** Illustrated by Brian Pinkney. Alfred A. Knopf/Borzoi Books, 1992. ISBN 0-679-91863-9. 122p. 7 and up. Fiction.

These ten original stories will give you goose bumps. They are ghost stories and horror stories of the kind told in the author's childhood home in the dark thirty, the half hour just before nightfall. Incorporating African American history and culture, the tales include stories from the days of slavery and from the twentieth-century civil rights movement. The final story is based on one of Patricia McKissack's childhood experiences. Brian Pinkney's scratchboard illustrations add just the right touch to these scary stories. *ALA Notable Children's Books, 1993; Coretta Scott King Writing Award, 1993; Newbery Honor Book, 1993; Notable 1992 Children's Trade Books in the Field of Social Studies.*

14.7   Rosen, Michael J., editor. **Home: A Collection of Thirty Distinguished Authors and Illustrators of Children's Books to Aid the Homeless.** HarperCollins/Charlotte Zolotow Books, 1992. ISBN 0-06-021789-8. 32p. All ages. Fiction.

Thirteen well-known authors and seventeen prominent illustrators have contributed stories, poems, and illustrations for this multicultural anthology. The theme is "home," and the proceeds support Share Our Strength (SOS) in its fight against homelessness. Even though it appears in the context of a poetic allusion to "Ali Baba and the Forty Thieves," some readers may find it offensive that the single representation of Arabs shows them as grinning thieves. *Notable 1992 Children's Books in the Field of Social Studies.*

14.8   Soto, Gary. **Baseball in April, and Other Stories.** Harcourt Brace Jovanovich, 1990. ISBN 0-15-205720-X. 111p. 10 and up (est). Fiction.

Like Gary Soto's poems, these eleven stories are filled with the details of daily life in a Mexican American community in Fresno, California. A big brother comes through at the right time; a boy tries to impress a girl with his knowledge of French; a mishap at a school talent show turns into a comic performance. Readers from all kinds of families and all kinds of neighborhoods will recognize something of themselves in the people depicted in these stories. A glossary of Spanish words is included. *Best Books for Young Adults, 1991.*

14.9   Tate, Eleanora E. **Front Porch Stories at the One-Room School.** Illustrated by Eric Velasquez. Bantam Skylark Books, 1992. ISBN 0-533-08384-8. 112p. 8 and up. Fiction.

Margie, who is a twelve-year-old African American girl, her father, and her seven-year-old cousin Ethel sit on the steps of the old one-room school and swap stories. Daddy does most of the telling, recalling growing up in Nutbush, Missouri, when Aunt Daisy was the teacher in the school. There are ghost stories, family stories, school stories, and town stories in this collection of ten tales. Middle graders will enjoy these yarns that beg to be read aloud.

14.10   Thomas, Joyce Carol, editor. **A Gathering of Flowers: Stories about Being Young in America.** Harper and Row, 1990. ISBN 0-06-026174-9. 236p. 11 and up. Fiction.

Covering such diverse settings as urban San Francisco, a Chippewa reservation, and a Latino barrio in Chicago, these eleven stories by authors from diverse backgrounds recount what it is like to grow up in the United States. Written by such well-known children's book authors as Lois Lowry, Gary Soto, and Jeanne Wakatsuki Houston, the stories are compassionate and moving accounts of life as experienced by young people from different backgrounds.

15 A Potpourri of Resources

This list of resources is not intended to be comprehensive. It includes materials that came to the attention of the committee members as we reviewed books for inclusion in this booklist. Although most of the books suggested for teachers have been published in the 1990s, many of the other listed resources provide information about useful materials published prior to that time. Wherever possible, addresses and phone numbers are listed for the resources; addresses and phone numbers for the publishers can be found in the Directory of Publishers. We hope that this list of resources will be a helpful starting point for readers just beginning to explore multicultural literature, and a reminder for others who are farther along on the journey.

Books for Teachers

Harris, Violet J., ed. *Teaching Multicultural Literature in Grades K–8.* Norwood, Mass.: Christopher-Gordon, 1992 (paper, 1993).

Lindgren, Merri V., ed. *The Multicolored Mirror: Cultural Substance in Literature for Children and Young Adults.* Fort Atkinson, Wis.: Highsmith Press, 1991.

Manna, Anthony L., and Carolyn S. Brodie, eds. *Many Faces, Many Voices: Multicultural Literary Experiences for Youth.* Fort Atkinson, Wis.: Highsmith Press, 1992.

Nieto, Sonia. *Affirming Diversity: The Sociopolitical Context of Multicultural Education.* New York: Longman, 1992.

Bibliographies and Guides

Khorana, Meena, comp. *The Indian Subcontinent in Literature for Children and Young Adults: An Annotated Bibliography of English-Language Books.* Bibliographies and Indexes in World Literature series, no. 32. Westport, Conn.: Greenwood Press, 1991.

Kruse, Ginny Moore, and Kathleen T. Horning, eds. *Multicultural Literature for Children and Young Adults,* 3d ed. Madison, Wis.: Cooperative Children's Book Center, 1991.

Miller-Lachman, Lyn. *Our Families, Our Friends, Our World: An Annotated Guide to Significant Multicultural Books for Children and Teenagers.* New Providence, N.J.: R. R. Bowker, 1992.

Schon, Isabel. *A Hispanic Heritage: A Guide to Juvenile Books about Hispanic People and Cultures*, series 1–4. Metuchen, N.J.: Scarecrow Press, 1980–91.

Slapin, Beverly, and Doris Seale. *Through Indian Eyes: The Native Experience in Books for Children,* 3d ed. Philadelphia: New Society Publishers, 1992.

Periodicals

Booklinks, 434 W. Downer, Aurora, IL 60506.

> A bimonthly magazine published by the American Library Association. Although not specifically concerned with multicultural literature, the magazine does include many relevant articles, activities, and reviews, and it often features works, authors, and artists of interest to multicultural literature proponents. The magazine offers themed annotated bibliographies, pieces focusing on book illustrations, and teaching ideas.

Faces (Cobblestone Publishing)

> For students in grades four to nine. This children's magazine with an anthropological perspective introduces readers to various cultures of diverse peoples around the world. It contains photographs, articles, stories, and suggested activities. The publisher also offers *Cobblestone*, a history magazine for young people that sometimes contains articles that are relevant to multicultural studies.

Harambee (Just Us Books)

> A newspaper for young readers published six times a year. The focus is on the African American experience. The newspaper contains information articles, photographs, learning activities, booklists, interviews, word lists, and the Captain Africa comic strip adventure.

Multicultural Review (Greenwood Publishing Group)

> Offers reviews of books and materials related to multiculturalism. Although not all material relates to elementary and middle schools, a substantial portion does, including reviews of children's books and curricular materials. Many of the ads are from small presses.

School Voices, 79 Leonard Street (Basement), New York, NY 10013.

> A New York City newspaper for parents, educators, and students that is published by a pro-equality, multiracial network of educators and parents.

Teaching Tolerance, Southern Poverty Law Center, 400 Washington Avenue, Montgomery AL 36104.

> Biannual, free to educators. The publication, first issued in spring 1992, focuses on diversity and tolerance and includes articles, reviews, news,

interviews, essays, and notes on resources. It is useful to teachers with an interest in multicultural education.

Tribal College: Journal of American Indian Higher Education, Paul Boyer, Editor, Tribal College, 2509 Montgomery Way, Sacramento, CA 95818; 916-456-5234.

> Sponsored by a consortium of 26 Indian-controlled community colleges. The journal reaches an audience of experienced American Indian instructors, administrators, and policymakers.

Classroom Resources

Children's Museum, 200 Congress Street, Boston, MA 02210; 617-426-6500.

> Offers a variety of multicultural programs for K–8 teachers and their classes. The museum houses many multicultural resources, including exhibits, and has multimedia curricula kits available for a small fee. A multicultural summer institute is also offered.

Ethnic Arts & Facts, P.O. Box 20550, Oakland, CA 94620.

> Offers "culture kits" from Africa, Mexico, Peru, and Guatemala. The kits include cultural/historical overviews written by university scholars "who have lived within the culture" and contain authentic traditional artifacts, such as masks, baskets, cloth, and musical instruments. Maps, bibliographies, references, and suggested activities also are part of the kits. Additional artifacts and children's literature are also available. Unfortunately, the catalog fails to specify *which* African cultures are represented, although such information is given for other kits (e.g., Huichol Indians of Mexico).

Facing History and Ourselves, National Foundation, 25 Kennard Road, Brookline, MA 02146; 617-734-1111.

> Works with teachers throughout the country who want to examine ways of bringing important but controversial material into the classroom. The organization focuses on the Holocaust as a vehicle for understanding the complexity of human behavior. It has also published a curriculum guide, which is available for purchase.

JACP, 414 East Third Avenue, San Mateo, CA 94401; 800-874-2242.

> A nonprofit organization, currently in its nineteenth year, that specializes in Asian American materials, including books, games, audiovisual materials, and dolls. In addition, it reviews recent Asian American publications.

Massachusetts Global Education Program (MGEP), Winchester Public Schools, Winchester, MA 01890; 617-721-1257.

> Nonprofit organization that helps elementary and secondary schools improve their students' ability to deal with the changing world and

increase their skills and knowledge in such subjects as foreign languages, world history, world cultures, geography, and global issues. It offers programs, activities, and technical assistance. In addition, it has a summer institute and provides mini-grants to teacher developers.

Menkart, Deborah, and Catherine A. Sunshine, eds. *Caribbean Connections: Puerto Rico.* Classroom Resources for Secondary Schools series. Washington, D.C.: Network of Educators' Committees on Central America, 1990.

One of a series of resource packets on the Caribbean. This packet is designed to encourage teachers to incorporate material on Puerto Rico and Puerto Ricans into existing curricula. It uses interviews, oral histories, and other first-person accounts to show Caribbean history, as well as essays, musical lyrics, maps, and short stories by well-known Puerto Rican authors. Other titles in the series: *Overview of Regional History; Jamaica; Haiti; Trinidad and Tobago;* and *Caribbean Life in North America.*

Organization for Equal Education of the Sexes, P.O. Box 438, Dept. WA, Blue Hill, ME 04614; 207-374-2489.

Specializes in posters of women of all different backgrounds who have made a difference.

Perez-Selles, Maria, and Nancy Carmen Barra-Zuman. *Building Bridges of Learning and Understanding: A Collection of Classroom Activities on Puerto Rican Culture.* Andover, Mass.: Regional Laboratory for Educational Improvement of the Northeast and Islands, and New England Center for Equity Assistance (300 Brickstone Square, Suite 900, Andover, MA 01810), 1990.

A compilation of activities that integrate elements of Puerto Rican history and culture into the curriculum, K–8, in three major sections (Location and Migration; A Blend of Cultures; An Island Rich in Tradition). There are activities for all subject areas. The focus is on the Tainos, the original inhabitants, and on the Spanish, but the activities omit Puerto Rico's African heritage.

World Music Press, 11 Myrtle Avenue, P.O. Box 2565, Danbury, CT 06813; 203-748-1131.

Specializes in multicultural music publications and recordings for educators and in community outreach programs.

Small Publishers and Distributors

Most of the books we received came from the major "mainstream" publishers of children's books. Important contributions to multicultural literature, however, are also coming from small independent presses. The following list is not comprehensive, but includes those small presses that came to our attention during the committee's tenure. The directory by Kathleen Horning will prove invaluable for those seeking children's books from the small presses. See the Directory of Publishers for addresses and phone numbers of the publishers listed below.

Arte Público Press

> Bills itself as the "oldest and largest publisher of U.S. Hispanic literature." The press offers books for adults, children, and young adults and includes some work of Nicholasa Mohr. It also offers *Kikiriki* and *Tun-ta-ca-tun*, highly recommended collections of stories and poems in English and Spanish.

Black Butterfly Children's Books (produced by Writers and Readers Publishing)

> Focuses on "Black children's books" and books about children of color for all children. It has published books by Tom Feelings and by Eloise Greenfield and Jan Spivey Gilchrist, including *Nathaniel Talking.*

California Tomorrow

> An organization that publishes materials focusing on the tremendous diversity in California's schools. Books include *California Perspectives* and *Embracing Diversity.*

Children's Book Press

> A nonprofit organization that publishes multicultural literature and audiocassettes. A number of its books are bilingual (e.g., English/Spanish, English/Khmer, English/Korean). The press focuses on folktales and contemporary stories from "minority and new immigrant" cultures, including Eastern European cultures.

Good Books for Young Readers

> Offers books focusing on the Amish. Its fiction works provide insight into the daily lives and culture of this religious minority.

Hispanic Books Children's Catalog (Hispanic Books Distributors and Publishers)

> Lists Spanish-language versions of well-known books and other titles available in Spanish from various publishers.

Horning, Kathleen. *Alternative Press Publishers of Children's Books: A Directory,* 4th ed. Madison, Wis.: Friends of the Cooperative Children's Book Center, 1992.

> A good reference source for finding less well known publishers of quality books for children.

Just Us Books

> Specializes in books for young readers that focus on the African and African American experience. It publishes Afro-Bets Books, which fea-

ture concepts and information related to Africa and African Americans, including *Afro-Bets Book of Black Heroes* and *Afro-Bets ABC Book.* It also publishes *Harambee* (see Periodicals).

Lee and Low Books

A new small publisher of multicultural literature for young readers, launched in spring 1993. To date, it has published five realistic picture books featuring Latino (Mexican American, Guatemalan), Japanese American, and African American characters.

Multicultural Publishers Exchange (Highsmith Press)

An association of African, Hispanic, Asian-Pacific Islander, Native American, and white American small press publishers of multicultural books. It publishes an annual catalog listing books for children and young adults, adult resources and references, and curriculum materials.

New Society Publishers

A nonprofit, worker-controlled publishing house. It publishes a variety of books focusing on issues of peace, feminism, the environment, and civil rights, including children's books on peace and the nuclear arms race.

Oyate, 2702 Mathews Street, Berkeley, CA 94702; 510-848-6700.

An organization of Native Americans. It evaluates texts, resource books, and fiction; conducts workshops for educators; and distributes children's books written and illustrated by Native Americans. Write for a list of materials.

Savanna Books

Specializes in books about children of color.

Tundra Books

Publishes children's books reflecting Canada's multicultural population, including Native peoples and immigrants. It offers some books in French and some in Spanish.

Helaine Victoria Press

A nonprofit educational organization specializing in posters, postcards, and other educational materials that focus on women and social protest.

Clearinghouses

Clearinghouse for Immigrant Education (CHIME), National Coalition of Advocates for Students, 100 Boylston Street, Suite 737, Boston, MA 02116.

An interactive resource center and networking service that facilitates access to educational materials, organizations, and people concerned with effective education of immigrant students.

Educational Materials and Services Center (EMSC), 144 Railroad Avenue, Suite 107, Edmonds, WA 98020; 206-775-3582.

> A multicultural education clearinghouse featuring children's books, filmstrips and other audiovisual materials, and professional materials. It also publishes a newsletter, *Multicultural Leader,* featuring articles and reviews focusing on multicultural issues.

National Clearinghouse for Bilingual Education (NCBE), Center for Applied Linguistics, 1118 22nd Street, N.W., Washington, DC 20037; 800-321-NCBE.

> Provides information on any aspect of bilingual education. It also publishes a free bi-monthly newsletter, *Forum.*

Agencies, Centers, and Other Organizations

Congreso Boricua, Puerto Rican Congress of New Jersey, 515 South Broad Street, Trenton, NJ; 609-989-8888.

> A statewide agency serving the community development needs of New Jersey's Puerto Rican and Latino populations. The congress has developed bilingual curriculum resources and also provides a multitude of other services to the educational community.

Council on Interracial Books for Children, 1841 Broadway, New York, NY 10023; 212-757-5339.

> Publishes a newsletter, the *Bulletin,* from time to time. This nonprofit organization was founded by writers, librarians, teachers, and parents in 1966. It promotes anti-racist and anti-sexist children's books and other materials which affirm diversity. It publishes lesson plans, resource materials, and curriculum guides, and it has developed a series of filmstrips on child care, racism and sexism in children's books, and stereotypes.

Educators for Social Responsibility, 23 Garden Street, Cambridge, MA 02138; 617-492-1764.

> A national teachers' organization that offers curricula and professional development addressing the socially significant controversies of the nuclear age. It publishes many curricula and sponsors workshops and conferences. Its membership includes teachers at all school levels.

Equity Institute, 6400 Hollis Street, Suite 15, Emoryville, CA 94608; 415-658-4577.

> A nonprofit national agency that specializes in multicultural organizational development. It works with universitites, schools, community groups, and corporations on issues of racism, sexism, anti-Semitism, and discrimination based on sexual orientation, social class, age, or disabilities.

Everyone's Books, 71 Elliot Street, Brattleboro, VT 05301; 802-254-8160.

> A bookstore focusing on multicultural books for children. It also publishes a quarterly newsletter of book reviews and sells parenting and educational books as well.

Learning Alliance, 494 Broadway, New York, NY 10012; 212-226-7171.

> A nonprofit independent organization that creates innovative educational programs and organizing activities. The alliance works with social change groups to provide information and resources on a variety of issues, such as ecology, diversity, health, and women's issues.

Multicultural Project for Communication and Education, 71 Cherry Street, Cambridge, MA 02139; 617-492-1063.

> Publishes a periodic newsletter with information of interest to educators. It provides training and has published *Caring for Children in a Social Context: Eliminating Racism, Sexism, and Other Patterns of Discrimination*, as well as other fine multicultural materials.

National Association for Bilingual Education (NABE), Union Center Plaza, Third Floor, 810 First Street, N.E., Washington, DC 20001-4205; 202-898-4205.

> A professional association founded in 1975 to address the educational needs of language minority students.

National Association for Multicultural Education (NAME), c/o Dr. Rose Duhon, Office of the Dean, Southern University, P.O. Box 9983, Baton Rouge, LA 70813; 504-771-2290.

> A professional organization founded in 1990 to promote multicultural education in the United States.

National Association of Black School Educators (NABSE), 2816 Georgia Avenue, N.W., Washington, DC 20001; 202-483-1549.

> A professional association that works to enhance and facilitate the education of Black children. It holds a national conference, publishes a newsletter, *Newsbriefs*, and sponsors the Educational Development Program, which consists of a demonstration school, a research and development institute, and the NABSE Foundation.

National Institute against Prejudice and Violence, 31 South Greene Street, Baltimore, MD 21201; 410-328-5170; FAX 410-328-7551.

> A national center dedicated to research and action against prejudice and intergroup conflict.

National Women's History Project, 7738 Bell Road, Windsor, CA 95492-8518; 707-838-6000.

> Publishes and sells educational materials focusing on women's history, including posters, display kits, videos, and curriculum materials.

Network of Educators on Central America (NECA), 1118 22nd Street, N.W., Washington, DC 20037; 202-429-0137; FAX: 202-429-9766.

> Formed in 1986 by teachers' committees from a dozen cities. It provides information for teachers and students on Central America and the Caribbean and has developed a number of resources on the quincentenary in both English and Spanish. It publishes many curricula and sponsors workshops.

New England Center for Equity Assistance (NECEA), 300 Brickstone Square, Suite 900, Andover, MA 01810.

> An assistance center that offers a catalogue of nonprofit resources, *Media Matters*, which is available on loan at no charge.

Traprock Peace Center, Woolman Hill, Keets Road, Deerfield, MA 01342; 413-773-7427.

> Works with educators and other community people to help bring peace issues into the curriculum. This resource center publishes *The Traprock Report* and *Teachable Moments,* both available for a small fee. It also sponsors a yearly conference and has a great many curricula for loan.

U.S. Committee for UNICEF, Information Center on Children's Cultures, 331 E. 39th Street, New York, NY 10016.

> Publishes a wealth of information on books and other educational materials with an international perspective, including the celebration of holidays. It also has sample lesson plans.

Award-Winning Books

The following award-winning books are annotated in *Kaleidoscope* and can be located in the text according to the annotation number that follows each listing.

For All Ages

Ada, Alma Flor. *The Gold Coin.* Notable 1991 Children's Trade Books in the Field of Social Studies. (9.62)

Anderson, David A./SANKOFA, reteller. *The Origin of Life on Earth: An African Creation Myth.* Coretta Scott King Illustration Award, 1993. (9.1)

Belting, Natalia M. *Moon Was Tired of Walking on Air.* Notable 1992 Children's Trade Books in the Field of Social Studies. (9.68)

Birdseye, Tom, adapter. *A Song of Stars: An Asian Legend.* Notable 1990 Children's Trade Books in the Field of Social Studies. (9.32)

Bryan, Ashley. *All Night, All Day: A Child's First Book of African-American Spirituals.* Coretta Scott King Illustration Honor Book, 1992. (2.2)

Bryan, Ashley. *Sing to the Sun.* Notable 1992 Children's Trade Books in the Field of Social Studies. (1.5)

Burgie, Irving. *Caribbean Carnival: Songs of the West Indies.* Notable 1992 Children's Trade Books in the Field of Social Studies. (2.3)

Cassedy, Sylvia, and Kunihiro Suetake, trans. *Red Dragonfly on My Shoulder.* ALA Notable Children's Books, 1993. (1.7)

Cox, Clinton. *Undying Glory: The Story of the Massachusetts 54th Regiment.* Notable 1991 Children's Trade Books in the Field of Social Studies. (7.3)

Cummings, Pat, comp. and ed. *Talking with Artists: Conversations with Victoria Chess, Pat Cummings, Leo and Diane Dillon, Richard Egielski, Lois Ehlert, Lisa Campbell Ernst, Tom Feelings, Steven Kellogg, Jerry Pinkney, Amy Schwartz, Lane Smith, Chris Van Allsburg and David Wiesner.* ALA Notable Children's Books, 1993; Boston Globe–Horn Book Nonfiction Award, 1992; NCTE Orbis Pictus Honor Book, 1993. (2.4)

Durrell, Ann, and Marilyn Sachs, eds. *The Big Book for Peace.* Jane Addams Award, 1991; ALA Notable Children's Books, 1991; Notable 1990 Children's Trade Books in the Field of Social Studies. (14.3)

Ekoomiak, Normee. *Arctic Memories.* NCTE Orbis Pictus Honor Book, 1991; Notable 1990 Children's Trade Books in the Field of Social Studies. (4.4)

Goble, Paul. *Dream Wolf.* Notable 1990 Children's Trade Books in the Field of Social Studies. (9.24)

Goble, Paul. *Love Flute.* ALA Notable Children's Books, 1993; Notable 1992 Children's Trade Books in the Field of Social Studies. (9.6)

Greenfield, Eloise. *Night on Neighborhood Street.* ALA Notable Children's Books, 1992; Coretta Scott King Writing Honor Book, 1992; Notable 1991 Children's Trade Books in the Field of Social Studies. (1.11)

Joseph, Lynn. *Coconut Kind of Day: Island Poems.* Notable 1990 Children's Trade Books in the Field of Social Studies. (1.14)

Lester, Julius, reteller. *Further Tales of Uncle Remus: The Misadventures of Brer Rabbit, Brer Fox, Brer Wolf, the Doodang, and Other Creatures.* ALA Notable Children's Books, 1991; Notable 1990 Children's Trade Books in the Field of Social Studies. (9.26)

Lewis, Richard. *All of You Was Singing.* ALA Notable Children's Books, 1992; Notable 1991 Children's Trade Books in the Field of Social Studies. (9.9)

Lomas Garza, Carmen (as told to Harriet Rohmer). *Family Pictures/Cuadros de Familia.* ALA Notable Children's Books, 1991. (4.17)

Martinez, Alejandro Cruz. *The Woman Who Outshone the Sun: The Legend of Lucia Zenteno/La Mujer que Brillaba Aún Más que el Sol: La Leyenda de Lucía Zenteno.* ALA Notable Children's Books, 1992. (9.47)

McKissack, Patricia C. *The Dark Thirty: Southern Tales of the Supernatural.* ALA Notable Children's Books, 1993; Coretta Scott King Writing Award, 1993; Newbery Honor Book, 1993; Notable 1992 Children's Trade Books in the Field of Social Studies. (14.6)

McKissack, Patricia C. *A Million Fish . . . More or Less.* Notable 1992 Children's Trade Books in the Field of Social Studies. (11.49)

Mollel, Tololwa M. *The Orphan Boy: A Maasai Story.* ALA Notable Children's Books, 1992; Notable 1991 Children's Trade Books in the Field of Social Studies. (9.11)

Oughton, Jerrie. *How the Stars Fell into the Sky: A Navajo Legend.* Notable 1992 Children's Trade Books in the Field of Social Studies. (9.13)

Roop, Peter, and Connie Roop. *Ahyoka and the Talking Leaves.* Notable 1992 Children's Trade Books in the Field of Social Studies. (12.14)

Rosen, Michael J., ed. *Home: A Collection of Thirty Distinguished Authors and Illustrators of Children's Books to Aid the Homeless.* Notable 1992 Children's Trade Books in the Field of Social Studies. (14.7)

San Souci, Robert. *Sukey and the Mermaid.* ALA Notable Children's Books, 1993. (9.53)

Soto, Gary. *Neighborhood Odes.* Notable 1992 Children's Trade Books in the Field of Social Studies. (1.22)

Younger Readers

Aardema, Verna. *Anansi Finds a Fool: An Ashanti Tale.* Notable 1992 Children's Trade Books in the Field of Social Studies. (9.18)

Aardema, Verna, reteller. *Borreguita and the Coyote: A Tale from Ayutla, Mexico.* Notable 1991 Children's Trade Books in the Field of Social Studies. (9.19)

Aardema, Verna, reteller. *Traveling to Tondo: A Tale of the Nkundo of Zaire.* ALA Notable Children's Books, 1992; Notable 1991 Children's Trade Books in the Field of Social Studies. (9.20)

Alexander, Lloyd. *The Fortune-Tellers.* ALA Notable Children's Books, 1993; Boston Globe–Horn Book Honor Picture Book, 1993; Notable 1992 Children's Trade Books in the Field of Social Studies. (9.63)

Bruchac, Joseph, and Jonathan London. *Thirteen Moons on Turtle's Back: A Native American Year of Moons.* Notable 1992 Children's Trade Books in the Field of Social Studies. (1.4)

Brusca, María Cristina. *On the Pampas.* Notable 1991 Children's Trade Books in the Field of Social Studies. (4.3)

Bunting, Eve. *The Wall.* ALA Notable Children's Books, 1991; Notable 1990 Children's Trade Books in the Field of Social Studies. (11.9)

Crews, Donald. *Bigmama's.* ALA Notable Children's Books, 1992. (6.4)

Demi. *The Empty Pot.* Notable 1990 Children's Trade Books in the Field of Social Studies. (9.65)

Dorros, Arthur. *Abuela.* ALA Notable Children's Books, 1992; Notable 1991 Children's Trade Books in the Field of Social Studies. (11.16)

Dorros, Arthur. *Tonight Is Carnaval.* Notable 1991 Children's Trade Books in the Field of Social Studies. (3.3)

Dragonwagon, Crescent. *Home Place.* Notable 1990 Children's Trade Books in the Field of Social Studies. (11.17)

Ehlert, Lois. *Moon Rope: A Peruvian Tale/Un Lazo a la Luna: Una Leyenda Peruana.* ALA Notable Children's Books, 1993. (9.4)

Eisenberg, Phyllis Rose. *You're My Nikki.* Notable 1992 Children's Trade Books in the Field of Social Studies. (11.18)

Gerson, Mary-Joan, reteller. *Why the Sky Is Far Away: A Nigerian Folktale.* Notable 1992 Children's Trade Books in the Field of Social Studies. (9.5)

Grifalconi, Ann. *Osa's Pride.* Notable 1990 Children's Trade Books in the Field of Social Studies. (11.21)

Hill, Elizabeth Starr. *Evan's Corner.* Notable 1991 Children's Trade Books in the Field of Social Studies. (11.26)

Hoffman, Mary. *Amazing Grace.* ALA Notable Children's Books, 1992; Notable 1991 Children's Trade Books in the Field of Social Studies. (11.27)

Howard, Elizabeth Fitzgerald. *Aunt Flossie's Hats (and Crab Cakes Later).* Notable 1991 Children's Trade Books in the Field of Social Studies. (11.29)

Hudson, Wade. *Jamal's Busy Day.* Notable 1991 Children's Trade Books in the Field of Social Studies. (11.30)

Ikeda, Daisaku. *The Cherry Tree.* Notable 1992 Children's Trade Books in the Field of Social Studies. (11.34)

Isadora, Rachel. *At the Crossroads.* ALA Notable Children's Books, 1992; Notable 1991 Children's Trade Books in the Field of Social Studies. (11.35)

Johnson, Angela. *When I Am Old with You.* ALA Notable Children's Books, 1991; Coretta Scott King Writing Honor Book, 1991; Notable 1990 Children's Trade Books in the Field of Social Studies. (11.40)

Joseph, Lynn. *An Island Christmas.* Notable 1992 Children's Trade Books in the Field of Social Studies. (3.5)

Kendall, Russ. *Eskimo Boy: Life in an Inupiaq Eskimo Village.* Notable 1992 Children's Trade Books in the Field of Social Studies. (4.14)

Knutson, Barbara, reteller. *How the Guinea Fowl Got Her Spots: A Swahili Tale of Friendship.* Notable 1990 Children's Trade Books in the Field of Social Studies. (9.8)

Mahy, Margaret. *The Seven Chinese Brothers.* ALA Notable Children's Books, 1991; Notable 1990 Children's Trade Books in the Field of Social Studies. (9.45)

Martin, Ann. *Rachel Parker, Kindergarten Show-off.* Notable 1992 Children's Trade Books in the Field of Social Studies. (11.48)

McMillan, Bruce. *Eating Fractions.* ALA Notable Children's Books, 1993. (5.10)

Medearis, Angela Shelf. *Dancing with the Indians.* Notable 1991 Children's Trade Books in the Field of Social Studies. (11.50)

Mennen, Ingrid, and Niki Daly. *Somewhere in Africa.* Notable 1992 Children's Trade Books in the Field of Social Studies. (4.19)

Pinkney, Gloria Jean. *Back Home.* ALA Notable Children's Books, 1993; Notable 1992 Children's Trade Books in the Field of Social Studies. (11.56)

Polacco, Patricia. *Chicken Sunday.* ALA Notable Children's Books, 1993; Notable 1992 Children's Trade Books in the Field of Social Studies. (11.57)

Polacco, Patricia. *Mrs. Katz and Tush.* Notable 1992 Children's Trade Books in the Field of Social Studies. (11.58)

Ringgold, Faith. *Tar Beach.* ALA Notable Children's Books, 1992; Caldecott Honor Book, 1992; Coretta Scott King Illustration Award, 1992. (11.61)

Roth, Susan L. *The Story of Light.* Notable 1990 Children's Trade Books in the Field of Social Studies. (9.14)

Say, Allen. *Tree of Cranes.* ALA Notable Children's Books, 1991; Notable 1991 Children's Trade Books in the Field of Social Studies. (11.66)

Shelby, Anne. *We Keep a Store.* Notable 1990 Children's Trade Books in the Field of Social Studies. (11.69)

Vá, Leong. *A Letter to the King.* Notable 1991 Children's Trade Books in the Field of Social Studies. (9.67)

Wahl, Jan. *Little Eight John.* Coretta Scott King Illustration Honor Book, 1992. (9.57)

Waters, Kate, and Madeline Slovenz-Low. *Lion Dancer: Ernie Wan's Chinese New Year.* Notable 1990 Children's Trade Books in the Field of Social Studies. (3.9)

Williams, Karen Lynn. *Galimoto.* Notable 1990 Children's Trade Books in the Field of Social Studies. (11.75)

Williams, Karen Lynn. *When Africa Was Home.* Notable 1991 Children's Trade Books in the Field of Social Studies. (11.76)

Williams, Sherley Anne. *Working Cotton.* ALA Notable Children's Books, 1993; Caldecott Honor Book, 1993; Coretta Scott King Illustration Honor Book, 1993; Notable 1992 Children's Trade Books in the Field of Social Studies. (11.77)

Williams, Vera B. *"More More More," Said the Baby: Three Love Stories.* ALA Notable Children's Books, 1991; Caldecott Honor Book, 1991. (10.11)

Wilson, Beth P. *Jenny.* Notable 1990 Children's Trade Books in the Field of Social Studies. (11.78)

Winter, Jeanette. *Diego.* Notable 1991 Children's Trade Books in the Field of Social Studies; Parents Choice Award, 1991. (6.28)

Middle-Grade Readers

Berck, Judith. *No Place to Be: Voices of Homeless Children.* ALA Notable Children's Books, 1992. (4.2)

Bunting, Eve. *Summer Wheels.* Notable 1992 Children's Trade Books in the Field of Social Studies. (12.1)

DeArmond, Dale, reteller. *The Boy Who Found the Light: Eskimo Folktales.* Notable 1990 Children's Trade Books in the Field of Social Studies. (9.70)

Drummond, Allan. *The Willow Pattern Story.* Notable 1992 Children's Trade Books in the Field of Social Studies. (9.37)

Everett, Gwen. *Li'l Sis and Uncle Willie: A Story Based on the Life and Paintings of William H. Johnson.* ALA Notable Children's Books, 1993; Notable 1992 Children's Trade Books in the Field of Social Studies. (6.7)

Golenbock, Peter. *Teammates.* Notable 1990 Children's Trade Books in the Field of Social Studies. (6.9)

Hooks, William H. *The Ballad of Belle Dorcas.* Notable 1990 Children's Trade Books in the Field of Social Studies. (9.42)

Hoyt-Goldsmith, Diane. *Arctic Hunter.* Notable 1992 Children's Trade Books in the Field of Social Studies. (4.10)

Hoyt-Goldsmith, Diane. *Pueblo Storyteller.* Notable 1991 Children's Trade Books in the Field of Social Studies. (4.11)

Hoyt-Goldsmith, Diane. *Totem Pole.* Notable 1990 Children's Trade Books in the Field of Social Studies. (3.4)

Jenness, Aylette. *Families: A Celebration of Diversity, Commitment, and Love.* Notable 1990 Children's Trade Books in the Field of Social Studies. (5.6)

Keegan, Marcia. *Pueblo Boy: Growing Up in Two Worlds.* Notable 1991 Children's Trade Books in the Field of Social Studies. (4.13)

Kidd, Diana. *Onion Tears.* Notable 1991 Children's Trade Books in the Field of Social Studies. (12.8)

Lankford, Mary D. *Hopscotch around the World.* Notable 1992 Children's Trade Books in the Field of Social Studies. (5.7)

Mollel, Tololwa M. *A Promise to the Sun: An African Story.* Notable 1992 Children's Trade Books in the Field of Social Studies. (9.12)

Paterson, Katherine. *The Tale of the Mandarin Ducks.* ALA Notable Children's Books, 1991; Boston Globe–Horn Book Picture Book Award, 1991; Notable 1990 Children's Trade Books in the Field of Social Studies. (9.49)

Peters, Russell M. *Clambake: A Wampanoag Tradition.* Notable 1992 Children's Trade Books in the Field of Social Studies. (3.6)

Price, Leontyne. *Aïda.* ALA Notable Children's Books, 1991; Coretta Scott King Illustration Award, 1991. (2.9)

Rappaport, Doreen. *Escape from Slavery: Five Journeys to Freedom.* Notable 1991 Children's Trade Books in the Field of Social Studies. (7.12)

Regguinti, Gordon. *The Sacred Harvest: Ojibway Wild Rice Gathering.* Notable 1992 Children's Trade Books in the Field of Social Studies. (4.20)

Reynolds, Jan. *Himalaya: Vanishing Cultures.* Notable 1991 Children's Trade Books in the Field of Social Studies. (4.21)

Reynolds, Jan. *Sahara: Vanishing Cultures.* Notable 1991 Children's Trade Books in the Field of Social Studies. (4.22)

Rosen, Michael J. *Elijah's Angel: A Story for Chanukah and Christmas.* Notable 1992 Children's Trade Books in the Field of Social Studies. (3.8)

Say, Allen. *El Chino.* Notable 1990 Children's Trade Books in the Field of Social Studies. (6.23)

Sewall, Marcia. *People of the Breaking Day.* Notable 1990 Children's Trade Books in the Field of Social Studies. (7.13)

Shetterly, Susan Hand, reteller. *Raven's Light: A Myth from the People of the Northwest Coast.* Notable 1991 Children's Trade Books in the Field of Social Studies. (9.15)

Stanley, Fay. *The Last Princess: The Story of Princess Ka'iulani of Hawai'i.* Notable 1991 Children's Trade Books in the Field of Social Studies. (6.25)

Stolz, Mary. *Go Fish.* Notable 1991 Children's Trade Books in the Field of Social Studies. (12.15)

Tate, Eleanor E. *Thank You, Dr. Martin Luther King, Jr.!* Notable 1990 Children's Trade Books in the Field of Social Studies. (12.17)

Taylor, Mildred D. *Mississippi Bridge.* Notable 1990 Children's Trade Books in the Field of Social Studies. (12.18)

Van Laan, Nancy, adapter. *The Legend of El Dorado: A Latin American Tale.* Notable 1991 Children's Trade Books in the Field of Social Studies. (9.16)

Volkmer, Jane Anne, reteller. *Song of the Chirimia: A Guatemalan Folktale/La Musica de la Chirimia: Folktale Guatemalteco.* Notable 1990 Children's Trade Books in the Field of Social Studies. (9.56)

Wells, Ruth. *A to Zen: A Book of Japanese Culture.* Notable 1992 Children's Trade Books in the Field of Social Studies. (4.26)

Williams, Sheron. *And in the Beginning. . . .* Notable 1992 Children's Trade Books in the Field of Social Studies. (9.17)

Wisniewski, David. *Sundiata: Lion King of Mali.* ALA Notable Children's Books, 1993; Notable 1992 Children's Trade Books in the Field of Social Studies. (6.29)

Wood, Ted (with Wanbli Numpa Afraid of Hawk). *A Boy Becomes a Man at Wounded Knee.* Notable 1992 Children's Trade Books in the Field of Social Studies. (3.10)

Zhensun, Zheng, and Alice Low. *A Young Painter: The Life and Paintings of Wang Yani—China's Extraordinary Young Artist.* ALA Notable Children's Books, 1992. (6.31)

Older Readers

Anastos, Phillip, and Chris French. *Illegal: Seeking the American Dream.* Best Books for Young Adults, 1992. (8.1)

Armstrong, Jennifer. *Steal Away.* ALA Notable Children's Books, 1993; Best Books for Young Adults, 1993. (13.2)

Berry, James. *Ajeemah and His Son.* ALA Notable Children's Books, 1993; Best Books for Young Adults, 1993; Boston Globe–Horn Book Fiction Award, 1993; Notable 1992 Children's Trade Books in the Field of Social Studies. (13.3)

Buss, Fran Leeper (with Daisy Cubias). *Journey of the Sparrows.* Jane Addams Award, 1992; Notable 1991 Children's Trade Books in the Field of Social Studies. (13.6)

Choi, Sook Nyul. *The Year of the Impossible Goodbyes.* ALA Notable Children's Books, 1992; Best Books for Young Adults, 1992. (13.8)

Collier, James Lincoln. *Duke Ellington.* Notable 1991 Children's Trade Books in the Field of Social Studies. (6.3)

Davis, Ossie. *Just like Martin.* Notable 1992 Children's Trade Books in the Field of Social Studies. (13.9)

Dorris, Michael. *Morning Girl.* Scott O'Dell Award for Historical Fiction, 1993. (13.10)

Fairman, Tony. *Bury My Bones but Keep My Words: African Tales for Retelling.* Notable 1992 Children's Trade Books in the Field of Social Studies. (9.71)

Fradin, Dennis Brindell. *Hiawatha: Messenger of Peace.* Notable 1992 Children's Trade Books in the Field of Social Studies. (6.8)

Freedman, Russell. *An Indian Winter.* ALA Notable Children's Books, 1993; Best Books for Young Adults, 1993; Notable 1992 Children's Trade Books in the Field of Social Studies. (7.4)

Fritz, Jean, Katherine Paterson, Patricia McKissack, Fredrick McKissack, Margaret Mahy, and Jamake Highwater. *The World in 1492.* ALA Notable Children's Books, 1993; Notable 1992 Children's Trade Books in the Field of Social Studies. (7.5)

Glenn, Mel. *My Friend's Got This Problem, Mr. Candler: High School Poems.* Notable 1991 Children's Trade Books in the Field of Social Studies. (1.10)

Gordon, Sheila. *The Middle of Somewhere: A Story of South Africa.* Jane Addams Honor Book, 1991. (12.3)

Hamanaka, Sheila. *The Journey: Japanese Americans, Racism, and Renewal.* Jane Addams Honor Book, 1991; Best Books for Young Adults, 1991; Notable 1990 Children's Trade Books in the Field of Social Studies; Recommended Books for Reluctant Young Adult Readers, 1991. (7.6)

Hamilton, Virginia. *Cousins.* ALA Notable Children's Books, 1991; Best Books for Young Adults, 1991. (12.6)

Hart, Philip S. *Flying Free: America's First Black Aviators.* Notable 1992 Children's Trade Books in the Field of Social Studies. (6.10)

Haskins, James. *Black Dance in America: A History through Its People.* Best Books for Young Adults, 1991; Coretta Scott King Writing Honor Book, 1991. (2.6)

Haskins, James. *Thurgood Marshall: A Life for Justice.* Notable 1992 Children's Trade Books in the Field of Social Studies. (6.11)

Haskins, Jim. *Against All Opposition: Black Explorers in America.* Notable 1992 Children's Trade Books in the Field of Social Studies. (6.12)

Haskins, Jim. *One More River to Cross: The Stories of Twelve Black Americans.* Best Books for Young Adults, 1993; Notable 1992 Children's Trade Books in the Field of Social Studies. (6.13)

Haskins, Jim. *Outward Dreams: Black Inventors and Their Inventions.* Notable 1991 Children's Trade Books in the Field of Social Studies. (6.14)

Hirschfelder, Arlene B., and Beverly R. Singer, comps. *Rising Voices: Writings of Young Native Americans.* Notable 1992 Children's Trade Books in the Field of Social Studies. (14.4)

Houston, James. *Drifting Snow: An Arctic Search.* Notable 1992 Children's Trade Books in the Field of Social Studies. (13.15)

Jacobs, Francine. *The Tainos: The People Who Welcomed Columbus.* Notable 1992 Children's Trade Books in the Field of Social Studies. (7.9)

Katz, William Loren. *Breaking the Chains: African-American Slave Resistance.* Best Books for Young Adults, 1991. (7.10)

Lyons, Mary E. *Letters from a Slave Girl: The Story of Harriet Jacobs.* ALA Notable Children's Books, 1992; Best Books for Young Adults, 1993. (13.16)

Lyons, Mary E. *Sorrow's Kitchen: The Life and Folklore of Zora Neale Hurston.* Recommended Books for Reluctant Young Adult Readers, 1991. (6.16)

Lyons, Mary E., comp. *Raw Head, Bloody Bones: African-American Tales of the Supernatural.* Notable 1991 Children's Trade Books in the Field of Social Studies. (9.74)

McKissack, Patricia C., and Fredrick McKissack. *Sojourner Truth: Ain't I a Woman?* ALA Notable Children's Books, 1993; Best Books for Young Adults, 1993; Boston Globe–Horn Book Nonfiction Award, 1993; Coretta Scott King Writing Honor Book, 1993. (6.17)

Mazzio, Joan. *The One Who Came Back.* Recommended Books for Reluctant Young Adult Readers, 1993. (13.17)

Moore, Yvette. *Freedom Songs.* Notable 1991 Children's Trade Books in the Field of Social Studies. (13.18)

Morey, Janet Nomura, and Wendy Dunn. *Famous Asian Americans.* Notable 1992 Children's Trade Books in the Field of Social Studies. (6.19)

Myers, Walter Dean. *The Mouse Rap.* Best Books for Young Adults, 1991. (13.19)

Myers, Walter Dean. *Now Is Your Time! The African-American Struggle for Freedom.* ALA Notable Children's Books, 1991; Best Books for Young Adults, 1992; Coretta Scott King Writing Award, 1992; NCTE Orbis Pictus Honor Book, 1992. (7.11)

Myers, Walter Dean. *The Righteous Revenge of Artemis Bonner.* Best Books for Young Adults, 1993. (13.20)

Myers, Walter Dean. *Somewhere in the Darkness.* ALA Notable Children's Books, 1993; Best Books for Young Adults, 1993; Boston Globe–Horn Book Fiction Honor Book, 1992; Newbery Honor Book, 1993; Recommended Books for Reluctant Young Adult Readers, 1993. (13.21)

Naidoo, Beverley. *Chain of Fire.* Best Books for Young Adults, 1991; Notable 1990 Children's Trade Books in the Field of Social Studies. (13.22)

Nye, Naomi Shihab, comp. *This Same Sky: A Collection of Poems from around the World*. ALA Notable Children's Books, 1993. (1.19)

Parks, Rosa (with Jim Haskins). *Rosa Parks: My Story*. ALA Notable Children's Books, 1993; Best Books for Young Adults, 1993; Recommended Books for Reluctant Young Adult Readers, 1993. (6.20)

Porter, A. P. *Jump at de Sun: The Story of Zora Neale Hurston*. Notable 1992 Children's Trade Books in the Field of Social Studies; Recommended Books for Reluctant Young Adult Readers, 1993. (6.21)

Rappaport, Doreen, reteller. *The Journey of Meng: A Chinese Legend*. Notable 1991 Children's Trade Books in the Field of Social Studies. (9.51)

Salisbury, Graham. *Blue Skin of the Sea: A Novel in Stories*. Best Books for Young Adults, 1992; Notable 1992 Children's Trade Books in the Field of Social Studies. (13.26)

Siegel, Beatrice. *The Year They Walked: Rosa Parks and the Montgomery Bus Boycott*. Notable 1992 Children's Trade Books in the Field of Social Studies. (7.14)

Soto, Gary. *Baseball in April, and Other Stories*. Best Books for Young Adults, 1991. (14.8)

Soto, Gary. *A Fire in My Hands: A Book of Poems*. Notable 1991 Children's Trade Books in the Field of Social Studies. (1.21)

Spinelli, Jerry. *Maniac Magee*. Boston Globe–Horn Book Fiction Award, 1990; Newbery Medal, 1991. (13.29)

Sullivan, Charles, ed. *Children of Promise: African-American Literature and Art for Young People*. Best Books for Young Adults, 1992. (2.10)

Tan, Amy. *The Moon Lady*. Notable 1992 Children's Trade Books in the Field of Social Studies. (11.72)

Trimble, Stephen. *The Village of Blue Stone*. Notable 1990 Children's Trade Books in the Field of Social Studies. (7.15)

Walter, Mildred Pitts. *Mississippi Challenge*. Coretta Scott King Writing Honor Book, 1993. (7.16)

Woodson, Jacqueline. *Maizon at Blue Hill*. Best Books for Young Adults, 1993; Notable 1992 Children's Trade Books in the Field of Social Studies. (13.35)

Yep, Laurence. *Tongues of Jade*. Notable 1991 Children's Trade Books in the Field of Social Studies. (9.76)

Directory of Publishers

Harry N. Abrams. Subsidiary of Times Mirror. Orders to: 120 Woodbine Street, Bergenfield, NJ 07621. 800-345-1359.

Arte Público Press. University of Houston, 4800 Calhoun, Houston, TX 77204-2090. 800-633-ARTE; FAX 713-743-2847.

Atheneum. Imprint of Macmillan. Orders to: 100 Front Street, Box 500, Riverside, NJ 08075. 800-257-5755.

Bantam Doubleday Dell. Orders to: 414 E. Gulf Road, Des Plaines, IL 60016. 800-223-6834.

Bantam Little Rooster Books. See Bantam Doubleday Dell.

Bantam Skylark Books. See Bantam Doubleday Dell.

Barron's Educational Series. P.O. Box 8040, 250 Wireless Boulevard, Hauppauge, NY 11788. 800-645-3476.

Black Butterfly Children's Books. Produced by Writers and Readers Publishing. Distributed by Publishers Group West, 4065 Hollis Street, Emeryville, CA 94608. 800-788-3123.

R. R. Bowker. 121 Chanlon Road, New Providence, NJ 07974. 800-521-8110. Orders to: P.O. Box 1001, Summit, NJ 07902-1001.

Boyds Mills Press. Division of Highlights Company. Distributed by St. Martin's Press, 175 Fifth Avenue, Room 1715, New York, NY 10010. 800-221-7945.

Boyds Mills Press/Caroline House. See Boyds Mills Press.

Boyds Mills Press/Wordsong. See Boyds Mills Press.

Bradbury Press. Imprint of Macmillan. Orders to: 100 Front Street, Box 500, Riverside, NJ 08075. 800-257-5755.

Candlewick Press. Distributed by Penguin USA. Orders to: 120 Woodbine Street, Bergenfield, NJ 07621. 800-526-0275.

Caroline House. Imprint of Green Hill. Distributed by National Book Network, 4720A Boston Way, Lanham, MD 20706-4310. 800-462-6420.

Carolrhoda Books. 241 First Avenue, N., Minneapolis, MN 55401. 800-328-4929.

Checkerboard Press. 30 Vesey Street, New York, NY 10007. 212-571-6300.

Children's Book Press. 6400 Hollis Street, Emeryville, CA 94608. 510-655-3395; FAX 510-655-1978. Distributed by Bookpeople, 7900 Edgewater Drive, Oakland, CA 94621. 800-999-4650.

Christopher-Gordon. 480 Washington Street, Norwood, MA 02062. 617-762-5577.

Chronicle Books. Division of Chronicle Publishing, 275 Fifth Street, San Francisco, CA 94103. 800-722-6657 (orders only).

Clarion Books. Imprint of Houghton Mifflin. Orders to: Wayside Road, Burlington, MA 01803. 800-225-3362.

Cobblehill Books. Imprint of Dutton Children's Books, a division of Penguin USA. Orders to: 120 Woodbine Street, Bergenfield, NJ 07621. 800-526-0275.

Cobblestone Publishing. 7 School Street, Peterborough, NH 03458. 603-924-7209.

Cooperative Children's Book Center. Orders to: Publication Sales, Wisconsin Department of Public Instruction, P.O. Box 7841, Madison, WI 53707-7841. 800-243-8782.

Thomas Y. Crowell. Imprint of HarperCollins Children's Books. Orders to: 1000 Keystone Industrial Park, Scranton, PA 18512. 800-242-7737.

Crown Publishing Group. Affiliate of Random House. Orders to: 400 Hahn Road, Westminster, MD 21157. 800-733-3000 (orders); 800-726-0600 (inquiries).

Delacorte Press. Division of Bantam Doubleday Dell. Orders to: 414 E. Gulf Road, Des Plaines, IL 60016. 800-223-6834.

Dial Books. Division of Penguin USA. Orders to: 120 Woodbine Street, Bergenfield, NJ 07621. 800-526-0275.

Dial Books for Young Readers. See Dial Books.

Dillon Press. Imprint of Macmillan. Orders to: 100 Front Street, Riverside, NJ 08705. 800-257-5755.

Doubleday. Division of Bantam Doubleday Dell. Orders to: Doubleday Consumer Services, P.O. Box 5071, Des Plaines, IL 60017-5071. 800-223-6834.

Doubleday Books for Young Readers. See Doubleday.

Dutton Children's Books. Division of Penguin USA. Orders to: 120 Woodbine Street, Bergenfield, NJ 07621. 800-526-0275.

Farrar, Straus and Giroux. 19 Union Square, W., New York 10003. 800-631-8571.

Four Winds Press. Imprint of Macmillan Children's Book Group. Orders to: 100 Front Street, Riverside, NJ 08705. 800-257-5755.

Friends of the Cooperative Children's Book Center. P.O. Box 5288, Madison, WI 53705-0288. 608-222-1867.

Good Books for Young Readers. P.O. Box 419, Main Street, Intercourse, PA 17534. 800-762-7171; FAX 717-768-3433.

Green Tiger Press. Imprint of Simon and Schuster, 1230 Avenue of the Americas, New York, NY 10020. 212-698-7000.

Greenwillow Books. Division of William Morrow. Orders to: 39 Plymouth Street, P.O. Box 1219, Fairfield, NJ 07007. 800-843-9389.

Greenwood Press. Division of Greenwood Publishing Group, 88 Post Road, W., P.O. Box 5007, Westport, CT 06881-5007. 800-225-5800 (orders only).

Harcourt Brace Jovanovich. Orders to: 6277 Sea Harbor Drive, Orlando, FL 32887. 800-225-5425.

Harcourt Brace Jovanovich/Gulliver Books. See Harcourt Brace Jovanovich.

Harcourt Brace Jovanovich/Odyssey Books. See Harcourt Brace Jovanovich.

Harper and Row. Division of HarperCollins. Orders to: 1000 Keystone Industrial Park, Scranton, PA 18512-4621. 800-242-7737 (800-982-4377 in Pennsylvania).

HarperCollins. Orders to: 1000 Keystone Industrial Park, Scranton, PA 18512-4621. 800-242-7737 (800-982-4377 in Pennsylvania).

HarperCollins/Willa Perlman Books. See HarperCollins.

HarperCollins/Charlotte Zolotow Books. See HarperCollins.

Highsmith Press. W5527, P.O. Box 800, Fort Atkinson, WI 53538-0800. 800-558-2110 for information; FAX 800-835-2329.

Hispanic Books Distributors and Publishers. 1665 West Grant Rd., Tucson, AZ 85745. 602-882-9484.

Henry Holt. Orders to: 4375 W. 1980, S., Salt Lake City, UT 84104. 800-488-5233.

Henry Holt/Red Feather Books. See Henry Holt.

Holiday House. 425 Madison Avenue, New York, NY 10017. 212-688-0085.

Houghton Mifflin. Orders to: Wayside Road, Burlington, MA 01803. 800-225-3362.

Hyperion Books for Children. Division of Disney Book Publishing. Distributed by Little, Brown. Orders to: 200 West Street, Waltham, MA 02254. 800-343-9204.

Just Us Books. 301 Main Street, Suite 22–24, Orange, NJ 07050. 201-676-4345.

Alfred A. Knopf. Subsidiary of Random House. Orders to: 400 Hahn Road, Westminster, MD 21157. 800-733-3000.

Alfred A. Knopf/Borzoi Books. See Alfred A. Knopf.

Lee and Low Books. 228 East 45th Street, 14th Floor, New York, NY 10017. 212-867-6155; FAX 212-338-9059. Distributed by Publishers Group West, 4065 Hollis Street, Emeryville, CA 94608. 800-788-3123.

Lerner Publications. 241 First Avenue, N., Minneapolis, MN 55401. 800-328-4929.

Lippincott Children's Books. Imprint of HarperCollins Children's Books. Orders to: 1000 Keystone Industrial Park, Scranton, PA 18512-4621. 800-638-3030.

Little, Brown. Division of Time Warner. Orders to: 200 West Street, Waltham, MA 02254. 800-759-0190.

Little, Brown/Joy Street Books. See Little, Brown.

Lodestar Books. Imprint of Dutton Children's Books, a division of Penguin Books. Orders to: Penguin USA, 120 Woodbine Street, Bergenfield, NJ 07621. 800-526-0275.

Longman. Division of Addison-Wesley. Orders to: 95 Church Street, White Plains, NY 1060l. 914-993-5000.

Lothrop, Lee and Shepard Books. Division of William Morrow. Orders to: 39 Plymouth Street, P.O. Box 1219, Fairfield, NJ 07007. 800-237-0657.

Lothrop, Lee and Shepard Books/Mulberry Books. See Lothrop, Lee and Shepard Books.

Margaret K. McElderry Books. Imprint of Macmillan Children's Books Group. Orders to: 100 Front Street, Riverside, NJ 08075. 800-257-5755.

Macmillan. Orders to: 100 Front Street, Riverside, NJ 08075. 800-257-5755.

Julian Messner. Imprint of Simon and Schuster, 1230 Avenue of the Americas, New York, NY 10020. 212-698-7000.

William Morrow. Orders to: Wilmor Warehouse, P.O. Box 1219, 39 Plymouth Street, Fairfield, NJ 07007. 800-237-0657.

Morrow Junior Books. See William Morrow.

Network of Educators' Committees on Central America. P.O. Box 43509, Washington, DC 20010-9509. 202-429-0137.

New Society Publishers. 4527 Springfield Avenue, Philadelphia, PA 19143. 215-382-6543.

North-South Books. Orders to: 1133 Broadway, Suite 1016, New York, NY 10010. 800-282-8257.

Northland Publishing. P.O. Box 1389, Flagstaff, AZ 86002. 800-346-3257.

Orchard Books. Division of Franklin Watts, 387 Park Avenue, S., New York, NY 10016. 800-672-6672.

Orchard Books/Richard Jackson Books. See Orchard Books.

Oyate. 2702 Mathews Street, Berkeley, CA 94702. 510-848-6700.

Philomel Books. Imprint of the Putnam Publishing Group. Orders to: 390 Murray Hill Parkway, East Rutherford, NJ 07073. 800-631-8571.

Picture Book Studio. Orders to: Simon and Schuster Children's Books, 15 Columbus Circle, New York, NY 10023. 800-223-2348; 800-223-2336 (orders only).

G. P. Putnam's Sons. Imprint of the Putnam Publishing Group. Orders to: 390 Murray Hill Parkway, East Rutherford, NJ 07073. 800-631-8571.

G. P. Putnam's Sons/Whitebird Books. See G. P. Putnam's Sons.

Rizzoli International Publications. 300 Park Avenue, S., New York, NY 10010. 800-462-2387.

Rizzoli International Publications/National Museum of American Art, Smithsonian Scholastic. See Rizzoli International Publications.

Savanna Books. 858 Massachusetts Avenue, Central Square, Cambridge, MA. 617-868-3423.

Scarecrow Press. Division of Grolier. Orders to: 52 Liberty Street, Box 4167, Metuchen, NJ 08840. 800-537-7107.

Scholastic. Orders to: P.O. Box 120, Bergenfield, NJ 07621. 800-325-6149 (orders only).

Scholastic/Apple Paperbacks. See Scholastic.

Scholastic/Cartwheel Books. See Scholastic.

Scholastic Hardcover Books. See Scholastic.

Scholastic Hardcover Books/Lucas Evans Books. See Scholastic.

Scholastic Hardcover Books/Byron Preiss–New China Pictures Books. See Scholastic.

Charles Scribner's Sons. Division of Macmillan. Orders to: 100 Front Street, Riverside, NJ 08075. 800-257-5755.

Sierra Club Books/Little, Brown. Distributed by Little, Brown. Orders to: 200 West Street, Waltham, MA 02254. 800-759-0190.

Sights Productions. P.O. Box 101, Mt. Airy, MD 21771. 410-795-4582.

Silver Burdett Press. Division of Paramount Publishing. Orders to: P.O. Box 2649, Columbus, OH 43216. 800-848-9500.

Simon and Schuster. 1230 Avenue of the Americas, New York, NY 10020. 212-698-7000.

Simon and Schuster Books for Young Readers. See Simon and Schuster.

Tambourine Books. Imprint of William Morrow. Orders to: Wilmor Warehouse, P.O. Box 1219, 39 Plymouth Street, Fairfield, NJ 07007. 800-237-0657 (customer service).

Tilbury House. Distributed by Consortium Book Sales and Distribution, 1045 Westgate Drive, St. Paul, MN 55114-1065. 800-283-3572.

Troll Associates. Subsidiary of Educational Reading Services, 100 Corporate Drive, Mahwah, NJ 07430. 800-526-5289.

Tundra Books. In Canada: University of Toronto Press, 5201 Dufferin St., Downsview, Ontario M3H 5T8; 416-667-7791; FAX 416-667-7832. In the U.S.: University of Toronto Press, 340 Nagel Dr., Buffalo, NY 14225; 716-683-4547.

Helaine Victoria Press. 911 N. College Avenue, No. 3, Bloomington, IN 47404. 812-331-0444.

Viking Penguin. Division of Penguin USA. Orders to: 120 Woodbine Street, Bergenfield, NJ 07621. 800-526-0275.

Walker and Company. Division of Walker Publishing, 720 Fifth Avenue, New York, NY 10019. 800-289-2553 (orders only).

Franklin Watts. Subsidiary of Grolier. Orders to: 5450 N. Cumberland Avenue, Chicago, IL 60656. 800-672-6672.

Whispering Coyote Press. 480 Newbury Street, Suite 104, Danvers, MA 01923. 508-281-4995.

Whispering Coyote Press/Treld Bicknell Books. See Whispering Coyote Press.

Albert Whitman. 6340 Oakton Street, Morton Grove, IL 60053. 800-155-7675.

Writers and Readers Publishing. 625 Broadway, 10th Floor, New York, NY 10012. 212-982-3158. Distributed by Publishers Group West, 4065 Hollis Street, Emeryville, CA 94608. 800-788-3123.

Author Index

Aardema, Verna, 9.18–9.20
Aaseng, Nathan, 7.1
Ada, Alma Flor, 9.62
Adler, David A., 6.1, 6.2
Adoff, Arnold, 1.1, 11.1
Albert, Burton, 11.2
Alexander, Lloyd, 9.63, 13.1
Allen, Judy, 11.3
Allison, Diane Worfolk, 1.2
Anastos, Phillip, 8.1
Ancona, George, 5.11
Anderson, David A., 9.1
Argueta, Manlio, 9.31
Armstrong, Jennifer, 13.2
Arnold, Caroline, 7.2
Ashley, Bernard, 11.4
Axworthy, Anni, 11.5

Barboza, Steven, 2.1
Begay, Shonto, 9.21
Beirne, Barbara, 4.1
Belpré, Pura, 9.22
Belting, Natalia M., 9.68
Berck, Judith, 4.2
Berry, James, 1.3, 13.3
Bierhorst, John, 9.69
Birdseye, Tom, 9.32
Blair, David Nelson, 13.4
Blanco, Alberto, 9.33
Bogart, Jo Ellen, 11.6
Bolden, Tonya, 13.13
Bond, Ruskin, 11.7
Booth, Coleen E., 13.5
Breckler, Rosemary K., 11.8
Brown, Tricia, 8.2
Bruchac, Joseph, 1.4
Brusca, María Cristina, 4.3, 9.34
Bryan, Ashley, 1.5, 2.2
Bunting, Eve, 11.9, 12.1
Burgie, Irving, 2.3
Buss, Fran Leeper, 13.6

Calhoun, Mary, 10.1
Carlson, Lori M., 14.1
Carlstrom, Nancy White, 1.6, 10.2, 14.2

Case, Dianne, 13.7
Cassedy, Sylvia, 1.7
Charles, Donald, 9.2
Cherry, Lynne, 11.10
Chocolate, Deborah M. Newton, 3.1
Choi, Sook Nyul, 13.8
Clifton, Lucille, 3.2, 11.11
Collier, James Lincoln, 6.3
Compton, Patricia A., 9.23
Cox, Clinton, 7.3
Crews, Donald, 6.4, 11.12
Cubias, Daisy, 13.6
Cummings, Pat, 2.4, 11.13, 11.14
Curtis, Gavin, 11.15

Dabovich, Lydia, 1.8
Daly, Niki, 4.19
Davis, Ossie, 13.9
DeArmond, Dale, 9.70
Dee, Ruby, 9.35
Delacre, Lulu, 2.5
Demi, 1.9, 6.5, 9.36, 9.64, 9.65
Denenberg, Barry, 6.6
Dixon, Ann, 9.3
Dorris, Michael, 13.10
Dorros, Arthur, 3.3, 11.16
Dragonwagon, Crescent, 11.17
Drummond, Allan, 9.37
Dunn, Wendy, 6.19
Durell, Ann, 14.3

Ehlert, Lois, 9.4
Eisenberg, Phyllis Rose, 11.18
Ekoomiak, Normee, 4.4
Emberley, Rebecca, 5.1
Everett, Gwen, 6.7

Fairman, Tony, 9.71
Falwell, Cathryn, 5.2
Fradin, Dennis Brindell, 6.8
Freedman, Russell, 7.4
French, Chris, 8.1
French, Fiona, 9.38
Fritz, Jean, 7.5

Gajadin, Chitra, 11.19
Garne, S. T., 5.3
Gerson, Mary-Joan, 9.5
Girion, Barbara, 13.11
Glenn, Mel, 1.10
Goble, Paul, 9.6, 9.24, 9.39, 9.40
Gogol, Sara, 12.2
Golenbock, Peter, 6.9
Gordon, Sheila, 12.3
Greenfield, Eloise, 1.11, 10.3–10.6, 11.20, 12.4
Greenspun, Adele Aron, 5.4
Grenquist, Barbara, 8.3
Grifalconi, Ann, 11.21

Hale, Sarah Josepha, 1.12
Hamanaka, Sheila, 7.6
Hamilton, Virginia, 9.72, 11.22, 12.5, 12.6
Hart, Philip S., 6.10
Haskins, Francine, 4.5, 11.23
Haskins, James, 2.6, 6.11
Haskins, Jim, 4.6, 6.12–6.14, 6.20, 7.7
Haugaard, Erik Christian, 13.12
Hauptly, Denis J., 4.7
Hausherr, Rosmarie, 5.5
Havill, Juanita, 11.24
Hayashi, Akiko, 11.25
Hernández, Xavier, 7.8
Hewett, Joan, 4.8
Higginsen, Vy, 13.13
Highwater, Jamake, 7.5
Hill, Elizabeth Starr, 11.26
Hill, Kirkpatrick, 13.14
Hillman, Elizabeth, 9.41
Hirschfelder, Arlene B., 14.4
Hoffman, Mary, 11.27
Hoig, Stan, 4.9
Hong, Lily Toy, 9.7
Hooks, William H., 9.42
Hort, Lenny, 11.28
Horton, Barbara Savadge, 10.7
Houston, James, 13.15
Howard, Elizabeth Fitzgerald, 11.29
Hoyt-Goldsmith, Diane, 3.4, 4.10, 4.11
Hudson, Wade, 11.30
Hughes, Libby, 6.15
Hughes, Shirley, 11.31
Hunter, Latoya, 4.12
Hurwitz, Johanna, 12.7

Ichikawa, Satomi, 11.32
Igus, Toyomi, 11.33

Ikeda, Daisaku, 9.43, 11.34
Isadora, Rachel, 11.35, 11.36

Jacobs, Francine, 7.9
Jenness, Aylette, 5.6
Johnson, Angela, 11.37–11.40
Johnson, Dolores, 11.41–11.43
Johnson, Ryerson, 11.44
Johnston, Tony, 11.45
Joosse, Barbara M., 10.8
Joseph, Lynn, 1.14, 3.5, 9.73

Katz, William Loren, 7.10
Keegan, Marcia, 4.13
Keller, Holly, 11.46
Kendall, Russ, 4.14
Kidd, Diana, 12.8
Kimmel, Eric A., 9.25
Knight, Margy Burns, 4.15
Knutson, Barbara, 9.8
Kraus, Joanna Halpert, 12.9
Kuklin, Susan, 8.4

Lacapa, Michael, 9.44
Lamb, Wendy, 14.5
Langstaff, John, 2.7
Lankford, Mary D., 5.7
Larrick, Nancy, 14.5
Lauture, Denizé, 1.15
Lee, Jeanne M., 11.47
Lester, Julius, 9.26
Lewington, Anna, 4.16
Lewis, Richard, 9.9
Linden, Ann Marie, 5.8
Livingston, Myra Cohn, 1.16
Lomas Garza, Carmen, 4.17
London, Jonathan, 1.4
Low, Alice, 6.31
Lyons, Mary E., 6.16, 9.74, 13.16

MacKinnon, Debbie, 5.9
Mado, Michio, 1.17
Mahy, Margaret, 7.5, 9.45
Martin, Ann, 11.48
Martin, Francesca, 9.10
Martin, Rafe, 9.46
Martinez, Alejandro Cruz, 9.47
Mathis, Sharon Bell, 1.18
Mayer, Marianna, 9.48
Mazzio, Joan, 13.17

McDermott, Gerald, 9.27
McKissack, Fredrick, 6.17, 7.5
McKissack, Patricia C., 6.17, 7.5, 11.49, 14.6
McMahon, Patricia, 4.18
McMillan, Bruce, 5.10
Medearis, Angela Shelf, 2.8, 11.50
Mennen, Ingrid, 4.19
Merrill, Jean, 11.51
Miller, Mary Beth, 5.11
Miller, Robert H., 6.18
Mills, Claudia, 11.52
Mollel, Tololwa M., 9.11, 9.12, 9.28
Moore, Yvette, 13.18
Mora, Pat, 11.53
Morey, Janet Nomura, 6.19
Morris, Ann, 5.12,
Myers, Walter Dean, 7.11, 12.10, 13.19–13.21

Naidoo, Beverley, 13.22
Namioka, Lensey, 12.11, 13.23
Nodar, Carmen Santiago, 11.54
Nye, Naomi Shihab, 1.19

O'Connor, Karen, 8.5
Orr, Katherine, 11.55
Oughton, Jerrie, 9.13

Parks, Rosa, 6.20
Paterson, Katherine, 7.5, 9.49
Pattison, Darcy, 9.50
Peters, Russell M., 3.6
Pinkney, Gloria Jean, 11.56
Pinkwater, Jill, 12.12
Polacco, Patricia, 11.57, 11.58
Porter, A. P., 3.7, 6.21
Poynter, Margaret, 8.6
Prather, Ray, 13.24
Price, Leontyne, 2.9

Rappaport, Doreen, 7.12, 9.51
Reddix, Valerie, 11.59
Regan, Dian Curtis, 12.13
Regguinti, Gordon, 4.20
Reynolds, Jan, 4.21, 4.22
Ringgold, Faith, 11.60, 11.61
Robinson, Margaret A., 13.25
Rodanas, Kristina, 9.52
Roe, Eileen, 11.62

Rohmer, Harriet, 9.66
Roop, Connie, 12.14
Roop, Peter, 12.14
Rosen, Michael J., 3.8, 14.7
Rosenberg, Maxine B., 5.13
Roth, Susan L., 9.14

Sabin, Louis, 6.22
Sachs, Marilyn, 14.3
Sage, James, 11.63
Sakai, Kimiko, 11.64
Salisbury, Graham, 13.26
Samton, Sheila White, 11.65
San Souci, Robert, 9.53
Say, Allen, 6.23, 11.66
Schmidt, Diane, 4.23
Schoberle, Cecile, 11.67
Scott, Ann Herbert, 11.68
Senna, Carl, 6.24
Serfozo, Mary, 10.9
Sewall, Marcia, 7.13
Shelby, Anne, 11.69
Shetterly, Susan Hand, 9.15
Siegel, Beatrice, 7.14
Sierra, Judy, 9.29
Singer, Beverly R., 14.4
Slier, Deborah, 1.20
Slovenz-Low, Madeline, 3.9
Smalls-Hector, Irene, 11.70, 11.71
So, Meilo, 9.54
Soto, Gary, 1.21, 1.22, 13.27, 13.28, 14.8
Spinelli, Jerry, 13.29
Stanley, Fay, 6.25
Stiles, Martha Bennett, 9.30
Stolz, Mary, 12.15, 12.16
Suetake, Kunihiro, 1.7
Sullivan, Charles, 2.10
Swentzell, Rina, 4.24

Tagore, Rabindranath, 1.23
Tan, Amy, 11.72
Tate, Eleanora E., 12.17, 14.9
Taylor, Mildred D., 12.18
Temple, Frances, 13.30
Thomas, Joyce Carol, 13.31, 14.10
Thompson, Peggy, 4.25
Torre, Betty L., 9.55
Trimble, Stephen, 7.15

Uchida, Yoshiko, 6.26

Vá, Leong, 9.67
Van Laan, Nancy, 9.16
Ventura, Cynthia L., 14.1
Volkmer, Jane Anne, 9.56

Wahl, Jan, 9.57, 9.58
Walker, Alice, 11.73
Walker, Paul Robert, 6.27
Walter, Mildred Pitts, 7.16, 11.74
Wanbli Numpa Afraid of Hawk, 3.10
Wang, Rosalind C., 9.59
Waters, Kate, 3.9
Watkins, Yoko Kawashima, 9.75
Weiss, Nicki, 10.10
Wells, Ruth, 4.26
Whelan, Gloria, 13.32
Williams, Karen Lynn, 11.75, 11.76
Williams, Sherley Anne, 11.77
Williams, Sheron, 9.17

Williams, Vera B., 10.11
Wilson, Beth P., 11.78
Wilson, Tona, 9.34
Winter, Jeanette, 6.28
Wisniewski, David, 6.29, 9.60
Wood, Ted, 3.10
Woodson, Jacqueline, 13.33–13.35
Wunderli, Stephen, 13.36

Yacowitz, Caryn, 9.61
Yee, Paul, 12.19
Yep, Laurence, 6.30, 9.76
Yolen, Jane, 1.24, 11.79
Young, Ruth, 10.12
Yu, Ling, 4.27

Zheng Zhensun, 6.31
Zimelman, Nathan, 11.80

Illustrator Index

Allen, Thomas B., 12.1
Allison, Diane Worfolk, 1.2
Anastos, Phillip, 8.1
Ancona, George, 5.11, 5.13
Andreasen, Dan, 13.7
Anno, Mitsumasa, 1.17
Arai, Tomie, 11.64
Asare, Meshack, 9.71
Axworthy, Anni, 11.5

Bacon, Paul, 6.9
Ballonga, Jordi, 7.8
Bang, Molly, 1.7
Barbour, Karen, 1.3
Begay, Shonto, 9.21
Beirne, Barbara, 4.1
Bent, Jennifer, 9.35
Bernstein, Michael J., 1.10
Binch, Caroline, 11.27
Bochak, Grayce, 1.23
Bodmer, Karl, 7.4
Bond, Higgins, 11.33
Brazell, Derek, 11.4
Brierley, Louise, 9.69
Brusca, María Cristina, 2.8, 4.3, 9.34
Bryan, Ashley, 1.5, 2.2, 2.7
Byard, Carole, 11.77
Byrd, Samuel, 1.16, 11.50

Casilla, Robert, 6.1, 6.2, 11.62
Chan, Harvey, 12.19
Charles, Donald, 9.2
Chen Ming-jeng, 4.27
Chen, Ju-Hong, 9.32, 9.59, 9.61
Cherry, Lynne, 11.10
Chesworth, Michael, 12.13
Clay, Wil, 9.57, 9.58
Club de Madras Virgin del Carmen of
    Lima, Peru, 3.3
Coalson, Glo, 11.68
Collins, Patrick, 7.9
Conklin, Paul S., 4.25
Cooper, Floyd, 11.51, 11.76
Cooper, Martha, 3.9
Crews, Donald, 6.4, 11.12

Cummings, Pat, 11.13, 11.14, 11.74, 12.15
Curtis, Gavin, 11.15

Dabovich, Lydia, 1.8
d'Amboise, Carolyn George, 2.1
Davis, Lambert, 9.72
de Kiefte, Kees, 12.11
DeArmond, Dale, 9.70
Deeter, Catherine, 11.73
DeJohn, Marie, 6.22
Delacre, Lulu, 2.5
Demi, 1.9, 6.5, 9.36, 9.64, 9.65
Desimini, Lisa, 9.13, 14.2
Dewey, Jennifer Owings, 7.15
Diaz, David, 1.22
Dillon, Diane, 1.6, 2.9, 9.49
Dillon, Leo, 1.6, 2.9, 9.49
Dodson, Liz Brenner, 4.6
Downing, Julie, 11.80
Drummond, Allan, 9.37

Ehlert, Lois, 9.4
Eitzen, Allan, 11.7
Ekoomiak, Normee, 4.4
Emberley, Rebecca, 5.1
Escofet, Josep, 7.8
Etre, Lisa, 5.3

Falwell, Cathryn, 5.2
Ford, George, 11.30
Frankel, Adrian, 11.8
French, Chris, 8.1
French, Fiona, 9.38

Geter, Tyrone, 11.70
Gilchrist, Jan Spivey, 1.11, 1.18, 3.2,
    10.3–10.6, 11.20
Ginsburg, Max, 12.18
Goble, Paul, 9.6, 9.24, 9.39, 9.40
Golembe, Carla, 9.5
Green, Jonathan, 1.15
Greenspun, Adele Aron, 5.4
Grifalconi, Ann, 11.21

Hamanaka, Sheila, 7.6, 9.23, 11.52, 12.7
Hanna, Cheryl, 11.1
Haskins, Francine, 4.5, 11.23
Hayashi, Akiko, 11.25
Hays, Michael, 11.11, 11.71
Hewett, Richard, 4.8, 7.2
Heyman, Ken, 5.12
Hillenbrand, Will, 9.20, 9.68
Himler, Ronald, 11.9
Hong, Lily Toy, 9.7
Houston, James, 13.15
Hu, Ying-Hwa, 1.20
Hughes, Shirley, 11.31
Humphries, Tudor, 11.3
Hyman, Trina Schart, 9.63

Ichikawa, Satomi, 11.32
Inouye, Carol, 9.55
Isadora, Rachel, 10.12, 11.35, 11.36

Jenness, Aylette, 5.6
Johnson, Dolores, 11.41–11.43, 11.78
Johnson, William H., 6.7

Kakkak, Dale, 4.20
Kastner, Jill, 11.18
Keegan, Marcia, 4.13
Keller, Holly, 11.46
Kendall, Russ, 4.14
Kleven, Elisa, 11.16
Knutson, Barbara, 9.8
Kuklin, Susan, 8.4

Lacapa, Michael, 9.44
Lang, Cecily, 11.53
Lavallee, Barbara, 10.8
Lee, Jeanne M., 11.47
Leonard, Richard, 6.18
Lessac, Frané, 2.3
Lilly, Charles, 7.12
Locker, Thomas, 1.4
Lomas Garza, Carmen, 4.17

Madama, John, 3.6
Maritz, Nicolaas, 4.19
Martin, Francesca, 9.10
Massey, Cal, 3.1
Mathers, Petra, 9.19
McDermott, Gerald, 9.27

McMillan, Bruce, 1.12, 5.10
Migdale, Lawrence, 3.4, 4.10, 4.11
Milone, Karen, 5.7
Miyake, Yoshi, 12.14
Montgomery, Lucy, 12.8
Morin, Paul, 9.11
Moser, Barry, 12.5

Narahashi, Keiko, 10.9, 11.63

O'Brien, Anne Sibley, 4.15
O'Brien, Michael F., 4.18
Olivera, Fernando, 9.47
Ong, Helen, 11.19
Orr, Katherine, 11.55
Ortega, José, 14.1

Parker, Edward, 4.16
Paterson, Diane, 11.54
Pinkney, Brian, 9.29, 9.42, 9.53, 9.73, 11.2, 14.6
Pinkney, Jerry, 1.1, 9.26, 11.17, 11.22, 11.56, 12.6
Polacco, Patricia, 11.57, 11.58
Politi, Leo, 11.45
Porter, Janice Lee, 3.7
Poydar, Nancy, 11.48

Ransome, James E., 11.28, 11.29, 11.37
Reade, Deborah, 7.15
Reisberg, Veg, 9.66
Revah, Patricia, 9.33
Reynolds, Jan, 4.21, 4.22
Ringgold, Faith, 11.60, 11.61
Ritz, Karen, 12.9
Robinson, Aminah Brenda Lynn, 3.8
Rodanas, Kristina, 9.52
Roth, Robert, 9.17
Roth, Susan L., 9.14
Russell, Lynne, 5.8

Sánchez, Carlos, 9.22
Samton, Sheila White, 11.65
Sauber, Robert, 9.48
Savadier, Elivia, 11.24
Say, Allen, 6.23, 11.66
Schields, Gretchen, 11.72
Schmidt, Diane, 4.23
Schoberle, Cecile, 11.67

Schutzer, Dena, 11.49
Sewall, Marcia, 7.13
Shannon, David, 9.46, 11.79
Shetterly, Robert, 9.15
Sieveking, Anthea, 5.9
Simmons, Elly, 9.31
So, Melio, 9.54
Soman, David, 11.38–11.40
Speidel, Sandra, 1.14, 11.26
Spurll, Barbara, 9.28
Stanley, Diane, 6.25
Steen, Bill, 4.24
Stevens, Janet, 9.25
Stevenson, Suçie, 10.2
Stock, Catherine, 3.5, 11.75
Stow, Jenny, 1.13

Thai, Ted, 8.2
Thomas, Larry, 9.30
Tseng, Jean, 9.45, 9.50, 9.75, 11.44, 11.59
Tseng, Mou-sien, 9.45, 9.50, 9.75, 11.44, 11.59

Vá, Leong, 9.67
Van Wright, Cornelius, 1.20

Velasquez, Eric, 13.22, 14.9
Vidal, Beatriz, 9.12, 9.16
Vitale, Stefano, 7.5
Volkmer, Jane Anne, 9.56

Waldman, Bryna, 9.18
Waldman, Neil, 9.62
Wallner, John, 9.41
Ward, John, 11.69
Watts, Jim, 9.3
Weiss, Nicki, 10.10
Wiesner, David, 9.76
Wildsmith, Brian, 9.43, 11.34
Williams, Vera B., 10.11
Wilson, Janet, 11.6
Wilson, Kathleen Atkins, 9.1
Winter, Jeanette, 6.28
Wisniewski, David, 6.29, 9.60

Yang Ming-Yi, 9.51
Yoshi, 4.26
Young, Ed, 9.9, 10.1, 10.7

Zheng Zhensun, 6.31

Subject Index

Abenaki Indians, 1.4
Abolition, 6.17, 7.10, 13.2
Abuse, 13.7
Adoption, 12.9
Adventure, 11.12, 13.1, 13.12, 13.17, 13.20, 13.23
Africa, 2.9, 3.1, 3.7, 4.19, 4.22, 6.6, 6.15, 6.29, 9.1, 9.5, 9.8, 9.10–9.12, 9.17, 9.18, 9.20, 9.25, 9.27–9.29, 9.35, 9.63, 9.71, 11.21, 11.35, 11.36, 11.75, 11.76, 12.3, 13.7, 13.22
African Americans, 1.1, 1.2, 1.11, 1.12, 1.15, 1.16, 1.18, 1.20, 2.2, 2.6–2.8, 2.10, 3.1, 3.2, 3.7, 3.8, 4.5, 4.12, 4.23, 5.2, 5.10, 5.13, 6.1, 6.3, 6.4, 6.7, 6.9–6.14, 6.16–6.18, 6.20, 6.21, 6.24, 7.3, 7.7, 7.10–7.12, 7.14, 7.16, 8.4, 9.26, 9.42, 9.53, 9.57, 9.58, 9.74, 10.3–10.6, 10.9, 10.12, 11.2, 11.11–11.15, 11.17, 11.18, 11.20, 11.22, 11.23, 11.26, 11.28–11.30, 11.33, 11.37–11.43, 11.49, 11.50, 11.56–11.58, 11.60, 11.61, 11.65, 11.69–11.71, 11.74, 11.77, 11.78, 12.4–12.6, 12.15–12.18, 13.2, 13.5, 13.9, 13.13, 13.16, 13.18–13.21, 13.24, 13.31, 13.33–13.35, 14.6, 14.9
African Canadians, 11.6
Aging, 11.40, 11.64
Ainus, 13.23
Alabama, 6.20, 7.14, 13.9
Alaska, 1.6, 4.10, 4.14, 9.3, 10.8, 11.68
Alcoholism, 13.33
Algonquin Indians, 9.46
Alphabet books, 4.26, 5.9
Anasazi Indians, 7.2, 7.15
Animals, 1.7, 1.9, 1.12, 1.17, 4.8, 9.4, 9.8, 9.10, 9.12–9.15, 9.18–9.31, 9.40, 9.41, 9.43, 9.49, 9.50, 9.54, 9.61, 9.70, 10.12, 11.3, 11.6, 11.14, 11.25, 11.32, 11.41, 11.45, 11.46, 11.67, 11.80
Anthologies, 1.9, 1.19, 1.20, 1.24, 9.68–9.76, 12.5, 14.1–14.10
Apache Indians, 9.44
Apartheid, 6.6, 6.15, 12.3, 13.22
Apartments, 11.26
Arawak Indians, 9.30
Architects, 9.64
Arctic, 4.4, 4.10, 10.8, 13.15

Argentina, 4.3, 9.34
Art/artists, 2.4, 2.10, 3.4, 4.11, 4.24, 6.7, 6.28, 6.31, 7.6, 9.61, 9.64, 11.44
Arts, performing, 2.1–2.3, 2.5–2.9, 4.1, 5.5, 13.5
Arts, visual, 2.4, 2.10, 6.7, 6.28, 6.31
Ashanti, 9.18
Asia, 1.7, 1.9, 1.17, 1.23, 4.6, 4.15, 4.18, 4.21, 4.25–4.27, 6.5, 6.31, 7.5, 8.5, 9.7, 9.23, 9.32, 9.36, 9.37, 9.41, 9.43, 9.45, 9.48–9.51, 9.54, 9.55, 9.59, 9.61, 9.64, 9.65, 9.67, 9.75, 10.7, 11.3, 11.5, 11.7, 11.8, 11.19, 11.25, 11.34, 11.44, 11.47, 11.51, 11.59, 11.66, 11.72, 11.80, 13.1, 13.8, 13.12, 13.23, 13.27, 13.32
Asian Americans, 3.9, 4.1, 6.19, 6.23, 6.26, 6.30, 7.6, 8.2, 8.4, 8.5, 9.76, 10.1, 11.8, 11.52, 11.64, 11.72, 12.2, 12.9, 12.11, 12.13
Athabascan Indians, 13.14
Aunts/uncles, 9.66, 9.73, 11.29, 11.53, 12.16, 13.18, 13.20
Australia, 12.8
Aviation, 6.10
Aymara Indians, 13.4
Aztecs, 9.9

Babies, 10.11
Baby-sitting, 11.42, 11.74
Bahamas, 11.79, 13.10
Baseball, 6.9, 6.22, 6.27, 11.15, 11.42, 12.10, 12.16
Bats, 9.12, 9.29
Bears, 10.12
Beauty/appearance, 9.46, 9.49, 9.54, 9.55
Bedtime, 1.6, 10.1, 11.28, 11.37
Bees, 11.41
Bicycles, 11.31, 12.1
Bilingual/multilingual books, 1.8, 1.17, 2.5, 4.4, 4.17, 4.26, 5.1, 6.28, 9.4, 9.31, 9.33, 9.47, 9.56, 9.66, 9.67, 11.62
Biography, 1.16, 2.4, 4.1, 4.5, 6.1–6.31, 7.11, 7.14, 11.12, 11.70, 13.16
Biracial families, 5.13, 11.1, 11.52, 12.9
Birds, 9.8, 9.54, 11.45, 11.46
Birth, 10.7
Birthdays, 11.31, 11.53

Black Britons, 1.3, 11.27
Board books, 10.3–10.6
Boats/boating, 1.23, 9.36, 11.65, 11.72
Bolivia, 13.4
Books/reading, 4.19, 13.4
Brazil, 4.16, 9.30, 11.10
British Columbia, 13.25
Buildings/structures, 4.15, 9.45, 11.9, 11.17
Bullfighting, 6.23

California, 1.21, 4.8, 8.5, 11.77, 14.8
Cambodia, 11.47
Cameroon, 9.29, 9.63, 11.21
Camouflage, 9.8
Camp, 11.14
Canada, 4.4, 13.14, 13.25
Caribbean, 1.3, 1.5, 1.13, 1.14, 2.3, 2.5, 3.5,
    4.7, 4.12, 5.8, 6.22, 6.27, 7.9, 8.3, 8.6,
    9.22, 9.38, 9.73, 9.74, 10.2, 11.46,
    11.54, 11.55, 11.79, 13.3, 13.10, 13.30,
    14.2
Carnaval, 3.3
Cats, 11.53, 11.58, 11.80, 12.12
Central America, 7.8, 8.6, 9.31, 9.56, 9.60,
    9.62, 9.66, 12.13, 13.6, 14.2
Ceremonies, 3.4, 3.6, 3.10
Chanukah, 3.8
Cherokee Indians, 9.14, 12.14, 13.20
Cheyenne Indians, 4.9
Chibcha Indians, 9.16
Chichewa text/terms, 11.76
China, 4.25, 6.5, 6.31, 9.7, 9.32, 9.36, 9.37,
    9.41, 9.45, 9.50, 9.51, 9.54, 9.55, 9.59,
    9.61, 9.64, 9.65, 9.67, 11.3, 11.72, 11.80,
    13.1
Chinese Americans, 3.9, 6.23, 6.30, 8.4,
    9.76, 11.72, 12.11, 12.13
Chinese Britons, 11.4
Chinese Canadians, 12.19
Chinese New Year, 3.9
Chinese text/terms, 9.67
Christmas, 2.5, 3.2, 3.5, 3.8, 11.66
City life, 1.3, 1.11, 4.2, 4.19, 4.23, 4.25,
    5.1, 7.8, 11.71, 12.12, 13.19
Civet cats, 9.20
Civil rights movement, 1.16, 6.6, 6.11, 6.15,
    6.20, 7.7, 7.14, 7.16, 13.9, 13.18, 14.6
Civil War (U.S.), 7.3
Cleanliness, 11.13
Cochiti Indians, 4.11
Cockroaches, 9.22
Codes, 7.1
Colombia, 9.16

Colorado, 7.2
Coming of age, 13.1, 13.17, 13.25, 13.30,
    14.10
Community, 1.11, 1.22, 5.1, 12.3, 13.22
Concept books, 5.1–5.13, 10.3
Connecticut, 13.35
Conservation/ecology, 4.16, 9.5, 11.3,
    11.10, 11.22, 11.55
Cookies, 11.45
Cotton, 11.77
Counting books, 4.6, 5.3, 5.8
Country life, 6.4, 11.69
Cousins, 11.52, 11.56, 12.2
Cowboys, 2.8, 4.3, 6.18
Coyotes, 9.13, 9.19, 9.21, 9.40
Creation stories, 9.1, 9.9, 9.13, 9.15, 9.17,
    9.68
Cuba, 8.3
Cuban Americans, 8.3

Dance, 2.1, 2.6, 11.47, 11.50
Desert life, 4.22, 9.33
Devils, 9.34
Diaries/journals/letters, 4.12, 4.18, 7.4,
    9.67, 11.5, 11.14, 11.51, 13.16
Dishes, 9.37
Dogs, 9.31, 11.6
Dragons, 9.41, 9.50, 9.61
Drought, 9.60, 11.22
Ducks, 9.49, 11.32

East (U.S.), 3.6, 4.1, 4.2, 7.3, 7.13, 11.16,
    11.61, 11.70, 13.18, 13.19, 13.34, 14.2
East Africa, 9.10, 9.11, 9.17, 9.28
Easter, 11.57
Egypt, 2.9
El Salvador, 9.31, 13.6
Elephants, 9.29, 9.30
Emotions, 11.73, 12.4
Employment/careers, 4.1, 11.18, 11.30,
    11.35
Endangered species, 11.3
England, 1.3, 11.4, 11.27, 11.31, 11.32
Eskimos—*See* Inuits
Explorers, 6.12, 6.18

Fairies, 9.72
Family life, 1.1, 1.11, 1.15, 3.6, 4.2, 4.5,
    4.12, 4.17, 4.18, 4.27, 5.4, 5.6, 5.13, 6.4,
    8.2, 8.5, 9.67, 9.73, 10.4, 10.6–10.8,
    10.10, 10.11, 11.1, 11.2, 11.6, 11.8,

11.13, 11.15, 11.17, 11.18, 11.20, 11.23, 11.24, 11.26, 11.28–11.30, 11.33, 11.35–11.40, 11.43–11.45, 11.52–11.56, 11.61, 11.62, 11.64, 11.66, 11.68, 11.69, 11.71–11.74, 12.4, 12.6, 12.11, 12.14–12.16, 13.7, 13.8, 13.10, 13.14, 13.15, 13.17, 13.21, 13.27–13.29, 13.31–13.33, 14.4, 14.8, 14.9

Fantasy, 13.1

Farm life, 11.22, 11.56, 11.77

Fathers/daughters, 5.4, 9.67, 11.35, 11.39, 12.14, 12.19

Fathers/sons, 1.15, 5.4, 10.4, 11.20, 11.28, 11.35, 12.19, 13.3, 13.9, 13.19, 13.21, 13.26

Fire, 9.2

Fish/fishing, 11.33, 11.49, 11.55, 11.80, 12.15, 13.26

Flight, 11.16, 11.61

Floods, 11.44

Florida, 6.4, 12.16, 13.24

Flutes, 9.6, 9.44, 9.56, 11.24

Folktales, 9.1–9.97, 13.31, 14.5

Food/eating, 4.20, 5.10, 8.4, 11.4, 11.29, 11.44, 11.45, 12.19

Football, 1.18

Fortune-telling, 9.63

Foster families, 13.21

Foxes, 9.4, 9.26, 11.25

French text/terms, 1.8

Friendship, 1.11, 3.8, 5.10, 9.54, 10.3, 10.12, 11.11, 11.31, 11.48, 11.65, 11.70, 11.73, 11.76, 12.1, 12.10, 12.17, 13.5, 13.28, 13.33, 13.34, 13.36

Games, 1.24, 5.7, 9.60

Geese, 11.44

Ghana, 9.18

Ghosts, 9.74, 14.6, 14.9

Gifts/wishes, 9.2, 9.6, 9.17, 9.34, 9.53, 9.70, 11.11, 11.53, 11.57, 11.72, 13.1

Goats, 11.67

Gods/goddesses, 9.1, 9.2, 9.35, 9.48, 9.60

Grandparents, 6.4, 11.1, 11.7, 11.15, 11.16, 11.21, 11.23–11.25, 11.27, 11.33, 11.36, 11.40, 11.54, 11.55, 11.59, 11.64, 11.72, 12.6, 12.15–12.17, 13.2

Growth/change, 9.66, 10.3, 10.7, 11.1, 11.4, 11.7, 11.46

Guatemala, 9.56, 12.13, 14.2

Gulf War, 6.24

Gymnastics, 4.23

Haiku, 1.7

Haiti, 13.30, 14.2

Hats, 9.66

Hawaii, 6.25, 13.26

Hawaiian text/terms, 6.25

Hearing disabilities, 5.11, 11.47

Himalayas, 4.21

Hindi text/terms, 4.6

Hispanic Americans/Latinos, 1.21, 1.22, 2.8, 4.8, 4.17, 8.3, 8.4, 10.10, 11.9, 11.16, 11.24, 11.53, 11.54, 11.62, 11.67, 12.7, 13.17, 13.27, 13.28, 14.8

Historical fiction, 11.70, 12.14, 12.19, 13.2–13.4, 13.8–13.10, 13.12, 13.16, 13.18, 13.20, 13.23, 13.36

History, North American, 2.6, 2.10, 3.10, 4.7, 4.9, 6.8, 6.12–6.14, 6.18, 6.25, 7.1–7.16, 8.3, 11.60, 11.79

History, South American, 6.2, 7.5

History, world, 4.15, 6.2, 6.5, 7.5, 8.5

Holidays/celebrations, 2.5, 3.1–3.10, 11.50, 11.57, 11.58, 11.66, 11.72, 14.4

Homelessness, 4.2, 11.34, 12.12, 13.12, 13.29, 14.7

Homosexuality, 13.33

Honesty, 9.65

Honey, 9.10

Hong Kong, 13.32

Horror stories, 14.6

Horses/riding, 4.8

Human rights, 13.30

Identity, 6.30, 11.27, 12.2, 12.8, 12.11, 12.17, 13.15, 13.25, 13.28, 13.29, 13.34, 13.35, 14.4

Illegal aliens, 8.1, 8.6, 13.6

Illness/death, 7.4, 7.9, 11.15, 11.19, 11.34, 11.54, 11.59, 11.64, 12.6, 12.8, 13.14, 13.34

Imagination, 1.2, 1.8, 11.6, 11.16, 11.61, 11.65

Immigrants/immigration, 4.12, 8.1–8.6, 9.76, 11.8, 12.2, 12.8, 12.9, 12.11, 12.19, 13.6, 13.32

Imprisonment, 6.26, 7.6, 13.12, 13.21

India, 1.23, 4.6, 9.48, 11.5, 11.7, 11.19

Indians—*See* Native Americans and also individual tribal entries

Insects, 11.51

Intergenerational stories, 3.8, 6.4, 9.11, 10.2, 11.1, 11.7, 11.15, 11.16, 11.21, 11.23–11.25, 11.27, 11.29, 11.33, 11.34, 11.36, 11.40, 11.42, 11.46, 11.53–11.55,

11.57–11.59, 11.64, 11.72, 12.6,
    12.15–12.17, 13.2
Interracial friendships, 11.48, 11.57, 11.58,
    11.65, 11.73, 11.76, 11.78, 12.1, 12.10,
    13.2, 13.11, 13.17, 13.27, 13.29, 13.35,
    13.36
Inuits, 4.4, 4.10, 4.14, 9.70, 10.8, 11.68, 13.15
Inuktitut text/terms, 4.4
Inupiaq text/terms, 4.10, 4.14
Inupiaqs, 4.10, 4.14
Inventors, 6.14
Iroquois Indians, 6.8, 13.11
Island life, 1.5, 1.13, 1.14, 3.5, 5.3, 5.8,
    10.2, 11.55, 13.26

Jamaica, 4.12, 9.38, 13.3
Japan, 1.7, 1.9, 1.17, 4.26, 9.23, 9.32, 9.43,
    9.49, 9.75, 11.25, 11.34, 11.44, 11.51,
    11.66, 13.12, 13.23, 13.27
Japanese Americans, 6.26, 7.6, 11.64
Japanese Britons, 11.32
Japanese text/terms, 1.17, 4.26, 13.27
Jealousy, 11.31
Jews, 3.8, 11.58
Judges, 6.11

Kampuchea—*See* Cambodia
Kindness, 9.62, 14.2
Kites, 11.59
Korea, 4.18, 13.8
Korean Americans, 4.1, 12.9
Kwanzaa, 3.1, 3.7

Lakota Indians, 3.10
Language, 12.14
Laotian Americans, 12.2
Latin America, 1.3, 1.5, 1.13, 2.3, 2.5, 3.3,
    4.3, 4.7, 4.12, 4.16, 5.3, 5.8, 6.2, 6.22, 6.27,
    7.8, 7.9, 8.3, 8.6, 9.2, 9.4, 9.16, 9.22, 9.30,
    9.31, 9.34, 9.38, 9.56, 9.60, 9.62, 9.66,
    9.68, 9.69, 9.74, 10.2, 11.10, 11.46, 11.54,
    12.13, 13.3, 13.4, 13.6, 13.30, 14.1, 14.2
Latinos—*See* Hispanic Americans/Latinos
Light, 9.3, 9.14, 9.15, 9.70
Lost children, 9.24, 9.52

Maasai, 9.11, 9.28
Magic, 9.31, 9.33, 9.35, 9.36, 9.39–9.43,
    9.45, 9.48, 9.49, 9.51–9.55, 9.59, 9.76,
    11.44, 12.5, 12.13

Malawi, 11.75, 11.76
Mali, 6.29
Mandan Indians, 7.4
Manual labor, 11.77
Maryland, 11.29
Massachusetts, 3.6, 7.3, 7.13
Mathematics, 5.10
Mayas, 9.56, 9.60, 12.13
Mermaids, 9.33, 9.53
Mexican Americans, 1.21, 1.22, 4.17,
    11.24, 11.53, 11.67, 13.17, 13.27, 13.28,
    14.8
Mexico, 6.28, 8.6, 9.9, 9.19, 9.33, 9.47,
    11.45, 13.6, 14.2
Mice, 9.22
Midwest (U.S.), 3.10, 4.20, 11.22, 14.9
Migrant workers, 11.77
Military figures, 6.24
Minnesota, 4.20
Mississippi, 7.16, 12.18
Missouri, 14.9
Moles, 9.4
Money, 11.70
Mongols, 6.5
Monsters, 9.28, 9.58, 9.72, 9.74
Mothers/daughters, 10.7, 10.8, 11.18,
    11.39, 11.43, 13.5, 13.13
Mothers/sons, 3.2, 9.57, 10.10, 11.6,
    11.36, 11.66, 11.68, 11.71, 13.28
Mountain life, 4.21
Moving, 11.38, 11.65
Multicultural theme, 1.10, 1.19, 1.24, 2.1,
    2.4, 3.8, 4.2, 4.15, 5.4–5.7, 5.9–5.13,
    7.5, 8.4, 9.72, 10.10, 10.11, 11.4, 11.31,
    11.41, 11.57, 11.58, 11.63, 11.73, 11.76,
    12.12, 13.27, 14.2, 14.3, 14.5, 14.7, 14.10
Music/songs, 2.2, 2.3, 2.5, 2.7–2.9, 4.1,
    5.5, 6.3, 9.9, 9.33, 9.44, 9.56, 10.5,
    10.12, 11.63, 12.11, 13.13, 13.31, 14.5
Mystery/detective stories, 13.17, 13.24
Myths/legends, 1.4, 9.1–9.3, 9.6. 9.9,
    9.13–9.17, 9.21, 9.32, 9.39, 9.40, 9.44,
    9.46–9.48, 9.52, 9.56, 9.60, 9.68, 9.70

National leaders, 1.16, 6.2, 6.5, 6.6, 6.15,
    6.25, 6.29, 7.7
Native Americans (North/South
    America), 1.4, 1.6, 3.4, 3.6, 3.10, 4.4,
    4.9–4.11, 4.13, 4.14, 4.20, 4.24, 6.8, 7.1,
    7.2, 7.4, 7.9, 7.13, 7.15, 9.3, 9.6, 9.9,
    9.13–9.16, 9.21, 9.24, 9.30, 9.39, 9.40,
    9.44, 9.46, 9.47, 9.52, 9.56, 9.60,
    9.68–9.70, 10.8, 11.50, 11.68, 11.79,

12.13, 12.14, 13.4, 13.10, 13.11, 13.14, 13.15, 13.20, 13.25, 13.35, 13.36, 14.4
Nature, 1.4, 1.6, 1.9, 1.17, 9.47, 9.68, 9.70
Navajo Indians, 7.1, 9.13, 9.21, 13.36
Navajo text/terms, 9.21
New Mexico, 4.11, 4.13, 4.24, 13.17
New York, 4.1, 4.2, 11.16, 11.61, 11.70, 13.18, 13.19, 13.34, 14.2
Ngoni, 9.10
Nicaragua, 9.66
Nigeria, 9.1, 9.5
Night, 1.6, 10.1
Nkundo, 9.20
Nootka Indians, 13.25
North Carolina, 11.56, 13.18

Ojibway Indians, 4.20
Ojibway text/terms, 4.20
Oklahoma, 4.9
Olympic Games, 6.1
Opera, 2.9
Orphans, 9.11, 12.16, 13.12, 13.29, 13.31
Oxen, 9.7

Pacific Northwest Indians, 9.15
Parades, 11.67
Peace/pacifism, 9.31, 14.3
Pearls, 9.55
Peru, 3.3, 9.2, 9.4
Pianos, 4.1
Plains Indians, 9.6, 9.24, 9.39, 9.40
Plants/gardening, 9.65, 11.7
Poetry, 1.1–1.24, 14.3–14.5, 14.7
Politics, 13.30
Pourquoi tales, 9.2, 9.4, 9.5, 9.7–9.12, 9.14, 9.30, 9.68
Poverty, 9.59, 13.6, 13.7, 13.15
Pride, 11.21
Pueblo Indians, 4.11, 4.13, 4.24, 7.2, 7.15
Puerto Ricans, 8.4, 12.7
Puerto Rico, 2.5, 4.7, 6.22, 6.27, 9.22, 11.54

Quebec, 4.4

Rabbits, 9.26–9.28
Race relations, 1.16, 6.6, 6.9, 6.10, 6.15, 6.20, 6.27, 7.6, 7.7, 7.10–7.12, 7.14, 7.16, 11.60, 12.2, 12.3, 12.17, 12.18, 13.7, 13.9, 13.11, 13.17, 13.18, 13.22, 13.24, 13.28

Rain, 10.9, 12.18
Rain forests, 4.16, 11.10
Ranch life, 4.3
Ravens, 9.15, 9.70
Realistic tales, 9.62–9.67
Refugees, 13.6, 13.8, 13.32
Rhyming text, 3.2, 5.8, 10.2–10.6, 10.10, 10.12, 11.13, 11.50
Rice, 4.20, 11.44
Riddles, 9.69
Romance/love, 9.6, 9.20, 9.22, 9.32, 9.37, 9.38, 9.42, 9.44, 9.46–9.51, 9.55, 9.56, 13.19
Royalty/nobility, 9.16, 9.41, 9.43, 9.48, 9.49, 9.51, 9.54–9.56, 9.61, 9.64, 9.65, 11.19, 11.47, 11.80, 13.1

Sahara, 4.22
School life, 1.10, 1.18, 4.12, 4.18, 8.2, 11.4, 11.27, 11.30, 11.41, 11.43, 11.48, 12.2, 12.7, 12.13, 13.25, 13.35, 14.9
Sea/seashore, 9.33, 9.55, 11.2, 11.55, 13.26, 13.32
Seasons, 1.1, 1.4, 1.9, 10.7
Seminole Indians, 11.50
Sexual harassment, 13.16
Shapes, 5.2
Sheep, 1.12, 9.19
Sherpas, 4.21
Short stories, 14.1–14.3, 14.5, 14.7, 14.8, 14.10
Siblings, 5.13, 9.43, 9.45, 9.46, 9.52, 10.6, 11.1, 11.6, 11.37, 11.39, 11.52, 11.62, 11.68, 11.74, 13.7, 13.14
Sign language, 5.11
Sioux Indians, 3.10
Size, 10.3
Slavery, 6.17, 7.10, 7.12, 7.16, 9.42, 11.60, 13.2, 13.3, 13.16, 14.6
Social life/customs, 3.1, 3.4, 3.6, 3.7, 3.9, 4.1–4.27, 7.2, 7.4, 7.5, 7.13, 7.15, 8.4, 8.5, 10.8, 11.36, 11.51, 11.66, 11.75, 13.10, 13.15, 13.23, 13.36, 14.6
South (U.S.), 1.15, 6.4, 6.7, 6.20, 7.14, 7.16, 9.57, 11.29, 11.56, 12.16, 12.18, 13.2, 13.9, 13.18, 13.24
South Africa, 4.19, 6.6, 6.15, 11.35, 11.36, 12.3, 13.7, 13.22
South America, 3.3, 4.3, 4.16, 6.2, 8.6, 9.2, 9.4, 9.16, 9.30, 9.34, 9.68, 9.69, 11.10, 13.4
South Carolina, 1.15, 6.7
South Dakota, 3.10

Southwest (U.S.), 4.9, 4.11, 4.13, 4.17, 4.24, 7.2, 7.15, 8.1, 9.52, 13.17
Space/privacy, 11.26
Spain, 6.23
Spanish text/terms, 1.8, 2.5, 3.3, 4.3, 4.17, 5.1, 6.28, 9.4, 9.19, 9.31, 9.33, 9.47, 9.56, 9.66, 11.16, 11.53, 11.62, 13.27, 13.28, 14.8
Spiders, 9.25
Spirituals, 2.2, 2.7
Sports, 1.18, 4.8, 4.23, 6.1, 6.9, 6.22, 6.23, 6.27, 9.60, 11.15, 11.42, 12.10, 12.11, 13.29
Spring, 10.7
St. Lucia, 11.55
Stars/sky, 9.1, 9.3–9.5, 9.7, 9.9, 9.11–9.15, 9.27, 9.32, 9.35, 9.41, 11.28
Stores/markets, 10.2, 11.69
Storms, 12.18
Storytelling, 9.71, 11.29, 11.49, 12.15, 14.9
Supernatural, 9.34, 9.57, 9.58, 9.72, 9.74, 14.6
Survival, 13.14, 13.16
Suspense, 9.76
Swahili, 9.8
Swahili text/terms, 3.1, 3.7
Swans, 9.43

Tails, 9.58
Taino Indians, 7.9, 11.79, 13.10
Taiwan, 4.27, 11.59
Tall tales, 11.49
Teen pregnancy, 13.33
Television, 13.5
Tewa Indians, 4.24
Tewa text/terms, 4.24
Texas, 4.17, 8.1
Theater, 11.27, 11.41
Thieves, 9.23, 9.62, 11.14
Tibet, 4.21
Tigers, 11.3
Tlingit Indians, 9.3
Toads, 9.21
Tobago, 3.5
Tools, 5.12
Toys, 9.52, 10.6, 10.12, 11.25, 11.75, 12.13
Track/field, 6.1
Traditional rhymes, 1.2, 1.8, 1.12, 1.13, 1.24
Trains, 11.12
Transkei, 11.36
Travel, 11.5, 11.36, 11.65

Treasure, 13.19, 13.20
Trees, 4.16, 11.7, 11.10, 11.34, 11.66
Trickster tales, 9.3, 9.8, 9.15, 9.18, 9.19, 9.21, 9.25, 9.27, 9.30, 9.36, 9.38–9.40, 9.70, 12.5
Trinidad, 1.14, 3.5, 9.73
Tsimshian Indians, 3.4
Tuaregs, 4.22
Turtles, 9.25, 9.30

Underground Railroad, 7.12, 11.60
Utah, 13.36

Vehicles, 10.2, 11.75, 12.18
Venezuela, 6.2
Vietnam, 13.32
Vietnam War, 11.9
Vietnamese Americans, 8.2, 8.5, 11.8
Vietnamese Australians, 12.8
Vietnamese text/terms, 11.8
Virginia, 13.2
Volcanoes, 9.31

Walls, 4.15, 9.45, 11.9
Wampanoag Indians, 3.6, 7.13
Wampanoag text/terms, 3.6, 7.13
War, 11.34, 13.4, 13.23
Washington (state), 3.4, 12.11
Washington, D.C., 4.5
West (U.S.), 1.21, 2.8, 3.4, 4.8, 6.18, 7.2, 8.5, 9.15, 11.77, 12.11, 13.20, 13.36, 14.8
West Africa, 9.27, 9.35
West Indies—*See* Caribbean
Whales, 9.30
Wildlife rescue, 11.32, 11.46
Witches, 9.72
Wolves, 9.23, 9.24, 9.26
Women's rights, 6.17
World War II, 6.26, 7.1, 7.6, 13.8
Writers/writing, 1.19, 1.21, 2.10, 6.16, 6.21, 6.26, 6.30, 9.67, 12.14

Yoruba, 9.1
Yukon, 13.14

Zaire, 9.20
Zapotec Indians, 9.47
Zuni Indians, 9.52

Title Index

A to Zen: A Book of Japanese Culture, 4.26
Abuela, 11.16
Abuelita's Paradise/El Paraíso de Abuelita, 11.54
Against All Opposition: Black Explorers in America, 6.12
Ahyoka and the Talking Leaves, 12.14
Aïda, 2.9
Ajeemah and His Son, 13.3
Aki and the Fox, 11.25
All Jahdu Storybook, The, 12.5
All Night, All Day: A Child's First Book of African-American Spirituals, 2.2
All of You Was Singing, 9.9
Amal and the Letter from the King, 11.19
Amazing Grace, 11.27
Anancy and Mr. Dry-Bone, 9.38
Anansi Finds a Fool: An Ashanti Tale, 9.18
Anansi Goes Fishing, 9.25
Ancient Cliff Dwellers of Mesa Verde, The, 7.2
And in the Beginning . . . , 9.17
Animals, The: Selected Poems, 1.17
Anni's India Diary, 11.5
Antonio's Rain Forest, 4.16
Arctic Hunter, 4.10
Arctic Memories, 4.4
Artist and the Architect, The, 9.64
At the Crossroads, 11.35
Aunt Flossie's Hats (and Crab Cakes Later), 11.29
Aunt Harriet's Underground Railroad in the Sky, 11.60

Baby-O, 10.2
Back Home, 11.56
Ballad of Belle Dorcas, The, 9.42
Baseball in April, and Other Stories, 14.8
Best Bug to Be, The, 11.41
Big Book for Peace, The, 14.3
Big Friend, Little Friend, 10.3
Bigmama's, 6.4
Birthday Basket for Tía, A, 11.53
Black Dance in America: A History through Its People, 2.6

Blacksmith and the Devil, The/El Herrero y el Diablo, 9.34
Blue between the Clouds, The, 13.36
Blue Skin of the Sea: A Novel in Stories, 13.26
Borreguita and the Coyote: A Tale from Ayutla, Mexico, 9.19
Boy and the Samurai, The, 13.12
Boy Becomes a Man at Wounded Knee, A, 3.10
Boy Who Found the Light, The: Eskimo Folktales, 9.70
Breaking the Chains: African-American Slave Resistance, 7.10
Brothers and Sisters, 5.13
Bury My Bones but Keep My Words: African Tales for Retelling, 9.71

Caribbean Carnival: Songs of the West Indies, 2.3
Chain of Fire, 13.22
Chancay and the Secret of Fire: A Peruvian Tale, 9.2
Cherry Tree, 11.7
Cherry Tree, The, 11.34
Chi-hoon: A Korean Girl, 4.18
Chicken Sunday, 11.57
Children of Clay: A Family of Pueblo Potters, 4.24
Children of Promise: African-American Literature and Art for Young People, 2.10
Chingis Khan, 6.5
City Kids in China, 4.25
Clambake: A Wampanoag Tradition, 3.6
Class President, 12.7
Clean Your Room, Harvey Moon, 11.13
Cleversticks, 11.4
Climbing Jacob's Ladder: Heroes of the Bible in African-American Spirituals, 2.7
Coconut Kind of Day: Island Poems, 1.14
Colin Powell: A Man of War and Peace, 6.24
Coming of the Bear, The, 13.23
Con Mi Hermano/With My Brother, 11.62
Count Your Way through India, 4.6

Cousins, 12.6
Cubans, 8.3
Curse of the Trouble Dolls, The, 12.13

Daddies, 5.4
Daddy and I . . . , 10.4
Dan Thuy's New Life in America, 8.5
Dancing with the Indians, 11.50
Daniel's Dog, 11.6
Dark Thirty, The: Southern Tales of the
    Supernatural, 14.6
Dark Way, The: Stories from the Spirit
    World, 9.72
Day Martin Luther King, Jr., Was Shot,
    The: A Photo History of the Civil
    Rights Movement, 7.7
Dear One, The, 13.33
Desert Mermaid, The/La Sirena del
    Desierto, 9.33
Diary of Latoya Hunter, The: My First
    Year in Junior High, 4.12
Diego, 6.28
Do like Kyla, 11.37
Dragon Kite of the Autumn Moon, 11.59
Dragonfly's Tale, 9.52
Dream Wolf, 9.24
Drifting Snow: An Arctic Search, 13.15
Drylongso, 11.22
Duke Ellington, 6.3

Eating Fractions, 5.10
El Chino, 6.23
Elephant's Wrestling Match, The, 9.29
Elijah's Angel: A Story for Chanukah
    and Christmas, 3.8
Emperor and the Nightingale, The, 9.54
Empty Pot, The, 9.65
Encounter, 11.79
Escape from Slavery: Five Journeys to
    Freedom, 7.12
Eskimo Boy: Life in an Inupiaq Eskimo
    Village, 4.14
Esmeralda and the Pet Parade, 11.67
Evan's Corner, 11.26
Everett Anderson's Christmas Coming, 3.2

Families: A Celebration of Diversity,
    Commitment, and Love, 5.6
Family in Taiwan, A, 4.27
Family Pictures/Cuadros de familia, 4.17
Famous Asian Americans, 6.19

Father and Son, 1.15
Fear the Condor, 13.4
Finding the Green Stone, 11.73
Fire in My Hands, A: A Book of Poems,
    1.21
First Pink Light, 11.20
Fish and Bones, 13.24
Flute Player, The: An Apache Folktale,
    9.44
Flying Free: America's First Black
    Aviators, 6.10
Fortune-Tellers, The, 9.63
Fourth Question, The: A Chinese Tale, 9.59
Freedom Songs, 13.18
Front Porch Stories at the One-Room
    School, 14.9
Further Tales of Uncle Remus: The
    Misadventures of Brer Rabbit, Brer
    Fox, Brer Wolf, the Doodang, and
    Other Creatures, 9.26

Galimoto, 11.75
Gathering of Flowers, A: Stories about
    Being Young in America, 14.10
Girl Who Loved Caterpillars, The: A
    Twelfth-Century Tale from Japan,
    11.51
Go Fish, 12.15
Going Live, 13.5
Gold Coin, The, 9.62
Golden Bear, 10.12
Golden Swan: An East Indian Tale of
    Love from *The Mahabharata*, 9.48
Goodbye, Vietnam, 13.32
Grandma's Baseball, 11.15
Great Adventure of Wo Ti, The, 11.80
Great Kapok Tree, The: A Tale of the
    Amazon Rain Forest, 11.10

Handtalk School, 5.11
Hard to Be Six, 11.1
Hiawatha: Messenger of Peace, 6.8
Himalaya: Vanishing Cultures, 4.21
Hoang Breaks the Lucky Teapot, 11.8
Home: A Collection of Thirty
    Distinguished Authors and
    Illustrators of Children's Books to
    Aid the Homeless, 14.7
Home Place, 11.17
Honey Hunters, The: A Traditional
    African Tale, 9.10
Hopscotch around the World, 5.7

House That Jack Built, The, 1.13
How Many Stars in the Sky?, 11.28
How My Family Lives in America, 8.4
How Raven Brought Light to People, 9.3
How the Guinea Fowl Got Her Spots: A
    Swahili Tale of Friendship, 9.8
How the Ox Star Fell from Heaven, 9.7
How the Stars Fell into the Sky: A
    Navajo Legend, 9.13

I Am a Jesse White Tumbler, 4.23
I Feel like Dancing: A Year with Jacques
    d'Amboise and the National Dance
    Institute, 2.1
I Make Music, 10.5
I Remember "121," 4.5
Iktomi and the Buffalo Skull: A Plains
    Indian Story, 9.39
Iktomi and the Ducks: A Plains Indian
    Story, 9.40
Illegal: Seeking the American Dream, 8.1
In for Winter, Out for Spring, 1.1
In the Eyes of the Cat: Japanese Poetry
    for All Seasons, 1.9
Indian Summer, 13.11
Indian Winter, An, 7.4
Invisible Thread, The, 6.26
Irene and the Big, Fine Nickel, 11.70
Island Baby, 11.46
Island Christmas, An, 3.5

Jade Stone, The: A Chinese Folktale, 9.61
Jamal's Busy Day, 11.30
James the Vine Puller: A Brazilian
    Folktale, 9.30
Jenny, 11.78
Jenny's Journey, 11.65
Jonathan and His Mommy, 11.71
Journey, The: Japanese Americans,
    Racism, and Renewal, 7.6
Journey of Meng, The: A Chinese
    Legend, 9.51
Journey of the Sparrows, 13.6
Jump at de Sun: The Story of Zora Neale
    Hurston, 6.21
Just like Martin, 13.9

Kenji and the Magic Geese, 11.44
Keys to My Kingdom, The: A Poem in
    Three Languages, 1.8

Koya DeLaney and the Good Girl Blues,
    12.4
Kwanzaa, 3.7

Las Navidades: Popular Christmas
    Songs from Latin America, 2.5
Last Princess, The: The Story of Princess
    Ka'iulani of Hawai'i, 6.25
Last Summer with Maizon, 13.34
Laura Loves Horses, 4.8
Leaving Morning, The, 11.38
Lee Ann: The Story of a
    Vietnamese-American Girl, 8.2
Legend of El Dorado, The: A Latin
    American Tale, 9.16
Let Freedom Ring: A Ballad of Martin
    Luther King, Jr., 1.16
Letter to the King, A, 9.67
Letters from a Slave Girl: The Story of
    Harriet Jacobs, 13.16
Li'l Sis and Uncle Willie: A Story Based
    on the Life and Paintings of William
    H. Johnson, 6.7
Light: Stories of a Small Kindness, 14.2
Lightning inside You, and Other Native
    American Riddles, 9.69
Lion Dancer: Ernie Wan's Chinese New
    Year, 3.9
Little Band, The, 11.63
Little Eight John, 9.57
Lorenzo, the Naughty Parrot, 11.45
Lost Garden, The, 6.30
Love, David, 13.7
Love Flute, 9.6
Luminous Pearl, The: A Chinese
    Folktale, 9.55

Magic Boat, The, 9.36
Magic Dogs of the Volcanoes/Los Perros
    Mágicos de los Volcanes, 9.31
Ma'ii and Cousin Horned Toad: A
    Traditional Navajo Story, 9.21
Maizon at Blue Hill, 13.35
Make a Joyful Sound: Poems for Children
    by African-American Poets, 1.20
Mama, Do You Love Me?, 10.8
Mama, I Want to Sing, 13.13
Maniac Magee, 13.29
Mary Had a Little Lamb, 1.12
Middle of Somewhere, The: A Story of
    South Africa, 12.3

Million Fish . . . More or Less, A, 11.49
Min-Yo and the Moon Dragon, 9.41
Mississippi Bridge, 12.18
Mississippi Challenge, 7.16
Moon Lady, The, 11.72
Moon Rope: A Peruvian Tale/Un Lazo a La Luna: Una Leyenda Peruana, 9.4
Moon Was Tired of Walking on Air, 9.68
Mop, Moondance, and the Nagasaki Knights, 12.10
"More More More," Said the Baby: Three Love Stories, 10.11
Morning Girl, 13.10
Mouse Rap, The, 13.19
Mrs. Katz and Tush, 11.58
My Doll, Keshia, 10.6
My First ABC, 5.9
My First Kwanzaa Book, 3.1
My Friend's Got This Problem, Mr. Candler: High School Poems, 1.10
My Grandpa and the Sea, 11.55

Navajo Code Talkers, 7.1
Neighborhood Odes, 1.22
Nelson Mandela: "No Easy Walk to Freedom," 6.6
Nelson Mandela: Voice of Freedom, 6.15
Night on Neighborhood Street, 1.11
No Place to Be: Voices of Homeless Children, 4.2
Nora's Duck, 11.32
Northern Lullaby, 1.6
Now Is Your Time! The African-American Struggle for Freedom, 7.11

On a Hot, Hot Day, 10.10
On Mother's Lap, 11.68
On the Pampas, 4.3
One More River to Cross: The Stories of Twelve Black Americans, 6.13
One of Three, 11.39
One Smiling Grandma: A Caribbean Counting Book, 5.8
One White Sail, 5.3
One Who Came Back, The, 13.17
Onion Tears, 12.8
Origin of Life on Earth, The: An African Creation Myth, 9.1
Orphan Boy, The: A Maasai Story, 9.11
Osa's Pride, 11.21

Outward Dreams: Black Inventors and Their Inventions, 6.14
Over the Green Hills, 11.36

Pacific Crossing, 13.27
Paper Boats, 1.23
People of the Breaking Day, 7.13
People of the Sacred Arrows: The Southern Cheyenne Today, 4.9
Perez and Martina: A Puerto Rican Folktale/Perez y Martina, 9.22
Petey Moroni's Camp Runamok Diary, 11.14
Pianist's Debut, A: Preparing for the Concert Stage, 4.1
Picture Book of Jesse Owens, A, 6.1
Picture Book of Simón Bolívar, A, 6.2
Pride of Puerto Rico: The Life of Roberto Clemente, 6.27
Promise to the Sun, A: An African Story, 9.12
Pueblo Boy: Growing Up in Two Worlds, 4.13
Pueblo Storyteller, 4.11
Puerto Rico: An Unfinished Story, 4.7

Rachel Parker, Kindergarten Show-off, 11.48
Rain Player, 9.60
Rain Talk, 10.9
Raven's Light: A Myth from the People of the Northwest Coast, 9.15
Raw Head, Bloody Bones: African-American Tales of the Supernatural, 9.74
Red Dog, Blue Fly: Football Poems, 1.18
Red Dragonfly on My Shoulder, 1.7
Reflections of a Black Cowboy: Book Four, Mountain Men, 6.18
Remarkable Journey of Prince Jen, The, 13.1
Rhinos for Lunch and Elephants for Supper! A Maasai Tale, 9.28
Righteous Revenge of Artemis Bonner, The, 13.20
Rising Voices: Writings of Young Native Americans, 14.4
River Dragon, The, 9.50
Roberto Clemente: Young Baseball Hero, 6.22
Rosa Parks: My Story, 6.20

Roses Sing on New Snow: A Delicious
    Tale, 12.19
Rough-Face Girl, The, 9.46

Sachiko Means Happiness, 11.64
Sacred Harvest, The: Ojibway Wild Rice
    Gathering, 4.20
Sahara: Vanishing Cultures, 4.22
San Rafael: A Central American City
    through the Ages, 7.8
Seven Chinese Brothers, The, 9.45
Shape Space, 5.2
Shortcut, 11.12
Silent Lotus, 11.47
Sing to the Sun, 1.5
Snow Country Prince, The, 9.43
Sojourner Truth: Ain't I a Woman?, 6.17
Somewhere in Africa, 4.19
Somewhere in the Darkness, 13.21
Song of Stars, A: An Asian Legend, 9.32
Song of the Chirimia: A Guatemalan
    Folktale/La Musica de la Chirimia:
    Folklore Guatemalteco, 9.56
Sorrow's Kitchen: The Life and Folklore
    of Zora Neale Hurston, 6.16
Steal Away, 13.2
Stealing Home, 12.16
Story of Light, The, 9.14
Street Rhymes around the World, 1.24
Sukey and the Mermaid, 9.53
Summer Wheels, 12.1
Sundiata: Lion King of Mali, 6.29

Tails of the Bronx: A Tale of the Bronx,
    12.12
Tailypo!, 9.58
Tainos, The: The People Who Welcomed
    Columbus, 7.9
Taking a Walk: A Book in Two
    Languages/Caminando: Un Libro en
    Dos Lenguas, 5.1
Taking Sides, 13.28
Tale of the Mandarin Ducks, The, 9.49
Tales from the Bamboo Grove, 9.75
Talking Walls, 4.15
Talking with Artists: Conversations with
    Victoria Chess, Pat Cummings, Leo
    and Diane Dillon, Richard Egielski,
    Lois Ehlert, Lisa Campbell Ernst,
    Tom Feelings, Steven Kellogg, Jerry
    Pinkney, Amy Schwartz, Lane Smith,

Chris Van Allsburg and David
    Wiesner, 2.4
Tall Boy's Journey, 12.9
Tar Beach, 11.61
Taste of Salt: A Story of Modern Haiti,
    13.30
Teammates, 6.9
Terrible EEK, The: A Japanese Tale, 9.23
Thank You, Dr. Martin Luther King, Jr.!,
    12.17
Things I Like about Grandma, 11.23
Thirteen Moons on Turtle's Back: A
    Native American Year of Moons, 1.4
This Is the Key to the Kingdom, 1.2
This Same Sky: A Collection of Poems
    from around the World, 1.19
Three Wishes, 11.11
Thurgood Marshall: A Life for Justice,
    6.11
Tiger, 11.3
To Ride a Butterfly: Original Stories,
    Poems, and Songs for Children by
    Fifty-two Distinguished Authors and
    Illustrators, 14.5
Tongues of Jade, 9.76
Tonight Is Carnaval, 3.3
Tools, 5.12
Totem Pole, 3.4
Toughboy and Sister, 13.14
Tower to Heaven, 9.35
Traveling to Tondo: A Tale of the
    Nkundo of Zaire, 9.20
Treasure Nap, 11.24
Tree of Cranes, 11.66
Two and Too Much, 11.74

Uncertain Journey, The: Stories of Illegal
    Aliens in *El Norte*, 8.6
Uncle Nacho's Hat/El Sombrero del Tío
    Nacho, 9.66
Undying Glory: The Story of the
    Massachusetts 54th Regiment, 7.3

Vatsana's Lucky New Year, 12.2
Village of Blue Stone, The, 7.15
Visit to Amy-Claire, A, 11.52

Wall, The, 11.9
Wave in Her Pocket, A: Stories from
    Trinidad, 9.73

We Keep a Store, 11.69
What Comes in Spring?, 10.7
What Instrument Is This?, 5.5
What Kind of Baby-sitter Is This?, 11.42
What Will Mommy Do When I'm at School?, 11.43
Wheels: A Tale of Trotter Street, 11.31
When Africa Was Home, 11.76
When I Am Old with You, 11.40
When I Dance, 1.3
When I Was Little, 11.33
When the Nightingale Sings, 13.31
Where Angels Glide at Dawn: New Stories from Latin America, 14.1
Where Does the Trail Lead?, 11.2
While I Sleep, 10.1
Why the Sky Is Far Away: A Nigerian Folktale, 9.5
Willow Pattern Story, The, 9.37
Woman of Her Tribe, A, 13.25
Woman Who Outshone the Sun, The: The Legend of Lucia Zenteno/La Mujer que Brillaba Aún Más que el Sol: La Leyenda de Lucía Zenteno, 9.47
Working Cotton, 11.77
World in 1492, The, 7.5

Yang the Youngest and His Terrible Ear, 12.11
Year of Impossible Goodbyes, 13.8
Year They Walked, The: Rosa Parks and the Montgomery Bus Boycott, 7.14
You're My Nikki, 11.18
Young Painter, A: The Life and Paintings of Wang Yani—China's Extraordinary Young Artist, 6.31

Zebra-Riding Cowboy, The: A Folk Song from the Old West, 2.8
Zomo the Rabbit: A Trickster Tale from West Africa, 9.27

Photo Credits

We wish to thank the following publishers for their gracious permission to reprint the photographs of book covers that appear on our photo pages.

Black Butterfly Children's Books
My Doll, Keshia by Eloise Greenfield; illustrated by Jan Spivey Gilchrist.

Borzoi Books
The Snow Country Prince by Daisaku Ikeda (translated by Geraldine McCaughrean); cover illustration by Brian Wildsmith used with permission of Alfred A. Knopf/Borzoi Books.

Boyds Mills Press
Chi-Hoon by Patricia McMahon; photographs by Michael F. O'Brien.
Paper Boats by Rabindranath Tagore; illustrated by Grayce Bochak.

Carolrhoda Books
Count Your Way through India by Jim Haskins; illustrated by Liz Brenner Dodson. All rights reserved.

Chronicle Books
Mama, Do You Love Me? by Barbara M. Joosse; cover illustration by Barbara Lavallee copyright 1991.

Clarion Books, an imprint of Houghton Mifflin Company
Shape Space by Cathryn Falwell; cover illustration copyright © 1992 by Cathryn Falwell.
Orphan Boy by Tololwa M. Mollel; cover illustration by Paul Morin copyright © 1991.
Dragonfly's Tale by Kristina Rodanas; cover illustration by Kristina Rodanas copyright © 1992.
Aunt Flossie's Hats (and Crab Cakes Later) by Elizabeth Fitzgerald Howard; cover illustration by James Ransome copyright © 1991.
The Wall by Eve Bunting; cover illustration by Ronald Himler © 1990.

Farrar, Straus and Giroux
Silent Lotus by Jeanne M. Lee; cover illustration © 1991 by Jeanne M. Lee.

Harcourt Brace Jovanovich
Aïda retold by Leontyne Price; cover illustration by Diane Dillon used with permission.
The Dark Way: Stories from the Spirit World retold by Virginia Hamilton; cover illustration by Lambert Davis used with permission.
Himalaya: Vanishing Cultures by Jan Reynolds; cover illustration used with permission.
In for Winter, Out for Spring by Arnold Adoff; cover illustration by Jerry Pinkney used with permission.
Moon Rope: A Peruvian Tale/ Un Lazo a La Luna: Una Leyenda Peruana by Lois Ehlert (translated by Amy Prince); cover illustration by Lois Ehlert used with permission.

Henry Holt and Company
Arctic Memories by Normee Ekoomiak; illustrations copyright © 1988 by Normee Ekoomiak.
Tailypo! retold by Jan Wahl; illustrations copyright © 1991 by Wil Clay.

Tower to Heaven retold by Ruby Dee; illustrations copyright © 1992 by Jennifer Bent.
The World in 1492 by Jean Fritz, Katherine Paterson, Patricia McKissack, Fredrick McKissack, Margaret Mahy, and Jamake Highwater; illustrations copyright © 1992 by Stefano Vitale.

Houghton Mifflin Company
El Chino by Allen Say; illustrations © 1990 by Allen Say.
Tree of Cranes by Allen Say; illustrations © 1991 by Allen Say.
Year of Impossible Goodbyes by Sook Nyul Choi; illustrations © 1991 by Sook Nyul Choi.

Hyperion Books for Children
Morning Girl by Michael Dorris; cover illustration © 1994 by Ellen Thompson.

Alfred A. Knopf
The Dark Thirty: Southern Tales of the Supernatural by Patricia McKissack; cover illustration copyright 1992 by Brian Pinkney.
Diego by Jonah Winter, translated by Amy Price; cover illustration © 1991 by Jeanette Winter.
Goodbye, Vietnam by Gloria Whelan; cover illustration © 1992 by David Levinson.
What Comes in Spring? by Barbara Savadge Horton; cover illustration © 1992 by Ed Young.

Lerner Publications Company
A Family in Taiwan by Ling Yu; cover photograph by Chen Ming-jeng. All rights reserved.

Little, Brown and Company
Jonathan and His Mommy by Irene Smalls; illustration copyright 1992 by Michael Hays.
Osa's Pride by Ann Grifalconi; illustration copyright 1990 by Ann Grifalconi.

William Morrow and Company
Ahyoka and the Talking Leaves by Peter and Connie Roop; cover illustration by Yoshi Miyake used with permission.
Hopscotch Around the World by Mary D. Lankford; cover illustration by Karen Milone used with permission.
Lightning inside You, and Other Native American Riddles compiled by John Bierhorst; cover illustration by Louise Brierley used with permission.
"More More More," Said the Baby: Three Love Stories by Vera B. Williams; cover illustration by Vera B. Williams used with permission.

Orchard Books
The Journey: Japanese Americans, Racism, and Renewal by Sheila Hamanaka; cover illustration © 1990.
The Middle of Somewhere: A Story of South Africa by Sheila Gordon; cover illustration © 1990.
A Taste of Salt: A Story of Modern Haiti by Frances Temple; cover illustration © 1992.
When Africa Was Home by Karen Lynn Williams; cover illustration by Floyd Cooper © 1991.
When I Am Old with You by Angela Johnson; cover illustration by David Soman © 1990.

Philomel Books
Father and Son by Denizé Lauture; cover illustration by Jonathan Green used with permission.
The Girl Who Loved Caterpillars: A Twelfth-Century Tale from Japan adapted by Jean Merrill; cover illustration by Floyd Cooper used with permission.

Editor

Rudine Sims Bishop is professor of education at The Ohio State University, where she teaches courses in children's literature. A graduate of West Chester University of Pennsylvania, Bishop also holds an M. Ed. from the University of Pennsylvania and an Ed.D. from Wayne State University in Detroit, where she was a participant in the Reading Miscue Research Project. She taught elementary school in Pennsylvania for a number of years, and for several years was on the faculty of the University of Massachusetts, where she directed a graduate-level teacher education program in reading, writing, and literature. Bishop has held a number of leadership positions in the National Council of Teachers of English, and is also an active member of the International Reading Association and the National Conference on Research in English. As a member of the American Library Association, she served on the 1992 Newbery Award Committee. Bishop has been a speaker at numerous conferences nationally and internationally, and is the author of many articles and chapters in professional journals and books. She is the author of *Shadow and Substance: Afro-American Experience in Contemporary Children's Fiction* and *Presenting Walter Dean Myers,* and is at work on a book on the evolution of African American children's literature.